The World of Eleanor of Aquitaine

The World of Eleanor of Aquitaine

LITERATURE AND SOCIETY IN SOUTHERN FRANCE BETWEEN THE ELEVENTH AND THIRTEENTH CENTURIES

Edited by
Marcus Bull and Catherine Léglu

THE BOYDELL PRESS

First published 2005
The Boydell Press, Woodbridge

ISBN 1 84383 114 7

The Boydell Press is an imprint of Boydell & Brewer Ltd
PO Box 9, Woodbridge, Suffolk IP12 3DF, UK
and of Boydell & Brewer Inc.
668 Mt Hope Avenue, Rochester, NY 14620, USA
website: www.boydellandbrewer.com

A CIP catalogue record for this title is available
from the British Library

Library of Congress Cataloging-in-Publication Data

The world of Eleanor of Aquitaine : literature and society in southern France between the eleventh and thirteenth centuries / edited by Marcus Bull and Catherine Léglu.

p. cm.

Includes bibliographical references.

ISBN 1–84383–114–7 (hardback : alk. paper)

1. France, Southern – Civilization – To 1500. 2. France, Southern – Intellectual life – To 1500. 3. Literature and society – France, Southern – History – To 1500. 4. Eleanor, of Aquitaine, Queen, consort of Henry II, King of England, 1122?–1204 – Influence. I. Bull, Marcus Graham. II. Léglu, Catherine. III. Title.

DC607.45.W67 2005

944'.71022 – dc22 2004008333

This publication is printed on acid-free paper

Typeset by Pru Harrison, Hacheston, Suffolk
Printed in Great Britain by
Antony Rowe Ltd, Chippenham, Wiltshire

Contents

Maps

Acknowledgements

The editors' principal thanks must go to the Colston Research Society. Without a generous subsidy by the Society, the April 2003 symposium on 'The World of Eleanor of Aquitaine', on which this present volume is based, could not have taken place. We would especially like to thank Professor Malcolm Anderson and John Harvey for their invaluable advice and encouragement, and Alison Calvert and Esther McLean for their administrative support. Boydell & Brewer were a great help throughout the process of planning and running the symposium, and we would like particularly to thank Caroline Palmer and Helen Barber. Annie Burnside and the staff of Clifton Hill House provided an excellent and friendly venue, and we were also greatly assisted by the staff of the University of Bristol Conference Office. We would like to thank the University of Bristol Centre for Medieval Studies for its support throughout the build-up to the conference and during it, especially Ad Putter (chair of the CMS) and Lyndsay Markham. The public lecture that forms part of the Colston Symposium format was a huge success, and attracted precisely the sort of broader audience that the Colston Research Society aims to reach. For this we would like to thank Barry Taylor for his excellent help with the publicity, as well as Birgit Beumers and Cardiff Museum and Art Galleries for their assistance with the poster. Finally, the present volume would not have been possible without the support and patience of our respective spouses and daughters. It is to them that it is dedicated.

Abbreviations

Actes Henri II	*Recueil des actes d'Henri II, roi d'Angleterre et duc de Normandie, concernant les provinces françaises et les affaires de France*, ed. L. Delisle and E. Berger, 4 vols. (Paris, 1909–27)
AHR	*American Historical Review*
AM	*Annales du Midi*
BdT	*Biographies des troubadours*, ed. J. Boutière and A.-H. Schutz with C.-I. Marrou, 2nd edn (Paris, 1964)
CCM	*Cahiers de civilisation médiévale*
CF	*Cahiers de Fanjeaux*
CN	*Cultura Neolatina*
Chanson	*La chanson de la croisade contre les Albigeois*, ed. and trans. E. Martin-Chabot, 3 vols. (Paris, 1931–61)
EHR	*English Historical Review*
FEW	*Französisches Etymologisches Wörterbuch*, ed. W. von Wartburg, 22 vols., 3 supplements and 15 unbound parts (Bonn, 1925–83)
HGL	*Histoire générale de Languedoc*, ed. C. Devic and J. Vaissete, rev. E. Roschach, A. Molinier et al., 16 vols. (Toulouse, 1872–1904)
LR	*Lexique roman, ou dictionnaire de la langue des troubadours*, ed. F. Raynouard, 6 vols. (Paris, 1838–44)
MGH SS	*Monumenta Germaniae Historica: Scriptores in Folio et Quarto*
MLR	*Modern Language Review*
PC	*Bibliographie der Troubadours*, ed. A. Pillet and H. Carstens (Halle, 1933; repr. New York, 1968)
PD	*Petit Dictionnaire Provençal–Français*, ed. E. Levy (Heidelberg, 1909)
PL	*Patrologiae cursus completus, series Latina*, ed. J-P. Migne, 221 vols. (Paris, 1844–64)
PSW	*Provenzalisches Supplement – Wörterbuch, Berichtigungen und Ergänzungen zu Raynouards 'Lexique Roman'*, ed. E. Levy, 8 vols. (Leipzig, 1894–1924; repr. Hildersheim, 1973)
R	*Romania*
RHC Oc	*Recueil des historiens des croisades: Historiens occidentaux*, ed. Académie des Inscriptions et Belles-Lettres, 5 vols. (Paris, 1844–95)
RHGF	*Recueil des historiens des Gaules et de la France*, ed. M. Bouquet, rev. L. Delisle, 24 vols. (Paris, 1840–1904)
RlR	*Revue des langues romanes*
RS	Rolls Series
ZrPh	*Zeitschrift für romanisiche Philologie*

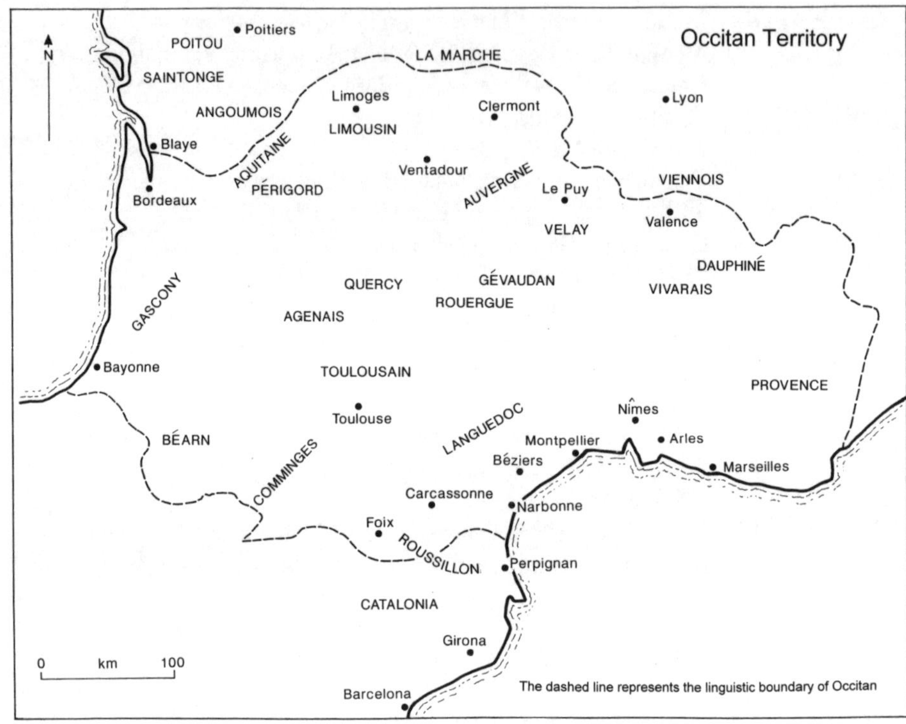

1. Southern France

Introduction

CATHERINE LÉGLU AND MARCUS BULL

As a woman, Eleanor of Aquitaine is a favourite answer to the question 'Which medieval person would you most like to meet?' She is often cited as an exemplary, albeit exceptional, individual, both in specific relation to her own time and in the general context of women's history. Given the continuing interest in Eleanor, which is evident both in medieval scholarship and in popular perceptions of the Middle Ages, and given too Bristol's long-standing links to Bordeaux and south-western France, it seemed natural that she should be the headline 'star' of an interdisciplinary conference organized by the University of Bristol's Centre for Medieval Studies on 'The World of Eleanor of Aquitaine: Literature and Society in Southern France between the Eleventh and Thirteenth Centuries'. The conference, held under the aegis of the Colston Research Society, took place on 8–10 April 2003. Eleanor lent her name to the colloquium, but the aim of the organizers was not to make her the sole, or even the main, object of attention. Indeed, their purpose was not to examine Eleanor of Aquitaine as a woman, a subject that is worthy of lengthy treatment, and has attracted playwrights, film-makers and novelists in equal measure.[1] It was rather to make use of this queen's life as a focal point in order to address, and to reassess, certain ideas about the regions and the times she inhabited. The aim was to explore a range of disciplinary perspectives and to consider various source types that are traditionally apportioned to discrete disciplinary domains. Thus, while many of the chapters collected in this volume to a greater or lesser degree examine aspects of Eleanor's career and reputation, these explorations form part of wider discussions about cultural, literary, intellectual, social, religious and political developments in southern France. The chronological range of the discussion, moreover, is not bounded by Eleanor's own lifetime, long as it was, but covers the generations before and after her so that the civilization of which Eleanor was part may be seen in a fuller context.

Eleanor's extraordinary longevity, mobility and fecundity make her a useful focal point for an examination of many of the wider social and cultural issues of her time. Using Eleanor as a leitmotif in this way is not without problems, however, for any re-examination of Eleanor's world runs up against the

1 Among the plethora of biographies and monographs, some of variable quality, may be cited a recent scholarly collection, *Eleanor of Aquitaine: Lord and Lady*, edited by Bonnie Wheeler and John Carmi Parsons (New York, 2002).

constraining effect of traditional categories and boundaries that complicate our understanding of both her individual experience and the cultural world in which she operated. Consider, for example, the geographical dimensions of her career, for these throw useful light on some of the difficulties involved. Despite the fact that she spent substantial portions of her life in Poitou, had sojourns across the Plantagenet empire, in England, Normandy and Anjou, and made significant journeys to places as far flung as Sicily, Antioch, Jerusalem and Castile, Eleanor is still perceived primarily in terms of her inherited title, interpreted as her region of birth and upbringing, the duchy of Aquitaine. Several of the contributors to this volume raise the issue of our modern attachment to notions of regional, even national, identity; and 'Aquitaine' is a case in point. It was, after all, more an administrative entity than a regional concept during this period. There is imprecision both in the geographical terminology and in the boundaries between various territorial circumscriptions. One illustration of this is the fact that the French-speaking county of Poitou is sometimes blended into 'Occitania', a modern term for those regions in which Occitan was spoken (despite the fact that the northernmost parts of the duchy of Aquitaine, the Saintonge, Poitou and Périgord, were not, predominantly, Occitanophone). Similarly 'Aquitaine' can be stretched to encompass Gascony (a separate duchy, which was inherited by the Aquitanian dukes in the eleventh century) and the northernmost Basque-speaking parts of the Pyrenees. There is also Toulouse to consider: not normally included within the boundaries of Aquitaine (though there were Carolingian precedents for its inclusion), it was nonetheless intimately connected to the duchy. Eleanor, indeed, embodied the potential for connectivity, for she inherited a claim to the county of Toulouse through her paternal grandmother Philippa – a claim that was at various stages to inform the policies of both Eleanor's husbands. Abutting the duchy's frontiers, Toulouse stood on the boundary between Gascony and the regions now known as the Languedoc. As we move south and east into this area, we enter a zone that scholars have traditionally differentiated from the Aquitanian/Gascon South-West: we are now in the 'Midi', the region sometimes perceived as the 'pure' South of troubadours, heresy, weak governance and lively urban civilization. Yet there is little evidence of organized heretical communities by the time we reach the eastern coastal regions now known as Provence, and the noble troubadour Raimbaut d'Orange (d.1173) held his court in the rural location of Courthézon.[2] We are also, once we reach the Roussillon and Provence, in regions under the direct influence of the counts of Barcelona. Clearly this contrast between the 'Midi' and its Aquitanian neighbour is overdrawn, if indeed it has any basis at all, and this is one of the issues that the contributors to this volume address. If we dissolve, or at least weaken, the traditional binary opposition between South and South-West, then Eleanor is able to serve as a point of entry into re-examinations of the whole area, seen either as a single entity or in its particular parts.

But there is a potential paradox. Eleanor was not in herself the 'southern

2 G. Brunel-Lobrichon and C. Duhamel-Amado, *Au Temps des troubadours: XIIe–XIIIe siècles* (Paris, 1997), pp. 193–211, esp. pp. 86–7 and 196–7.

woman' envisaged by modern authors of pulp romance and popular historical works. She was raised in a county that stood on the linguistic and social boundary between regions that are now viewed as 'northern' and 'southern' France. Indeed, despite the patronage of troubadours that even medieval writers fondly (and mistakenly) attributed to her, she probably did not speak Occitan. It is significant that the lyric poems attributed to Richard I, the son most directly implicated in Eleanor's Aquitanian inheritance and of all her children the one with whom she seems to have most identified, are composed in Poitevin. To deny the validity of regional distinctions may entail the same error as that of the radio DJ who recently described the Lancastrian singer Lisa Stansfield as 'Yorkshire's finest': these are more than formal or geographical niceties. Regional and linguistic issues are just one facet, but an important one, of the problem inherent in viewing the past through distorting and simplistic lenses, especially those that seek to establish straightforward oppositions, for example between 'north' and 'south'. Eleanor's career, interests and connections belie the utility of such stark binary divisions. Thus a theme running through several of the papers in this collection is the question of cultural perception and stereotyping – an issue made more complicated by the fact that from the 1150s Eleanor's Aquitaine became part of a wider political grouping that included areas, most notably England and Normandy, which had had relatively few links to the south of France up to that point. This political reordering brought about new opportunities for observers to construct comparisons and contrasts. How would the South fare in this new world of cross-currents and co-existence between discrete sociopolitical spheres? Were crude stereotypes available to be wheeled out and reiterated? Or would more nuanced ideas prevail? On the face of it, it might appear that a stock repertoire of images and associations linked to the South was ready and waiting for Eleanor's arrival on the northern scene through her marriage to Henry of Anjou (as, for that matter, with her earlier marriage to Louis VII of France). One thinks, for example, of the arch observations of the eleventh-century Burgundian historian Ralph Glaber describing the flood of vain, frivolous people from the Auvergne and Aquitaine, complete with funny clothes, hairstyles and manners, who accompanied Constance of Arles northwards when she married King Robert II of France.[3] Similarly, a Norman historian of the First Crusade, Ralph of Caen, seems on the face of it to be tapping into long-established and culturally entrenched stereotypes of the South when he describes the antagonism that northern French crusaders felt towards their southern colleagues.[4] But we should be wary of constructing a broad pattern on the basis of the few explicit references such as these that survive. As John Gillingham's chapter forcibly demonstrates, the views of the South that were formulated by the Anglo-Norman historians writing during and shortly after Eleanor's lifetime point to perceptions that were contingent and informed by immediate circumstances rather than conceived as simply variations on timeless themes. The South as seen by outsiders, then, becomes a more shifting quantity,

3 Ralph Glaber, *Opera*, ed. and trans. J. France, N. Bulst and P. Reynolds (Oxford, 1989), pp. 164–6.

4 'Gesta Tancredi', *RHC Oc*, III, 617 and 651.

thereby defying the sort of sweeping generalization that stereotyping feeds. As with medieval perceptions, so with more recent judgements: a similar protean quality emerges in John Gillingham's, Laurent Macé's and other chapters in the context of discussion of the historiographical stereotypes that have developed over the last century or so concerning the geographical extent of the spread of heresy, the mores of the regional nobility, the image and power of the counts of Toulouse, and even Eleanor herself.

Indeed, traditional generalizations about the South seem to be confounded at every turn. As Malcolm Barber's discussion of the Templar preceptory of Douzens reveals, even in the fairly restricted zone within which the first substantial Templar presence in the South developed its material and human resources, we encounter significant variations in terms of habitat and social structure. These obviate any resort to stock truisms about life in just one part of Languedoc; by extension the same is true of the South as a whole. Similarly we encounter both the inward- and the outward-looking. Barber's emphasis on the significance of the South to the Templars' expansion into western Europe as a whole is a reminder of the full part that this region played in contemporary international affairs – here specifically in terms of its receptiveness to the new concept of the Military Order and, behind that, in its enthusiasm for the crusading idea, as originally exemplified, of course, by the participation of Eleanor's great-great-uncle, Raymond of Saint-Gilles, and her grandfather, William IX of Aquitaine, in the First Crusade. Likewise, Daniel Callahan's chapter on the 'coronation' rituals used by the dukes of Aquitaine points on the one hand towards the exploitation of localized myths and ideologies in the use of the cult of St Valerie, behind which loomed the even greater regional cult of St Martial at Limoges. But on the other hand, it emerges that the Aquitanian rituals of power were part of a wider ideological system that was fortified by contacts with other centres of authority, such as the Capetian court, as well as by a shared indebtedness to the rhetorical and symbolic discourses of venerable Carolingian models.

Eleanor's career encompassed crusading, remarriage, the cultivation of lineage, imprisonment and a probably exaggerated role in literary patronage. This last is the basis of one of the most enduring scholarly and popular misconceptions surrounding Eleanor, her alleged patronage of troubadour poetry and her supposed self-fashioning as the Queen of the Courts of Love and Queen of the Troubadours. Ruth Harvey's chapter demolishes these myths totally, not in the spirit of robbing us of one of the most attractive facets of the traditional image of Eleanor, but rather in order to remind us of the many challenges that are involved in gaining a truer understanding of Eleanor's significance to her age. Again, stereotypes fall away and a more interesting, shifting and challenging picture takes their place. Similarly, Dan Power's paper points to how the mythifying process around Eleanor and her memory was in full swing as early as the thirteenth century, as evidenced by the hostile writings of Norman and Picard chroniclers whose barbed comments were in fact extensions of anecdotes that were already circulating in Eleanor's own lifetime. Women in prominent social positions are singularly vulnerable to mythification, and a figure such as the queen of two expanding dynasties would be no exception. Harvey and Power both allude to old readings of Eleanor as the model for heroines of *chansons de geste* or the troubadours' *domna*. It is more plausible that she, as a historical figure, was imagined by those who described her through the filter of strong-willed queens such as Blanchefleur in *Garin le Loherenc*, rebellious Saracen princesses (the 'exotic' woman of the South was a well-established type), or demonic matriarchs.[5] To say nothing, of course, of either Iseut or Guenevere. Would scholarly and popular works seeking to establish a true 'portrait' of Eleanor of Aquitaine be so detailed, or for that matter so intense, were their object Henry II? A feature of women's objectification is the emphasis on physical beauty, understood as an essential aspect of sexual reputation. Eleanor's combination of fecundity (as a Plantagenet) and suspected adultery (as a Capetian) make her compelling even for the modern descendants of those who transcribed rumours concerning her. Once again, Eleanor has been the victim of a preference for the lurid and simple over the uncertain and complex. The issue of what she may or may not have got up to with Raymond of Antioch during the Second Crusade exemplifies this perfectly. It is remarkable that even today scholars continue to debate whether or not Eleanor actually did have an incestuous liaison with her uncle – as if we can ever definitively know one way or the other – whereas the true significance of the scandal is what it reveals about the manner in which a fascinated fear of female sexuality readily surfaced when male writers were casting around for scapegoats. Myth-making, in other words, *in media res*.

A consideration of stereotypes and distorted views of distant figures and realms leads to the key role of oral and written report in informing chronicles. As we can see from the chapters by Richard Barber, John Gillingham, Ruth Harvey and Dan Power, reputation, acclaim and *rumor* (what may now be termed gossip), especially that variety circulating in writing, had a paradoxical role in developing the Plantagenet mystique. In Eleanor's particular case, this is complicated by the fact that the bulk of texts about the Midi were produced by outside observers, visitors and those who reported the travels of others. The potential for selectivity and self-imposed distortion is enormous. For example, John Gillingham's chapter reveals that reports by merchants who had contacts with the South could not have been utilized by the clerical authors of chronicles to anything like the same extent as information coming from pilgrims or diplomats. As a result, references to major ports with little political or religious significance scarcely feature in the extant narrative sources. This is just one illustration of the fact that the picture of Aquitaine that emerges from the available sources is partial and unsatisfyingly incomplete. Scholars have often had occasion to

5 J.-M. Berland, 'Les retrouvailles du vendredi saint: un episode orléanais dans Girart de Roussillon', in *La Chanson de Geste et le mythe carolingien: Mélanges René Louis*, 2 vols. (Saint-Père-sous-Vézelay, 1982), II, 845–64 (pp. 854–6); for a more cautious view, see W. M. Hackett, 'L'élément courtois dans le vocabulaire de *Girart de Roussillon*', *ibid.*, II, 729–33. On the 'Belle Sarrasine' motif, see J. Gilbert, 'The Practice of Gender in *Aucassin et Nicolette*', *Forum for Modern Language Studies* 33 (1997), 217–28; S. Kay, *The Chansons de Geste in the Age of Romance: Political Fictions* (Cambridge, 1994), pp. 25–48; and J. De Weever, *Sheba's Daughters: Whitening and Demonizing the Saracen Woman in Medieval French Epic* (New York, 1998). Also M. de Combarieu du Grès, *L'Idéal humain et l'expérience morale chez les héros des chansons de geste des origines à 1250*, 2 vols. (Aix-en-Provence and Paris, 1979), I, 404–11; L. Harf-Lancner, *Les Fées au Moyen Age: Morgane et Mélusine, la naissance des fees* (Paris, 1983), pp. 396–400.

remark that the sources for Eleanor herself are surprisingly exiguous; there are occasional clusters of evidence generated by particular phases of her public career, such as the Second Crusade and her rebellion against Henry II in 1173, but these only serve to remind us of how much more we would like to know about long periods of her life. An important point to note is that Eleanor is not alone in this respect. For example, we have a similarly fragmentary picture of another powerful southern woman of Eleanor's era, Ermengard of Narbonne.[6] Ermengard's patronage of troubadours is demonstrable, and what little evidence survives of her career points to genuine attempts to function as an autonomous *seigneur*. Like Ermengard, Eleanor is, in a sense, emblematic of the distorting and obscuring quality of the source base that characterizes the central medieval South in general.

Why the South is relatively poorly served by the extant sources – in particular historiographical narratives, for there are significant if chronologically and geographically uneven documentary survivals – is a question that has long exercised scholars. In an important article published in 1990, Thomas Bisson suggested that the functionalist written culture that arose in Occitania, a culture predominantly legalistic in its horizons and applications, developed in ways that 'inhibited' a historiographical textual flourishing of the sort that can be seen in contemporary England and parts of northern Europe. As Bisson observes: 'Fragmentation and divergence inhibited the production of finished or "official" works, the rare surviving examples of which seem less characteristic than the dispersed or incidental traces of a modestly utilitarian engagement with the past.'[7] Indeed, according to this view, the production of coherent, extended pieces of historiography or epic was something alien to the Occitan-speaking regions. These genres were much more the province of Catalonia, as well as of Anglo-Norman and French circles. Several explanations have been offered for this imbalance. For example, Ian Short has proposed, with specific reference to Gaimar's *Estoire des Engleis* (c.1138–40), that this work and by extension others like it were the product of a pragmatic context: a multilingual environment stimulated by aristocratic lay literacy, as exemplified by Gaimar's bicultural and literate patron Constance fitzGilbert.[8] This theory has a lot to commend it, but the problem is that it does not neatly extend to the circumstances surrounding the production of southern works. As Linda Paterson's chapter in this volume shows, the writing down of the *Canso d'Antioca* is a case in point. While multilingual contexts and the movement of elites as colonizers and settlers to new lands

6 For a recent treatment, see F. L. Cheyette, *Ermengard of Narbonne and the World of the Troubadours* (Ithaca, 2001).

7 T. N. Bisson, 'Unheroed Pasts: History and Commemoration in South Frankland before the Albigensian Crusade', *Speculum* 65 (1990), 281–308 (p. 308).

8 I. Short, 'Gaimar et les débuts de l'historiographie en langue française', in *Chroniques nationales et chroniques universelles: Actes du Colloque d'Amiens, 16–17 janvier 1988*, ed. D. Buschinger (Göppingen, 1990), pp. 155–63. See also J. Blacker, ' "Dame Custance la Gentil": Gaimar's Portrait of a Lady and her Books', in *The Court and Cultural Diversity: Selected Proceedings of the Eighth Triennial Congress of the International Courtly Literature Society, Queen's University, Belfast, 26 July – 1 August, 1995*, ed. E. Mullally and J. Thompson (Cambridge, 1997), pp. 109–20.

undoubtedly played an important role in stimulating literary effort, essentially in making patrons wish for texts in their preferred language, other factors should also be considered.

In his chapter, Laurent Macé suggests an explanation for the lack of extant chronicles produced in the circles of the counts of Toulouse. The key, he argues, is the fact that there were few clerics in the comital entourage. In addition, the abbeys with close ties to the counts were not active as centres of ideological production. This contrasts with the counts' near-neighbours in Provence and Catalonia, and even more with their northern counterparts. Instead of heroic narratives as the prime vehicle of comital self-fashioning, Macé points to the importance of troubadour poetry, as well as laudatory schemes based on heraldry and metaphor. The counts' emerging genealogical mystique is, he argues, 'a late attempt to catch up' with their Plantagenet cousins. By placing the court troubadour centre-stage, in a powerful development on existing work on the subject, Macé's argument connects with the chapters by Linda Paterson, William D. Paden and Ruth Harvey. The lesson to be drawn is that it is not critical to look for extended narratives (which either have not survived, or were never there in the first place); more is to be gained from examining other sources, reflecting different approaches to historiography and prestige. The value of this shift of perspective emerges, for example, from Linda Paterson's contribution, which explores the possibility that the principality of Antioch was the site of a unique cosmopolitan ferment, where crusaders' tales and existing local traditions could be melded, and where troubadours were able to find a receptive audience capable of understanding their words, if not their ideas. Texts produced in or around Antioch show oral interaction, and hint at the broader picture of communication of stories and reputations.

Paterson's exploration of the 'Antioch connection' in troubadour lyric also raises further considerations. The exact nature of 'literacy' in this period was highly variable, but the identification of a milieu open to textual composition in the principality of Antioch makes it possible to envisage Occitan narrative being performed, perhaps even composed, in Outremer. Patronage, after all, rests on more than a degree of literacy; it may also turn on a given figure's appreciation of the value and usefulness of cultural production. Thus Paterson's chapter, like Macé's, reveals the value of exploring the wider context that produces works of prestige and commemoration, looking beyond the chronicle material associated with Anglo-Norman, Capetian and Catalonian circles.

Linda Paterson's contribution also asks if questions of literacy were important for writers seeking to identify and court a suitable patron, and by extension what exactly literacy was understood to be in this period and context. Is it the ownership of books, the love of books, access to a library, or the ability to sign one's name? Is it, indeed, about books at all? It is well known that in this period wax tablets were used predominantly for drafting both short and lengthy texts, as well as making notes and schedules for a range of administrative purposes. One excellent illustration of the importance of tablets is provided by the working methods of Galbert of Bruges: this thoughtful historian of the crises that convulsed Flanders in 1127–28 began the process of imposing pattern and explanatory order on the chaos around him by carrying wax tablets on his person so that he could make notes wherever and whenever he could.[9] Eadmer and Orderic Vitalis are among other contemporary writers who have left us similar evidence for the importance of tablets in their literary endeavours.[10] These three men are, of course, prime representatives of the northern European historiographical flourishing, which we have just seen contrasts so starkly with conditions in southern France. But the broad lesson about the plurality of modes of literary expression is of more general application. To take another example of the different ways in which ideas could be committed to writing, *Liederblätter* (poems written on rolls of parchment) have been discovered from as late a period as the 1250s, and rolls (*rolets*) continued to be used until the early Renaissance as actors' scripts.[11] In other words, books as we understand them may not have been the key mode of transmission for texts. Furthermore, what many of our sources rely upon is the report of an interpreter, or of someone who can interpret events for a non-native observer or audience. In her recent study, Nicole Schulman has suggested that some of Peter of Vaux-de-Cernay's criticisms of the Languedoc and its people may result from deliberate 'misinformation' by one of his key sources, the bishop of Toulouse, Folc of Marseille.[12] Interpreters and translators do not inevitably act as neutral transmitters of information. *Rumor* may be created in writing as much as it is transcribed.

Laurent Macé's exploration of the 'lack of documents' reflects a southern culture that sought expression for political ideas in other ways (via songs, allegory, and 'secondary writing' media such as seals and coins).[13] Coins do not require written literacy of those who handle them. Macé cites material in which the seal of the count of Toulouse is said to show either a sun or a star. What the exact object represented was matters less than the essential action, that of recognizing and acknowledging the image as part of the comital emblem. Similarly, there is no need to 'look up' the significance of a star, a cross or a knight on horseback for its viewer to identify the image as a sign of the count's prestige. In a paper given at the colloquium but not published here, John Arnold explored the evidence for divergent and parallel concepts of written texts in thirteenth-century Languedoc. The Inquisition's emergent 'technology of power' stood as

9 R. H. Rouse and M. A. Rouse, 'Wax Tablets', *Language and Communication* 9 (1989), 175–91; J. Rider, *God's Scribe: The Historiographical Art of Galbert of Bruges* (Washington, DC, 2001), pp. 31–4. Evidence for the extensive use of wax tablets in Aragon (previously contested) is cited in J. Trenchs-Odena and M. J. Carbonell, 'Tablettes de cire aragonaises, XIIe–XVe siècles', *Bibliothèque de l'Ecole des Chartes* 151 (1993), 155–60.

10 M. T. Clanchy, *From Memory to Written Record: England 1066–1307*, 2nd edn (Oxford, 1993), pp. 118–19; M. J. Carruthers, *The Book of Memory: A Study of Memory in Medieval Culture* (Cambridge, 1990), pp. 195–6, 204–5.

11 R. H. Rouse, 'Roll and Codex: The Transmission of the Works of Reinmar von Zweter', in M. A. Rouse and R. H. Rouse, *Authentic Witnesses: Approaches to Medieval Texts and Manuscripts* (Notre Dame, 1991), pp. 13–29; G. A. Runnalls, 'The Medieval Actors' Rôles found in the Fribourg Archives', *Pluteus* 4–5 (1986–87), 5–67. For fragments of actors' rôles in Catalan and Occitan from Barcelona, Palma and Ille, see A. A. MacDonald, *La Passion Catalane-Occitane* (Geneva, 1999), pp. 276–87.

12 N. Schulman, *Where Troubadours were Bishops* (New York and London, 2001), pp. xxvi–ix.

13 Simon Franklin has placed coinage in the category of 'secondary writing', as a medium in which writing is found but where it does not play a primary role: *Writing, Society and Culture in Early Rus, c.950–1300* (Cambridge, 2002), pp. 47–70.

the culmination of written language's power to create social divisions.[14] On the other hand, Arnold argued, there existed concerns about the status of literacy among peasants and clerks alike.

It is perhaps otiose to rehearse the arguments concerning medieval literacy, and the status of vernacular as opposed to Latin reading and/or writing. Rather, as Roy Harris has pointed out in a recent publication, western scholarship is embedded in a literate culture, and views 'illiteracy' strictly in terms of a lack of access to discursive written materials, rather than an alternative. Writing is perceived as what he terms a 'phonoptic' mode ('visible speech').[15] Perceptions of writing are key to the modern concept of 'literacy'. A twelfth-century clerk would have been able to read and write numerals; musical notation would have been legible to many and used as both a support for memorized music and as a way of transmitting it. Discursive writing, especially creative writing, is the end-point of literacy.[16] In between, medieval culture knew a wide range of other literacies, some of which did not involve writing or reading at all. For example, a school-taught man would have used his hands in complex, often highly sophisticated ways. He would have been trained from childhood in *computus manualis*, calculating feast-days with his hands (a method also ascribed to shepherds). He would, until the thirteenth century, have calculated expenditure and accounts through finger-reckoning, or with the support of the abacus.[17] Singing was taught and memorized with the assistance of variations on the so-called Guidonian hand, a method of allocating notes and modes to parts of the hand.[18] Those clerks who wished to practise fortune-telling could have used geomancy, a technique of inscribing signs on sand or earth, or have read the palms of their or others' hands.[19] Beyond school-based technologies such as these (for which written treatises exist, and which may well have been learned by women too), there lay the intensive visual 'reading' skills of heralds, an emerging group in the late twelfth century, who were often not school-taught at all.[20] Seigneurial visual signs such as seals, coats of arms, coinage, and later developments such as the royal monogram, are not what a modern reader may accept as 'literacy', but they involve similar skills.[21] To quote Simon Franklin on the multilingual and multi-

14 For 'technology' as a term, see J. B. Given, *Inquisition and Medieval Society: Power, Discipline, and Resistance in Medieval Languedoc* (Ithaca, 1997); J. Arnold, *Inquisition and Power: Catharism and the Confessing Subject in Medieval Languedoc* (Philadelphia, 2001); see also his article, ' "A Man Takes an Ox by the Horn and a Peasant by the Tongue": Literacy, Orality and Inquisition in Medieval Languedoc', in *Learning and Literacy in Medieval England and Abroad*, ed. S. Rees-Jones (Turnhout, 2003), pp. 31–47.

15 R. Harris, *Rethinking Writing* (London, 2000), pp. 1–9, 23–4.

16 See *ibid.*, pp. ix–xi.

17 For an overview, see A. Murray, *Reason and Society in the Middle Ages* (Oxford, 1978), pp. 163–9, 195; P. Riché and D. Alexandre-Bidon, *L'Enfance au Moyen Age* (Paris, 1994), pp. 108–57.

18 *The New Grove Dictionary of Music and Musicians*, 2nd edn, rev. S. Sadie, executive ed. J. Tyrrell, 29 vols. (London, 2001), XXIII, 644–6 and X, 525.

19 For Occitan examples of geomancy and chiromancy, see P. Meyer, 'Traités en vers provençaux sur l'astrologie et la géomancie', *Romania* 26 (1897), 225–75. These texts are from the early fourteenth century.

20 O. Neubecker, *Heraldry: Sources, Symbols and Meaning*, trans. J. P. Brooke-Little and R. Tobler (London, 1988), pp. 10–15.

21 Harris, *Rethinking Writing*, pp. 161–83.

scriptural context of twelfth-century Rus (where no fewer than five scripts were used), 'participation in, or access to, the culture of the written word was far from being the exclusive preserve of technically literate people'. Meanwhile birch-bark letters discovered in Novgorod have enabled specialists to reconstruct the kind of pragmatic, confident writing practices that have been left without evidence in western Europe.[22] The contentious issue of orality, especially in relation to narrative, is only part of a complex field of communication and signs.

Such questions lead us back to the bodies that made up medieval society. A contribution to the Symposium by Kate Robson-Brown and Mark Horton, not included here, produced considerable discussion. Forensic technology, in particular the identification of mitochondrial DNA, enables researchers in the twenty-first century to identify kinship groups in cemeteries, where only written evidence or artefacts would have been of use beforehand. It is now, perhaps shockingly to some, possible to know what an individual ate (something that also tells us where they were raised), whether their lives were sedentary or burdened by hard manual labour, and how they died. The minutiae that chronicles and romances omit are increasingly available for scrutiny. As a result, some ethnic, gender and social stereotypes are under review. Malcolm Barber suggested in discussion that such methods, applied to remains at the Templar house of Douzens, would open new windows onto the complex social relationships his chapter reconstructs. Skeletons are eloquent fragments of the society they constituted, a new kind of 'text' to be consulted with due respect.

Can a received view of the 'South' change through this collection of papers? John Gillingham's chapter asks if the image created by the chroniclers of an unruly, heretical Aquitaine was politically motivated, or influenced by the fact that only bad news, especially concerning rebellion, travels. Literature can also play a part, as we can see in the twelfth-century *chansons de geste* of *Garin le Loherenc* and *Gerbert de Mez* (composed c.1130–60) depicting the vendettas between two rival lineages, the Lorrains and the (partly northern) Bordelais. The Lorrain cycle, which expanded over the next two centuries to include three more poems, was widely disseminated in Picard and Norman lands, and treats the 'South' as an area riven with destructive warfare, treachery and weak religious faith. Admittedly, both lineages are equally bloodthirsty and corruptible, but the Bordelais are cast as the villains of the piece from the outset, as a lineage of traitors.[23] For the anti-hero Fromont, lineage and region are closely allied: 'I was indeed born of the Bordelais; my best kinsmen are in those lands' (ll. 2128–9). The foul deeds of Fromont's uncle recur throughout the two poems as the reason for the Bordelais clan's commitment to treasonable behaviour (for example,

22 Franklin, *Writing, Society and Culture in Early Rus*, p. 4. On birch-bark letters, see pp. 36–40. Wax tablets were used too, pp. 42–7. The scripts used in Rus were Glagolitic, Cyrillic, Greek, Latin and Runic. There are also traces of Arabic, Turkic and Hebrew, pp. 83–119.

23 *Garin le Loherenc*, ed. A. Iter-Gittelman, 3 vols. (Paris, 1997) (see discussion of dating, I, 31); *Gerbert de Mez: chanson de geste du XIIe siècle*, ed. P. Taylor (Namur and Louvain, 1952). For one view of the nuanced portrayal of mischief in the cycle, see B. Guidot, 'La Partialité du trouvère est-elle discrètement infléchie dans *Garin le Loherain*?', in *Au Carrefour des routes d'Europe: La Chanson de geste: Xe Congrès international de la Société Rencesvals, Strasbourg, 1985*, Senefiance 20, 2 vols. (Aix-en-Provence, 1987), I, 601–27.

ll. 2169–75). The conflict is also repeatedly compared to the earlier, equally destructive north-south conflict between Charles Martel and Girart de Roussillon. In *Gerbert de Mez*, Fromont converts to the Saracen faith, an act of disloyalty that disgusts the Saracens who watch the ceremony (ll. 7577–633); his son breaks his religious vows twice in order to pursue revenge (ll. 9212–471 and 14624–735). This epic cycle, extant in over fifty complete and fragmentary versions, seems in some ways to crystallize a particular northern view of the South. Was it a reflection of existing attitudes, or did it influence reception of news and people from these treacherous regions?

This is just one of many issues that remain to be explored in relation to the world of Eleanor of Aquitaine, broadly conceived. In the plenary discussion that concluded the conference, the term that cropped up again and again was 'fluidity': fluidity, that is, as a catchword for the sorts of scholarly responses that are appropriate to the study of substantial, and sometimes unexpected, variety across time and space; and fluidity in terms of the methodological approaches that we can, and should, adopt in order to extend our understanding of the complex layerings of cultural and social spaces that we call the medieval South.

Eleanor of Aquitaine and the Media*

RICHARD BARBER

Royal scandals have been meat and drink to the media since classical times. Suetonius on the private lives of the Caesars or the 'secret history' of the Byzantine court as recorded by Procopius are as juicy as anything dished up by today's newspapers. And, despite the passage of time, Eleanor of Aquitaine is remembered today outside the dusty covers of the chronicles that record her doings, as a subject for romantic biographers, playwrights and television serials. A brief sketch of her dramatic career will explain why. Eleanor was probably born in 1122, and was heiress to vast estates, which amounted to much of the southern half of modern France. Her grandfather, William IX of Aquitaine, had been famed as one of the first troubadours. At fifteen, Eleanor was married to the king of France, Louis VII, a year older than herself. Ten years later, she insisted on accompanying him on crusade to Palestine, where her behaviour led to a fierce quarrel between them. On their journey home they were reconciled by the pope, but she was nonetheless divorced from Louis four years later, in 1152, on the grounds that they were too closely related. It was a political disaster for France. Within six weeks she had married Louis's most powerful vassal, Henry II, soon to be king of England and already duke of Normandy, by whom she had eight children. After Henry, the eldest surviving son, had been crowned king in his father's lifetime, he and two of his brothers rebelled against their father; Eleanor sided with her sons and was imprisoned by her husband, who took a mistress for whom he built a magnificent palace at Woodstock. On her husband's death, she emerged from fifteen years in captivity to become queen regent of England. When her son Richard was captured on his return from crusade in 1191, she played a major role in raising his ransom and negotiating his release, beside securing England for him in his absence. She died in retreat at the abbey of Fontevraud near the Loire valley, aged over eighty.

Scandals in the East, papal reconciliations, divorce, instant remarriage, rebellion – all this would have made superb copy for *Paris Match*, *Hello!*, and *Private Eye*, let alone the daily papers. But how do we know about Eleanor's doings, and how, as historians, can we disentangle her real identity from the gloss put on them by the media of the day? At least the sources are manageable; I sometimes wonder how a modern historian can ever hope to come to any conclusion, given the overwhelming mass of material at his or her disposal. David Starkey

* The Colston Research Society Public Lecture, delivered on 9 April 2003.

commented recently that the Tudor age was ideal for the historian, because one could hope to know enough, but not too much, while the medieval historian was always longing for more, and the modern historian for less. By contrast, all that we have in the way of contemporary records of Eleanor are brief chronicles, notes of important events from the pens of clerks, and the frigid records of royal government. And there is little enough material even from these sources: to print all the records and chronicle entries about Eleanor would take less than a hundred pages.

But that little, much fought over by historians, has not produced much agreement among them. How can we begin to examine the ways in which her image was shaped for future generations, with such a relatively small amount of information to hand?

With some difficulty, is the answer: much of her image today is the product of later historical and literary imagination. That process, too, is part of my brief today: I want to explore, however, not the fantasies of the nineteenth and twentieth century but the roots of the later stories about Eleanor in contemporary histories. So our starting point must be the men who wrote about Eleanor in her own day.

Fleet Street is still the symbolic shorthand for the modern press, even though much of the glory has departed, and the journalists are to be found elsewhere. It is within the bounds of the medieval city of London, and perhaps we should start our explorations in the same place. The legendary Fleet Street tavern of El Vino's, where unprintable scandal was talked and printable stories were jotted down in the twentieth century, had its equivalent in twelfth-century London. William FitzStephen wrote one of the first biographies of Thomas Becket, the martyred archbishop of Canterbury; he evidently knew it well, for he gives it a three-star write-up in his description of London:

> There is in London upon the river's bank, amid the wine that is sold from ships and wine-cellars, a public cookshop. There daily, according to the season, you may find food of all kinds, roast, fried and boiled dishes, fish great and small; the coarser for the poor, the more delicate for the rich, such as venison and birds of all sizes. If friends, weary with travel, should come unexpectedly to visit the citizens of London, and do not want to wait hungrily until fresh food is bought and cooked, they hurry to the riverside shop and everything they could want is there. However many knights and foreigners are coming into the city or leaving it, whatever the hour of day or night, those who are arriving need not go hungry for long, and those who are leaving need not miss their dinner: for they go in and choose whatever they want. A cookshop of this kind is an essential part of city life.[1]

Let us imagine – and before the stricter historians among you groan inwardly at the prospect of yet another romantic reinvention of Eleanor, I promise that this is my only indulgence in this direction – let us imagine that we are among the throng in the cookshop, an ideal place to meet those who come on whatever business to the

1 William FitzStephen, *Norman London*, trans. H. E. Butler (London, 1934, repr. New York, 1990), p. 52.

city, whether that of the government, the Church or simply the social life of the court. We will learn a good deal about Eleanor from them, but we will also find out much about them and how they view the queen. And it is appropriate that we should meet them, not in the scriptorium where they set down their knowledge, but in the kind of place where they would have garnered their information. For this is essentially a society where such information is transmitted by word of mouth. Writing at the royal court is for accounting, for the business of royal government; in monasteries it is for learning and for the study of the scriptures. There is some truth in Robert Fawtier's portrait of twelfth-century chroniclers as men 'who most often had only the common talk of the day on which to rely for their knowledge of public affairs. Their position was not very different from that of the modern journalist, hearing only what those better informed wish him to know, and more often reporting inaccurate news than the reverse.'[2] He points out that in the Middle Ages, the concept of open government was unknown, and that the great officials whom we still call 'secretaries of state' are the descendants of men whose job was to keep the secrets of medieval rulers.

So the men we shall meet in the cookshop are not at the heart of affairs, though some are closer to it than others. Our first visitor is in clerical garb, and is also a royal official; in an age when literacy was the preserve of the Church, the business of government was carried on by members of the clergy. He is the absentee parson of Howden in Yorkshire, and author of two chronicles, one under his own name, Roger of Howden, and one simply called *The Deeds of King Henry and King Richard*. The *Deeds* is in the form of year-by-year entries, and preceded the more literary version that Howden produced in the early 1190s. Neither version has a great deal to say about Eleanor, for their talk is of official business, of diplomacy and the king's government, though all they can tell us is what has happened, not why it has happened. Eleanor, as far as they are concerned, is merely part of the king's entourage. Of *The Deeds of King Henry and King Richard*, the great Victorian historian William Stubbs wrote: 'In a work like the present we miss much that we might have desired. There is none of the life or of the colouring of history; there is no "word-painting", or grouping of characters, or pictorial effects; there is none of the philosophy of history, no speculations on principles.'[3] What Howden gives us is an account of the business of the realm, of the deeds and acts of its rulers.

In these two chronicles, Eleanor's marriage to Henry is recorded; the later account discreetly emphasizes the dynastic implications of her divorce and remarriage by noting that she and Louis had only two daughters, while her union with Henry produced both sons and daughters. It was not until his third marriage that Louis had the much-desired son, Philip Augustus. The chaos that could ensue if there was no son to inherit is shown by the civil war in England over the claim of Henry II's mother Matilda to be queen in her own right. This fear was – in political terms – ground enough for Louis to divorce Eleanor. Henry likewise was anxious for a son to secure the succession, even though the customs in

2 R. Fawtier, *The Capetian Kings of France: Monarchy and Nation 987–1328*, trans. L. Butler and R. J. Adam (London, 1960), p. 6.

3 *Gesta Regis Henrici Secundi*, ed. W. Stubbs, RS 49, 2 vols. (London, 1867), I, xiii.

England and Normandy were more relaxed, and his mother had indeed claimed the throne in her own right. The brief paragraph on the divorce in the later chronicle reminds us of the matters of state that lay behind Eleanor's marriages. Other writers were to take a very different view.

From her marriage until 1173, Eleanor scarcely figures in Howden's chronicles. With her re-entry into politics in that year, as instigator of her son's rebellion, she is briefly the centre of attention, but disappears at once into the obscurity of her prison. After the death of his eldest son Henry the young king, Henry II attempted to make peace with his surviving sons, and Eleanor's presence at the Christmas court at which the reconciliation took place is noted. Her release in 1185 in an attempt to curb Richard's independence by forcing him to hand over Aquitaine to his mother is another official occasion; but it is not until her final release on the death of Henry in 1189 that she becomes a major figure in the narrative. It is she who secures England for Richard on his father's death, and there is the briefest acknowledgement of her personal history in the note that she freed many of those imprisoned by Henry. Howden reports – and he could have heard her say it – that she knew herself how unpleasant prisons were, and how a most cheerful (*jocundissimam*) lifting of the spirits accompanied release from prison.

Roger of Howden accompanied Richard on crusade, and he tells us of Eleanor's travels to Spain and Sicily in order to arrange Richard's marriage to Berengaria of Navarre. Eleanor's activities in England, defending Richard's interests after his capture on his way back from crusade, are described; but once she withdraws from the world of government, we learn nothing more, partly because Howden himself seems to have been out of England, on business at the papal court, on his return from crusade. As a result, her death is not even noted.

The next guest at our medieval El Vino's has not come far: Ralph of Diss, or Diceto, is a canon of St Paul's, a few hundred yards away. Being based in London, he has close contacts with Henry's court, though he does not hold an official position. As a writer, he is erudite, attempting to provide a universal history for English readers, but he is also more vivid than Howden. Ralph of Diss travelled south, for he seems to have known southern France personally. His chronicle includes a detailed description of the town of Angers, and he follows this with an account of the customs of the people of Aquitaine, as if these were recollections of a journey. Alas, he does not help us with Eleanor, who is simply a cypher in the genealogy of the Angevin royal family for most of his chronicle, as her divorce, remarriage and the birth of her children are recorded in one-line entries. Only when she emerges from prison in 1189, when her third son, Richard, inherits the throne, is there the barest comment: he quotes a line from the *Prophecies of Merlin*, written some fifty years earlier, to the effect that 'the eagle of the broken covenant shall rejoice in her third nesting'.[4] He briefly notes her political activity in Richard's absence, but tells us nothing about his view of her.

Roger of Howden and Ralph of Diss were in London regularly, and it is easy to underestimate the degree to which medieval people travelled. Henry himself was

[4] Geoffrey of Monmouth, *The History of the Kings of Britain*, trans. L. Thorpe (Harmondsworth, 1966), p. 174.

a prodigious, restless traveller, and Eleanor in her seventies went from England to Navarre, on to Sicily and home by way of Rome in the space of a year. Travellers often relied on the hospitality of monasteries, and such men could have ridden from the London cookshop to Canterbury in a day, on the way to Henry's domains on the Continent. Thus the monks of Canterbury, at the heart of the religious administration of England, were well placed to obtain information about events in both England and Normandy. Gervase of Canterbury, like most monastic chroniclers, is concerned as much about the affairs of Christ Church as the wider sweep of politics, but he is nonetheless a valuable witness. His information has something of the flavour of travellers' tales, the gossip recounted when a passing magnate enjoyed the abbey's hospitality. In contrast to Howden's dry calculation of the dynastic implications of Eleanor's divorce, he offers an account that relates the episode to the character of those involved. He regards the divorce as obtained by 'much labour and artificial oaths',[5] and tells us that there was a quarrel between Louis and Eleanor 'over something which happened on their pilgrimage, about which it is better to be silent',[6] which led to the divorce. He does not seem to regard it as motivated by Eleanor's failure to bear a son. He then tells us that Eleanor sent messengers secretly to Henry telling him that she was free to marry, and reports that 'it was said that she had brought about the contrived divorce by her ingenuity'.[7] Henry hastened to meet her and the desired marriage quickly took place.

Gervase notes that in 1154 Eleanor was crowned at the same time as Henry; this was by no means always the case. His subsequent entries record the birth of children and their marriages, until Eleanor's involvement in her sons' revolt. Here again Gervase gives details that sound like something he has been told: we learn that she disguised herself as a man to follow her sons, and was captured, while they escaped. Gervase, who may have met Eleanor in the 1190s, comments that she was a prudent enough woman, of very noble birth, but – and this may well be monkish prejudice – she was inconstant (*instabilis*). In 1185, he claims that it was at the petition of Baldwin, archbishop of Canterbury, that Eleanor was released; though Gervase may have exaggerated the influence of Canterbury in that decision.

Our traveller might well have found hospitality on the other side of the Channel at the great abbey at Mont-Saint-Michel, particularly if he landed at Cherbourg. Mont-Saint-Michel was visited regularly by the dukes of Normandy, and for most of Henry's reign the abbot was Robert of Torigni, who had already begun to write history before he became head of the abbey. He was in touch with many important figures, and met Henry and Eleanor on a number of occasions: he was sponsor to Eleanor's second daughter at her baptism at Domfront in 1161. He also met Louis of France when he came on pilgrimage to Mont-Saint-Michel in Henry's company. He is very favourably inclined towards Henry, who gave generously to the abbey. As a historian, he is particularly interested in diplomatic

5 Gervase of Canterbury, *Historical Works*, ed. W. Stubbs, RS 73, 2 vols. (London, 1879–80), I, 149.

6 *Ibid.*

7 *Ibid.*

affairs, treaties and alliances and the shifting balance of power between kingdoms.

What he records, however, is a little like a visitor's book: of his twenty or so entries relating to the queen, half are simply notes of her presence in Normandy or her travels to and from the duchy, such as the occasions when the royal Christmas court was held at Cherbourg, Falaise or Le Mans and both king and queen were present. His perspective is in this respect very local, rather as a regional newspaper today will still give good coverage to a royal visit. Even when Eleanor is taken under guard to England in 1173, he makes no comment on her status as a captive, despite the fact that he had briefly noted her rebellion one year earlier. He died in 1185, before Eleanor's release from captivity.

Robert's account of Eleanor's divorce from Louis is very formal, and notes only the church ritual involved: he says that a quarrel had arisen between them, and 'in Lent, at Beaugency, having been given the sacrament in the presence of the archbishops and bishops, they were separated on the authority of the Christian Church because of their consanguinity'.[8] As to her marriage to Henry, he hedges his bets: Henry married her either *repentino*, on the spur of the moment, or *praemeditato consilio*, according to a pre-arranged plan. Evidently different versions of the story were in circulation already.

Other monasteries far from the centres of power also had their historians, and they too show us how news travelled outside the capital and court. William, canon of the priory at Newburgh in Yorkshire, wrote his history at the request of the Cistercian abbot of Rievaulx: the Cistercians themselves were forbidden to undertake such literary activity. William read widely, and compiled the early part of his work from a number of written sources, as well as from conversations. As to the latter, he names his informants in many cases, and we can see him at work, questioning visitors and gleaning any stories that are relevant to his book, including anything on the supernatural, which was evidently one of his interests. He almost certainly knew and used Roger of Howden's work, and he also had access to the newsletters giving an account of major events, particularly in wartime, an innovation that Richard I used to keep royal officials and bishops in the provinces informed of what was happening. These become a regular source for chronicle entries, often being copied in their entirety; William, however, prefers to abstract them.

He has relatively little to say about Eleanor, but he does provide some new information, of exactly the type that might come from a conversation with a traveller. Although he is writing forty years after the event, his account of Eleanor's divorce is interesting, as it does not rely obviously on previous writers, but seems to reflect what was said about Eleanor in the 1190s. In his version, which may derive in part from William of Tyre,[9] Eleanor's beauty overwhelms Louis, and when he declares his intention of setting out on crusade, she says that she will not be left at home, but intends to set out for battle in his company. He is unable to resist her request, but because of her example, many other nobles took

8 Robert of Torigni, *Chronicle*, in *Chronicles of the Reigns of Stephen, Henry II, and Richard I*, ed. R. Howlett, RS 82, 4 vols. (London, 1884–89), IV, 164.

9 See pp. 21–2 below.

their wives with them, and a multitude of women occupied the chaste Christian castles in the East, causing a scandal. On the return of the royal couple to France, their initial passion gradually cooled, and a divorce was discussed; Newburgh reports that 'she was greatly offended by the king's strict morals, and pleaded that she had married a monk, not a king'.[10] It was also said that she had in mind marriage to the duke of Normandy, and that it was she who had thought up and obtained the divorce. After judgement was pronounced, she married the duke of Normandy almost in secret, lest anyone prevent the marriage.

This was written in Eleanor's lifetime, in 1196–98, when she had retired to the abbey of Fontevraud, but that does not necessarily give the account authority; it is more interesting in that it shows how she had become an almost legendary figure in her own lifetime. Her supposed insistence on going to war was later to be embroidered into a parade on horseback in which she and her companions dressed as Amazons, and the insistence on the effect of her beauty on Louis was to be the cue for endless romantic daydreams on the part of her biographers. But after this opening scene, Eleanor all but disappears from view; we learn only that she was behind her sons' flight to the French court in 1173, and that she played some part in government in Richard's absence. Perhaps there were no travellers with good tales to tell about her later years; perhaps William simply did not realize the extent of her political influence, though if he used Howden's work he could scarcely have failed to do so.

Good stories and an often highly imaginative approach are even more prominent in the work of Richard of Devizes. Richard was a monk at St Swithun's, Winchester, a Benedictine house that had perhaps become somewhat worldly in outlook, and recent studies of his chronicle have noted strong similarities with contemporary romances. It is very much a literary exercise, even if its subject is ostensibly history; he is rhetorical, sarcastic and dramatic, widely read in the classics, and his book does not really resemble any of the other historical works we have so far discussed. I suspect that the writing of a chronicle was for him a substitute for more secular literary ambitions, which, as a monk, he hesitated to indulge. But he can be discreet, and because we have what is almost certainly his original manuscript, we can watch him at work. He mentions Eleanor incidentally a couple of times in the early pages of his book, but when she brings Berengaria of Navarre from Spain to marry Richard, she steps into the limelight for a moment, and he has this to say:

> Queen Eleanor, an incomparable woman, beautiful yet virtuous, powerful yet gentle, humble yet keen-witted, qualities which are most rarely found in a woman, who had lived long enough to have had two kings as hushands and two kings as sons, still tireless in all labours, at whose ability her age might marvel, brought with her the daughter of the king of the Navarrese . . .[11]

Against this entry, in the margin, emphasized by a penwork border, he writes:

10 William of Newburgh, *Historia Rerum Anglicarum*, in *Chronicles of the Reigns of Stephen, Henry II, and Richard I*, I, 92–3.

11 Richard of Devizes, *Chronicle*, ed. and trans. J. T. Appleby (London, 1963), p. 25.

> Many know what I would that none of us knew. This same queen, during the time of her first husband, was at Jerusalem. Let no one say any more about it.[12]

But he cannot leave the matter be; he adds, outside the border, as a separate paragraph:

> I too know it well. Be silent!

Richard of Devizes, who may well have seen Eleanor at the council of Winchester in 1191, clearly admired her, and was reluctant to discuss the stories about her behaviour on crusade, partly because his chronicle has Richard as its hero, and Eleanor's role is as the hero's mother; anything that detracts from her detracts also from Richard. He offers us another portrait of her, in the conventional aspect of the lady having pity on her subjects, though this may have been genuine enough, if we remember her comment when she liberated prisoners at the death of Henry. In 1192, he adds another marginal note:

> That matron, worthy of being mentioned so many times, Queen Eleanor, was visiting some cottages that were part of her dower, in the diocese of Ely. There came before her from all the villages and hamlets, wherever she went, men with women and children, not all of the lowest orders, a people weeping and pitiful, with bare feet, unwashed clothes, and unkempt hair. They spoke by their tears, for their grief was so great that they could not speak. There was no need for an interpreter, for more than what they wanted to say could be read on the open page [of their faces].[13]

Eleanor discovers the cause of their grief: the bishopric of Ely is under interdict because of a dispute between its bishop and the archbishop of Rouen, and no church services can be held. The dead lie unburied in the fields, and on learning of this the queen hastens to London, where she brings about a reconciliation between the quarrelling clerics. Of the deeper political issues behind the excommunication of the bishop, better known as William Longchamp, chancellor of England, we learn nothing.

Even if royal newsletters were not yet commonplace, there is some evidence that newsletters circulated between monasteries. These may have originated in letters concerning the affairs of the individual monastic orders, but seem to have broadened in scope to take in political and other news. Another chronicler whom we can watch at work is Ralph of Coggeshall; a manuscript in the British Library looks very like his first draft, and once again the margins are extensively used. We can see from the handwriting that some groups of items have been added as marginalia at different places in the text, evidently as some new source of information became available. The first part of his chronicle is a brief set of annals, and it is only after 1187 that we learn more about Eleanor than simply the genealogical notices of marriage and birth of her children. But these entries are only concerned with the great events of government, Eleanor's late-flowering political career, and add nothing to our assessment of her character.

12 *Ibid.*, pp. 25–6.
13 *Ibid.*, p. 59.

*

So far, we have been looking at Eleanor through Anglo-Norman eyes; but until her divorce she had lived in France and visited the Holy Land. The gossip in our London cookshop might not have reached as far afield as this, but there was the same network of monasteries and travellers in France. There are intriguing touches in the account of Lambert of Wattrelos, a monk of Cambrai, who made a note of the divorce of Eleanor and Louis; he tells us that he was writing the chronicle more or less simultaneously with the events he records, so this is valuable testimony. According to him, Louis picked a childish (*puerilis*) quarrel with Eleanor, which lasted from the time when they were on crusade until the year of the divorce. Louis then imprudently gathered 'certain people of the kingdom', told them his private thoughts, and following their ill-advised counsel, forswore her and completely deserted her. Eleanor, whom Lambert describes as *moesta*, grieved, at this news, at once returned to her own lands, where she soon married Henry.[14] Louis, furious at his own political miscalculation, launched an attack on Henry's lands, though peace was soon made. Cambrai was a wealthy self-governing merchant city, not over-friendly to the kings of France, and Lambert's story may reflect the general attitude of the townspeople to the French monarchy. He also confirms Eleanor's reputation for beauty, calling her *perpulcra*, very lovely.

We also find local information again, in the Chronicle of Tours, which describes Eleanor's journey south as a desperate flight, in which she had to avoid capture by both Theobald of Blois and by Geoffrey of Anjou, Henry's younger brother. Chroniclers further afield were only interested in the shock caused by her marriage to Henry Plantagenet, if indeed they ever knew the story of her escape from two would-be suitors.

If Lambert is sure that the blame for the divorce lay with Louis, we get a very different account from the one historian from Palestine who describes the key episode in Antioch that undoubtedly lay at the heart of the dispute. This is William, archbishop of Tyre, who held high office in the service of the kings of Jerusalem from the 1160s onwards. Although his knowledge of the doings of Eleanor and Louis in the East could well have come from eye-witnesses, it is at a distance, and second-hand. This is what he has to say of the events of 1147:

> For many days Raymond, prince of Antioch, had eagerly awaited the arrival of the king of the Franks . . . [for he] had conceived the idea that by his aid he might be able to enlarge the principality of Antioch. With this in mind, therefore, even before the king started on the pilgrimage, the prince had sent to him a large store of noble gifts and treasures of great price in the hope of winning his favor. He also counted greatly on the interest of the queen with the lord king; for she had been the king's inseparable companion on his pilgrimage. She was Raymond's niece, the eldest daughter of Count William of Poitou, his brother.[15]

14 Lambert of Wattrelos, 'Annales Cameracenses', *MGH SS*, XVI, 522.

15 William of Tyre, *A History of Deeds Done Beyond the Sea*, trans. E. A. Babcock and A. C. Krey, 2 vols. (New York, 1943), II, 179.

Raymond attempts, by gifts and arguments, to persuade Louis to help him to conquer the neighbouring cities:

> Raymond had already more than once approached the king privately in regard to the plans which he had in mind. . . . The king, however, ardently desired to go to Jerusalem to fulfil his vows, and his determination was irrevocable. When Raymond found that he could not induce the king to join him, his attitude changed. Frustrated in his ambitious designs, he began to hate the king's ways; he openly plotted against him and took means to do him injury. He resolved also to deprive him of his wife, either by force or by secret intrigue. The queen readily assented to this design, for she was a foolish woman. Her conduct before and after this time showed her to be, as we have said, far from circumspect. Contrary to her royal dignity, she disregarded her marriage vows and was unfaithful to her husband. As soon as the king discovered these plots, he took means to provide for his life and safety by anticipating the designs of the prince. By the advice of his chief nobles, he hastened his departure and secretly left Antioch with his people. . . His coming had been attended with pomp and glory; but fortune is fickle, and his departure was ignominious.
>
> Some people attribute this outcome to the king's own base conduct. They maintain that he received his just deserts because he did not accede to the request of a great prince from whom he and his followers had received kind treatment. This is of especial interest, because these persons constantly affirm that if the king would have devoted himself to that work, one or more of the above-named cities might easily have been taken.[16]

This all sounds very persuasive and detailed, but there are undercurrents, which hint that all is not what it seems: notice that William of Tyre talks of Eleanor's conduct 'before and after this time', and his views may have been coloured by the subsequent divorce, because he was writing at least twenty years later. And he makes it clear that there are other versions of the story in circulation, in which Louis is more to blame than Eleanor. We shall return to this crucial account later.

Eleanor, so far, has had few supporters; it is a change to read the splendid piece of rhetoric, studded with biblical echoes and sprinkled with allusions to the supposed prophecies of Merlin, penned by a monk in Poitiers soon after the news of Eleanor's capture in 1173 reached that city, which was the centre of her own government in south-west France. It paints a picture of Eleanor as a wronged captive, deprived of her companions and advisers, and urges her to escape to her loyal subjects in the south:

> Tell me, o eagle of the two heads, where wert thou when thy nestlings flew from their nest and dared to raise their talons against the king of the north? For thou hast stirred them up, so we have heard, to bring sore affliction on their father. Therefore hast thou been removed from thy land and led into a country which thou knewest not. The great ones of thy lands have betrayed thee with soft words. Thy harp also is turned to mourning, and thy organ into the voice of them that weep. Once tender and delicate, thou didst enjoy a royal freedom, thou wert surfeited with riches, young girls surrounded thee playing on the

16 *Ibid.*, II, 180.

> tambourine and the harp, singing pleasant songs. . . . Why dost thou now trouble thy heart with daily tears? Return, o captive, return to thy cities, if thou mayest; else weep with King David and say: 'Woe is me, that I sojourn in Mesech, that I dwell in the tents of Kedar!', for thou livest among an unknown and coarse people. Weep again and always, and say: 'My tears have been my meat day and night', while they continually say unto thee, 'Where are thy servants? Where are thy counsellors?' Cry aloud, spare not, lift up thy voice like a trumpet, that thy children may hear it. For the day draws nigh when they shall set thee free and thou shalt return to thy lands.[17]

This is Eleanor as an idealized symbol of the lost independence of Aquitaine, a kind of *princesse lointaine* for whom her people long. It may tell us more about the writer than the subject, but it is nonetheless an essential part of her image: divorced, imprisoned and cut off from political life, she was nonetheless the ruler of Aquitaine, and even Henry could not revoke her grant of those lands to her son Richard. He had to release her from captivity to accomplish this in 1185.

Our next group of witnesses should be able to show us something of Eleanor as a person, because they all knew her, either as clerics, courtiers or members of her entourage. The first of these, whose testimony we have at second-hand, would not, I think, have been found in a public cookshop in London, however. For this story comes from one of the earliest biographers of St Bernard, leading light of the Cistercian order and a hugely influential figure in the political and philosophical world of twelfth-century France. The writer could only have learnt of the conversation that he reports from Bernard or Eleanor themselves. Bernard was trying to make peace between Louis and Theobald of Blois in 1144, and Eleanor had set herself against this. He tried to persuade her to withdraw her opposition, and in the course of the conversation, she complained of the fact that she was still childless. Bernard proposed a deal: if she changed her mind, he would pray for her. The saint's reputation was such that Eleanor accepted, and she duly bore a daughter a little over a year later.

If St Bernard or his biographer were not to be found at our London table, John of Salisbury, one of the great scholars of the twelfth century, might well have been present, though he spent much of his life on the Continent. It is our good fortune that he was at the court of Pope Eugenius III when Louis and Eleanor visited Rome on their way home from Jerusalem in October 1149, the wounds of their recent quarrel still evidently festering. John's discreet evidence as to the nature of the quarrel is obviously derived from sources in the French royal entourage, but it is clear that there were already factions forming for and against the queen. Louis had arrived at Antioch in Syria with his army in disorder, and Raymond of Antioch's hospitality had been a welcome respite from the arduous march to Jerusalem. John describes the sequel:

> But whilst they remained there to console, heal and revive the survivors from the wreck of the army, the attentions paid by the prince to the queen, and his constant, indeed almost continuous, conversation with her, aroused the king's

17 Continuator of Richard le Poitevin, *RHGF*, XII, 420.

> suspicions. These were greatly strengthened when the queen wished to remain behind, although the king was preparing to leave, and the prince made every effort to keep her, if the king would give his consent. And when the king made haste to tear her away, she mentioned their kinship, saying that it was not lawful for them to remain together as man and wife, since they were related in the fourth and fifth degrees. Even before their departure a rumour to that effect had been heard in France, where the late Bartholomew bishop of Laon had calculated the degrees of kinship; but it was not certain whether the reckoning was true or false. At this the king was deeply moved; and although he loved the queen almost beyond reason he consented to divorce her if his counsellors and the French nobility would allow it. There was one knight amongst the king's secretaries, called Thierry Galeran, a eunuch whom the queen had always hated and mocked, but who was faithful and had the king's ear like his father's before him. He boldly persuaded the king not to suffer her to dally longer at Antioch, both because 'guilt under kinship's guise could lie concealed',[18] and because it would be a lasting shame to the kingdom of the Franks if in addition to all the other disasters it was reported that the king had been deserted by his wife, or robbed of her. So he argued, either because he hated the queen or because he really believed it, moved perchance by widespread rumour. In consequence, she was torn away and forced to leave for Jerusalem with the king; and, their mutual anger growing greater, the wound remained, hide it as best they might.[19]

On their arrival at the papal court, Eugenius, evidently forewarned of all this

> reconciled the king and queen, after hearing severally the accounts each gave of the estrangement begun at Antioch, and forbade any future mention of their consanguinity: confirming their marriage, both orally and in writing, he commanded under pain of anathema, that no word should be spoken against it and that it should not be dissolved under any pretext whatever. This ruling plainly delighted the king, for he loved the queen passionately, in an almost childish way. The pope made them sleep in the same bed, which he had had decked with priceless hangings of his own; and daily during their brief visit he strove by friendly converse to restore love between them.[20]

John of Salisbury says at the outset of his book that 'I shall, by the help of God, write nothing but what I myself have seen and heard and know to be true, or have on good authority from the testimony or writings of reliable men'; and his modern editors have generally agreed that he achieved his aim. It is easy to read into his account more criticism of Eleanor than is actually there; what he is saying is that the queen may have been indiscreet in her liking for her uncle's company, but that the accusations against her were from a very hostile source. Louis is shown as pliable and unsure of himself, easily swayed by advisers, and Eleanor as headstrong and capable of bearing a grudge. For once, for a moment, we may have caught a real glimpse of our elusive central character.

By contrast with the sober John of Salisbury, Gerald of Wales and his friend

18 Ovid, *Heroides*, iv.38.

19 John of Salisbury, *Historia Pontificalis*, ed. and trans. M. Chibnall (Edinburgh, 1956), p. 52.

20 *Ibid.*, p. 54.

Walter Map would have been entirely at home in a London tavern, and a circle of fascinated listeners would have soon gathered round this fiery Welshman and his companion from the English side of the Marches. Gerald was as good a hater as one could wish to find. Descended from the Welsh princess Nest, as beautiful and controversial as Eleanor herself, he was an ardent advocate of all things Welsh, and attempted to have the see of St David's, to which he was elected in 1199, raised to an archbishopric; Eleanor confirmed his election, but the king vetoed the appointment. He had a particular grudge against the whole Angevin brood after his disappointment over the bishopric. His letters and autobiography are self-justifying, but he is an eloquent and powerful writer, and his vitriolic portrait of Henry II is all the more persuasive because of his skill with words. He it is who makes the most damning accusations about Eleanor: if there had been libel lawyers in the twelfth century, they would have made their fortune from his soberly entitled book called *On the Instruction of a Prince*, in which Henry and his family are basically held up as an example of how not to rule. He accuses Henry of being a womanizer; after the queen was incarcerated in 1174, he took Rosamund Clifford as his mistress, and publicly flaunted his relationship with her. Of Eleanor he has even worse things to say: she was seduced, according to him, by Geoffrey of Anjou, Henry's father, who warned his son on several occasions not to marry her, because he had slept with her himself. And he demands as a parting shot, 'How could a fortunate generation spring from such a coupling?'[21]

Walter Map simply confirms this gossip for us. He is, by the way, one of the few people for whom Gerald of Wales has a good word to say. He too had Welsh blood, but preferred to take the Norman side. His book *On the Trifles of the Court* is a lightweight mixture of reminiscence, marvellous stories and pen-portraits of the court and its life: the latter, and his depiction of Henry, bring the king and his world vividly to life. Sadly, he does not have much to add to Gerald's gossip about Eleanor, for he gives us much the same story:

> Eleanor, the Queen of France, cast glances of unholy love on Henry, son of Matilda. She was the wife of that most pious King Louis, but she managed to secure an unlawful divorce and married Henry, and this in spite of the charge secretly made against her that she had shared Louis's bed with Henry's father Geoffrey. Support for this charge is found in the circumstance that their offspring was 'cut off on the steps of the throne' and came to nothing.[22]

William FitzStephen tells us that all ranks of society frequented our cookshop, including knights; and if Gerald of Wales would have held us by his invective, whether we liked it or not, it would have been a pleasure to meet William Marshal. The Marshal is one of the very few knights for whom an autobiography survives, and it is evident that he regarded Eleanor with great affection. William Marshal dictated his story to a minstrel in his last years, and it gives us a unique view of chivalric life. William's career was to some extent made in Eleanor's service. In 1168, his uncle, Patrick earl of Salisbury, had been entrusted with

21 Gerald of Wales, *De Principis Instructione Liber*, in *Opera*, ed. J. S. Brewer, J. F. Dimock and G. F. Warner, RS 21, 8 vols. (London, 1861–91), VIII, 300.

22 Walter Map, *De Nugis Curialium*, trans. F. Tupper and M. Bladen Ogle (London, 1924), p. 297.

safeguarding the queen as she made her way through territory in the hands of the rebel lord of Lusignan; they were ambushed, Patrick was killed, and William, after a fierce fight, was captured. The queen, however, escaped, and ransomed William, showering gifts of horses, armour and money on him when he was released.

He was later tutor in arms to the younger Henry, and remained loyal to him during his rebellion against his father. At the young king's death William took on the crusading vow made by the dying man. When he returned to England after the elder Henry's death, he found Eleanor freed, and discreetly alludes to her captivity by saying that 'she was more at ease than she was accustomed to be'. Like Eleanor, his career lay in high politics from then on, and we see Eleanor in a different guise, as lady of England, in the later pages of his biography.

Most, if not all, the major figures who wrote about Eleanor in the twelfth century have now had their say. It is time to analyse what we have heard from them, and to assess how these chroniclers and writers of memoirs, the media of the day, viewed Eleanor. It is at best a distant view: Antonia Gransden has called this the 'golden age of historiography in England', but this can only be true relative to what had gone before. Good historiography does not mean good biography; and if there is a new sense of the individual in the air, it scarcely affects our writers. This development of the sense of the individual is a striking feature of twelfth-century civilization in the West; at its most extreme we see it in the cult of chivalry, with its emphasis on individual prowess, as typified by the biography of William Marshal.

Little of this new attitude comes through to the chroniclers. We have seen how in their eyes, at the simplest level, Eleanor is part of the royal genealogy, wife in turn of the kings of France and England, a pawn in a male world, whose duty is to provide heirs. Her failure to produce a male heir for Louis is probably the real reason behind her divorce; serial marriage in quest of a male heir is so common in medieval royal biographies as to pass almost without comment. This aspect of her life is most prominent in the chroniclers remote from the centre of affairs. Little more comes to their ears about Eleanor than the birth or marriage of her children: this is the dry world of the court circular.

At the next level, she is a focal point of the gossip and intrigues at court, renowned for her beauty, variously judged as frivolous, light-headed and wanton. Here we have to tread with caution: there is a very good case to be made that most, if not all, of the gossip about her stems from the French court after her divorce, an attempt by those loyal to Louis to justify the incredible political folly of his actions. At a stroke, Louis handed half his domains to his most powerful vassal, soon to become a king in his own right. The stories about her affairs with the prince of Antioch or the count of Anjou, or even her future husband Henry Plantagenet, are therefore probably to be discounted. Or am I perhaps falling into the same trap, in a different form, of reading twelfth-century history in twenty-first-century terms? I think not: propaganda was understood in the twelfth century better than the novel idea of romantic love. I am aware that this is a lenient reading, which, in Professor Shippey's splendid phrase, declares that there is no smoke without smoke.

But I think that there is a much more important piece of information about Eleanor to be gleaned from the stories of the quarrel in Antioch. The key to this lies in the queen's conversation with St Bernard. Eleanor is shown as taking a determined political stance over Theobald of Blois, and the saint has to resort to spiritual bribery, if you like, to dissuade her. The same political element may well be present in her dealings with Raymond of Antioch. Steven Runciman, in his magisterial history of the crusades, is positive about this:

> Queen Eleanor was far more intelligent than her husband. She saw at once the wisdom of Raymond's scheme; but her passionate and outspoken support of her uncle only roused Louis's jealousy.[23]

In other words, Eleanor's stance was not romantic but realistic, not personal but political. This reading would tie in well with the third aspect of Eleanor that comes down to us, on which I have perhaps dwelt too little: it is her unspectacular but patient work to preserve the peace in England in Richard's absence, and after his captivity, to raise his ransom.

My final piece of evidence is not Eleanor as viewed by the media, but Eleanor using the media for her own purposes. In 1191, she wrote a letter to the pope, whom she knew personally, pleading for his assistance in obtaining the release of Richard from captivity. It begins with an extraordinarily striking phrase, much beloved of romantic biographers of Eleanor, but never, as far as I know, closely analysed by scholars. Instead of the usual preamble, 'Eleanor, by the grace of God, queen of England', she begins, 'Eleanor, in the wrath of God, queen of England'.[24] Royal letters were as a matter of course written by trained clerks, though rarely with such style. *Ira dei* is a biblical echo, and the letter could have been penned for her by one of the great letter writers of the age, Peter of Blois. This is Eleanor manipulating the media, presenting herself as a forlorn figure worthy of the utmost sympathy, whether she is doing so directly or indirectly. For we need to ask what the relationship between the queen and the writer of her letter might have been. Was it that between a modern president and his speechwriter, coining a soundbite that echoes round the world within hours? Perhaps; but no president will deliver a speech that does not reflect something of his own feelings, and in that *ira dei* I like to think that we have either Eleanor's own words or the words of someone who captured her feelings exactly.

So in the end I have fallen neatly into the trap of everyone who writes about Eleanor, of fantasizing gently about a clearly outstanding and extraordinary character. Eleanor lies under the grey vaults of the abbey church of Fontevraud; her austere effigy holds a stone book, a book that has been replaced at least once, and that is blank. I hope I have offered a possible text for those unwritten leaves of her life.

23 S. Runciman, *A History of the Crusades*, 3 vols. (Harmondsworth, 1978), II, 279.

24 Thomas Rymer, *Foedera, Conventiones, Litterae, et Acta Publica*, ed. A. Clarke and F. Holbrooke, 7 vols. (London, 1816–69), I:i, 56.

Eleanor of Aquitaine, the Coronation Rite of the Duke of Aquitaine and the Cult of Saint Martial of Limoges[1]

DANIEL F. CALLAHAN

The twelfth-century Limousin chronicler Geoffrey of Vigeois included in his regional chronicle a brief account of the investiture ceremony in which the young Richard the Lionheart in June 1172 became duke of Aquitaine. According to Geoffrey,

> King Henry gave to Richard by the will of his mother Eleanor the duchy of Aquitaine. First at Saint-Hilaire of Poitiers on the Sunday after Pentecost, according to custom, he was raised onto the seat of the abbot [traditionally the counts of Poitou were the abbots of the house of Saint-Hilaire]; but also he was offered by Bishops Bertram of Bordeaux and John of Poitiers a lance with a banner. Then Richard, coming to Limoges, was received into the city in a procession, was adorned with the ring of Saint Valerie [who was venerated as the first martyr of Aquitaine] and was proclaimed new duke by all.[2]

Later, probably in that century, there was inserted into a manuscript of the cathedral chapter of Saint-Etienne of Limoges an *ordo* of ceremonies to be used at the inauguration of the dukes of Aquitaine.[3] Appended to it in the early thirteenth century was a commentary on this *ordo*.[4] Poitiers no longer has a place in

1 A much earlier version of this chapter was presented at the Fifteenth International Congress on Medieval Studies at Western Michigan University in 1980. I wish to thank Professor Elizabeth A. R. Brown for her comments on that paper and for the subsequent assistance of her articles on Eleanor of Aquitaine in helping me think through this material in greater depth.

2 Geoffrey of Vigeois, 'Chronica', Bk 1 c. 37, *RHGF*, XII, 442–3. 'Tempore illo Rex Henricus senior filio Richardo ex voluntate matris Aquitanorum tradidit Ducatum. Post haec apud S. Hilarium Pictavis Dominica post Pentecosten, juxta consuetudinem, in Abbatis sedem elevatur: sed a Bertramno Burdegalensi et Joanne Pictavensi Praesulibus lancea ei cum vexillo praebetur. . . . Procedenti tempore Richardus Lemovicas veniens, in urbe cum processione suscipitur, annulo S. Valeriae decoratur, novusque Dux ab omnibus proclamatur.' See the comments on this ceremony in J. Gillingham, *Richard I* (New Haven and London, 1999), p. 40.

3 On this insertion, see the *RHGF* edition [as above], p. 442 n. b. Besly edited it from a manuscript of Saint-Etienne of Limoges. See A. Richard, *Histoire des comtes de Poitou 778–1204*, 2 vols. (Paris, 1903), II, 183.

4 Richard, *Histoire des comtes*, II, 152–3, esp. p. 153 n. 1.

the rite for everything is now performed at Limoges. The new duke was to receive a mantle of silk, a small crown – similar, it would seem, to that used in a comparable rite employed at Rouen for the duke of Normandy in 1199 – the ducal banner, sword and spurs, all in addition to the ring of Saint Valerie.[5] As Schramm pointed out, the rite is based on 'the Roman, that is the "German", ordo fitted to local conditions and omitting the specifically royal privileges like anointing'.[6] It is important to note that the new duke was to swear to protect the church of Limoges as his predecessors had done. In the commentary on the *ordo* there is a reference to the purported first dukes of Aquitaine living in the first century and ruling from Limoges.[7] The commentator wishes to emphasize that the new duke is to follow in the traditions established by the first.

Yet the dukes of Aquitaine, in fact, never had their principal center in Limoges, nor had they always been particularly interested in the affairs of the Limousin church. Long before the Plantagenets arrived in Aquitaine as rulers, the dukes had great trouble controlling the lords of the Limousin, and more often than not they had to be content with only nominal recognition of their ducal authority.[8] Long before the Limousin became a battle stage for the struggles between Henry II and his sons in the 1170s and 1180s, the lords of the Limousin, including the viscount of Limoges, had pursued their independent ways.[9] Louis VII as duke of Aquitaine while married to Eleanor had problems with the region.[10] Some warriors from the Limousin had joined their sovereign on the Second Crusade, but there was considerably less enthusiasm for the enterprise in the region than there had been for the First Crusade.[11] Henry II experienced the enmity of these inhabitants on his first visit in 1152 when a fight broke out in Limoges between the townspeople and some of the men of Henry's entourage.[12] As punishment, the new duke destroyed the walls of the *castrum*. Moreover, he would have to enter the region on a number of occasions during his life to quell uprisings.[13] Richard, in turn, spent much time as ducal leader fighting the lords of

5 See the comments of P. Schramm on this *ordo* in *A History of the English Coronation* (Oxford, 1937), pp. 48–9.

6 *Ibid*., p. 49.

7 See Richard, *Histoire des comtes*, II, 151–3 for the influence of the new *vita* of St Valerie on these developments.

8 Still of great value are the two volumes of Alfred Richard. These works should be used in conjunction with the recent pieces of Jane Martindale as gathered in the collection of her essays entitled *Status, Authority and Regional Power: Aquitaine and France, 9th to 12th Centuries* (Aldershot, 1997).

9 Remaining basic are the articles of S. Painter, 'Castellans of the Plain of Poitou in the Eleventh and Twelfth Centuries' and 'The Lords of Lusignan in the Eleventh and Twelfth Centuries', in *Feudalism and Liberty: Articles and Addresses of Sidney Painter*, ed. F. A. Cazel, Jr (Baltimore, 1961), pp. 17–89.

10 Richard, *Histoire des comtes*, II, 151–3.

11 See E.-R. Labande, 'Dans l'Empire Plantagenêt', ch. 5 of *Histoire du Poitou, du Limousin et des Pays Charentais*, ed. E.-R. Labande (Toulouse, 1976), p. 134. For the participation of individuals from the Limousin on the First Crusade, M. G. Bull, *Knightly Piety and the Lay Response to the First Crusade: The Limousin and Gascony, c.970–1130* (Oxford, 1993).

12 Geoffrey of Vigeois, 'Chronica', Bk 1 c. 54, *RHGF*, XII, 438.

13 See esp. W. L. Warren, *Henry II* (Berkeley and Los Angeles, 1973), pp. 146, 589–93.

the Limousin. It was there in 1199 that he lost his life.[14] The region's reputation for turbulence and lack of affection for the dukes of Aquitaine was without question deserved.

Yet even with this turmoil and animosity as a background, some in Limoges clearly sought identification with the duke. This chapter will examine some of the principal means employed by the churchmen of Limoges in seeking to achieve this objective and some of the reasons why this connection served Henry, Eleanor and Richard so well.

One of the principal means of identification between Limoges and the dukes of Aquitaine came from what is called the Aurelian legend.[15] This tale of St Martial, the first bishop of Limoges, purportedly by his disciple and episcopal successor Aurelian, appeared in the mid to late tenth century. It replaced a Carolingian *vita* that had made Martial a disciple of St Peter and a missionary to Gaul in the first century.[16] In fact, according to Gregory of Tours, Martial was one of a number of missionaries, including St Denis, sent from Rome in the third century.[17] The Aurelian *vita* greatly expanded the role of Martial in Gaul and made him an immediate disciple of Christ. By the early eleventh century this *vita* was amplified further by the monk Adhemar of Chabannes to make Martial an apostle of Christ sent by God to convert all of Gaul.[18]

Just as the role of the saint grows in these *vitae*, so too does that of the first duke of Aquitaine, Stephen. He appears as a minor figure in the Carolingian *vita* and was not even mentioned by name.[19] By the eleventh century he is the master of all Gaul who participates with the apostle in the conversion of his lands.[20] He is even desirous of converting the Germans and extending Roman control in the north.[21] *And* he the first duke is buried in Limoges at the house of religious established by St Martial.[22]

The role of St Valerie also grows in the legend, but she is not nearly so important as Martial or the duke, at least initially. She appears in the Carolingian *vita* as an early convert of St Martial.[23] She leaves her fiancé in order to remain a virgin for Christ, and she donates land for the tomb of the saint in return for the privilege of being buried near him.[24] Charles de Lasteyrie in his early twentieth-

14 See the excellent account of his death, with a discussion of the sources, in Gillingham, *Richard I*, pp. 323–34.

15 On the Aurelian legend, D. Callahan, 'The Sermons of Ademar of Chabannes and the Cult of St. Martial of Limoges', *Revue Bénédictine* 86 (1976), 251–95 and more recently R. Landes, *Relics, Apocalypse, and the Deceits of History: Ademar of Chabannes, 989–1034* (Cambridge, Mass., 1995), pp. 54–67.

16 Callahan, 'The Sermons', p. 253.

17 Gregory of Tours, *Historia Francorum*, MGH *Scriptores Rerum Merovingicarum*, I.I:i, 22–3.

18 Callahan, 'The Sermons', pp. 258–61.

19 C. Bellet, *L'Ancienne Vie de saint Martial et la prose rythmée* (Paris, 1897), pp. 43–50.

20 Callahan, 'The Sermons', pp. 261–2.

21 *Ibid.*, p. 272.

22 *Vita Prolixior*, in *De probatis Sanctorum Vitis*, ed. L. Surius, 12 vols. (Cologne, 1618), VI, 365–74, esp. cc. 14–27, pp. 368–74.

23 Bellet, *L'Ancienne Vie*, pp. 43–50.

24 *Ibid.*

century study of the monastery of Saint-Martial is probably correct when he suggests that the real Valerie was a pious donor in the Merovingian period who wished to be buried near the saint.[25] In order to explain the tomb the religious invented the tale of the holy virgin. In the Aurelian legend she becomes a martyr when her angry fiancé, Duke Stephen, whom she no longer wishes to marry, has her beheaded.[26] By the late tenth century her remains were moved to a priory of the monastery of Saint-Martial outside of Limoges at Chambon.[27] A *vita* of Valerie was written incorporating much of the Aurelian material but also including some new items, such as her picking up her head after her martyrdom and bringing it to St Martial, in much the same fashion as St Denis is supposed to have carried his head.[28] Professor Gabrielle Spiegel has pointed out in an article on the cult of St Denis that the *cephalorie*, or headless saint who carries his head, was important in medieval France. It is, however, only one of many similarities between the saints of the Aurelian legend and those connected with the cult of St Denis.[29]

A great deal more of Valerie's background appears in a lengthy *vita* of the saint from the last half of the twelfth century, probably prepared to celebrate a new church commemorating the saint in Limoges and undoubtedly written to make a connection with Eleanor of Aquitaine.[30] In this *vita* the saint's noble roots, which are scarcely mentioned in the Aurelian legend, are fully disclosed. She appears as the daughter of the Roman nobleman Leocadius, a relative of Augustus whom the emperor sent to Gaul to be its ruler.[31] Tiberius confirmed him as ruler and Limoges as his center of power, where he settled with his wife Susanna and daughter Valerie.[32] Following local customs, according to this *vita*, he took the title of duke.[33] When he died, the Emperor Claudius sent another lieutenant of imperial lineage to Gaul to succeed Leocadius and to marry the heiress Valerie, in what would seem as good feudal fashion. This individual was

25 C. de Lasteyrie, *L'Abbaye de Saint-Martial de Limoges: Etude historique et archéologique, précédée de recherches nouvelles sur la vie du saint* (Paris, 1901), pp. 19–20.

26 *Vita Prolixior*, cc. 12–13, pp. 367–8.

27 Lasteyrie, *L'Abbaye*, p. 19.

28 See the writings of M.-M. Gauthier on the cult of St Valerie, esp. 'La légende de sainte Valérie et les émaux champlevés de Limoges', *Bulletin de la Société Archéologique et Historique du Limousin* 86 (1955), 35–80.

29 G. Spiegel, 'The Cult of Saint Denis and Capetian Kingship', in her *The Past as Text: The Theory and Practice of Medieval Hagiography* (Baltimore, 1997), pp. 138–62.

30 Lasteyrie, *L'Abbaye*, pp. 18–19. For a detailed examination of the growth of the cult of St Valerie, see Gauthier, 'La légende', pp. 35–80, and especially the final paragraph on p. 80 on the possible commissioning of reliquaries of the saint by Eleanor of Aquitaine. On this new *vita*, see Richard, *Histoire des comtes*, II, 151–2.

31 *Catalogus codicum hagiographicorum latinorum antiquiorum bibliothecae nationalis Parisiensis*, ed. Société des Bollandistes, 4 vols. (Brussels, 1889–93), II, 2: '. . . misit in Gallias procuratorem Leocadium, qui erat ex ejus genere, ut describeret Galliam et tributum acciperet in Romanorum potestatem'.

32 *Ibid.*, p. 3: 'Hic [Tiberius] supradictum Leocadium in principatu Galliarum constituit. Qui Leocadius cum uxore sua, nomine Susanna, ab urbe Roma veniens, Lemovicam civitatem, quae primatum tenebat super civitates Galliarum, constituit sibi sedem . . . Qui filiam, nomine Valeriam de uxore sua suscipiens . . .'

33 *Ibid.*: 'Quem Galli principes ducem appellaverunt consuetudine linguae suae.'

Stephen, who accompanied Claudius to Britain and shared in the honors.[34] When he returned to Gaul, the new duke selected a count for Poitiers named Archadius.[35] By so doing the writer of this *vita* obviously intended to place Poitiers under the control of Limoges and diminish the stature of the former.

The new *vita* also undermines the position of another city in Aquitaine. Gregory of Tours in his history of the Franks mentions a certain Leocadius as a leading senator in Gaul in the late third century.[36] As a resident of Bourges the senator welcomed to that community a disciple of the group of third-century missionaries to Gaul, among whose number were Martial and Denis. Leocadius eventually became a central figure in the legend that grew up around that welcomed disciple, namely St Ursin, the first bishop of Bourges.[37] As Monsignor Duchesne pointed out in his studies of the early bishops of Gaul, it was common to borrow ideas or even characters from other legends in the development of the French *vitae* in the Middle Ages.[38] The new *vita* of Valerie utilized the person of Leocadius as a means of giving further authenticity to these amplifications of the Aurelian legend and at the same time diminishing the importance of Bourges, the seat of the metropolitan of Limoges and a traditional center of much importance in Merovingian and Carolingian Aquitaine.

The reference to Carolingian Aquitaine leads to a second connection between Limoges and the duke of Aquitaine, namely the Carolingian ties that the monks of Saint-Martial sought to publicize throughout the Middle Ages. The Carolingian connection appears in a number of ways. One must remember that Carolingian Aquitaine was a large, somewhat amorphous kingdom embracing much of the area of modern France south of the Loire and west of the Rhône. It was a region where Pepin the Short fought long and ferociously, where Charlemagne had established his son Louis the Pious as king and where Louis, in turn, would place his sons Pepin and subsequently Charles as rulers. In the year 855 Charles the Bald had his second son Charles the Child, age eight, crowned king of Aquitaine in Limoges.[39] Here was the precedent that churchmen in Limoges would later cite for its role as the proper place for the inauguration of the duke. It

34 *Ibid.*: 'Claudius vero imperator misit in Gallias Stephanum principem in loco ejus, jussitque secundum Romanorum legem Valeriam sibi desponsari et uxorem eam duci, tributumque Gallorum in romanam ditionem exigi et totius ejusdem regionis esse procuratorem. Desponsata est ergo Valeria eidem juveni Stephano duci, genere Augustorum nobili et romana dignitate praeclaro fastuque mundialis gloriae sublimato. In illis diebus Claudius Caesar expeditionem fecit contra Britannos, habuitque secum in exercitu Stephanum, sponsum Valeriae, cum multitudine Gallorum.'

35 *Ibid.* 'Stephanus vero dux cum reverteretur ab imperatore Claudio cum legionibus Gallorum, edicto Caesaris civitatem Pictavis, quam Julius Caesar primum condiderat et ex nomine amici ducis sui, qui in bello recenti caesus fuerat, Pictavo eam vocaverat, de priori loco in aptiorem, quae nunc est, mutavit positionem, praefecitque in ea ex genere suo militem romanum proconsulem Archadium, quem Galli sua lingua comitem nuncupare coeperunt.'

36 Gregory of Tours, *Historia Francorum*, I.I:i, 24.

37 L. Duchesne, *Fastes épiscopaux de l'ancienne Gaule*, 3 vols. (Paris, 1894–1900), II, 100–24 and 130–7.

38 *Ibid.*, pp. 110–17.

39 Adhemar of Chabannes, *Chronicon*, ed. R. Landes, G. Pon and P. Bourgain, Corpus Christianorum Continuatio Mediaeualis 129 (Turnhout, 1999), p. 137.

made little difference that the coronation of Louis the Pious as king of Aquitaine occurred in Rome in 781 or that that of his son Pepin took place in Aachen in 817. Limoges was the first site in Aquitaine used for this purpose. It also made little difference that Charles the Child's burial at his death in 866 was at Saint-Sulpice in Bourges, the city that was much more the center of Aquitaine in the late ninth century.[40] It seemed, moreover, to make little difference that the coronation of Louis the Stammerer in 867 and later Louis, the son of the West Frankish King Lothar, in 979 as kings of Aquitaine took place elsewhere.[41] For the churchmen of Limoges the coronation of Charles the Child established the true precedent.

Another Carolingian is said to have done a special favor for the churchmen residing at the tomb of St Martial. In 765, according to the chronicle of Adhemar of Chabannes, Pepin the Short bestowed upon them the golden banner of Duke Waiffre of Aquitaine, which the Frankish king had won in battle.[42] The idea clearly was that the ruler of Aquitaine was the advocate of the house, the defender of its patron and its lands and a central member of the family of St Martial.[43] Carl Erdmann long ago pointed out the great significance of the banner in his study of the origins of the idea of crusade.[44] He offers examples from Fleury and Conques. As he indicates, banners seem to have made their appearance as symbols of advocacy around 1000, which would have made this gift one of the very earliest, if Pepin actually did make such a presentation.

Still another Carolingian whom the monks of Saint-Martial sought to connect with their past in a special manner was Louis the Pious. In 833 the former king of Aquitaine granted to this monastery, according to a false charter concocted in the tenth or eleventh century, large amounts of land, including the *castrum* of Limoges.[45] This purported donation sought to bring the viscount of Limoges under the control of the monks, a matter that did not go unchallenged.

A third tie between Limoges and the dukes of Aquitaine, in addition to the Aurelian and Carolingian connections, is that which became fully manifest in the second half of the twelfth century – namely, the similarity in the relationship between Limoges and the duke as compared to that between Saint-Denis and the Capetian king. The parallels, at least as envisioned by the monks of Saint-Martial and the Plantagenets, are numerous.[46] This chapter has examined the emphasis on the apostolic origins of the cult, the primacy over Gaul, the *cephalorie*, the possession of a special banner and important Carolingian grants,

40 L. Auzias, *L'Aquitaine carolingienne, 778–987* (Toulouse and Paris, 1937), pp. 355–6 and 370.

41 On the later coronation, *ibid.*, pp. 511–15.

42 Adhemar, *Chronicon*, p. 71.

43 On the family of St Martial, D. Callahan, 'When Heaven Came down to Earth: The Family of St. Martial of Limoges and the "Terrors of the Year 1000" ', in *Portraits of Medieval and Renaissance Living: Essays in Memory of David Herlihy*, ed. S. K. Cohn, Jr and S. A. Epstein (Ann Arbor, 1996), pp. 245–58.

44 C. Erdmann, *The Origins of the Idea of Crusade*, trans. M. W. Baldwin and W. Goffart (Princeton, 1977), pp. 35–56.

45 On this false charter, Lasteyrie, *L'Abbaye*, pp. 41–50.

46 Particularly valuable on this point is the recent essay by E. A. R. Brown, 'Eleanor of Aquitaine Reconsidered: The Woman and Her Seasons', in *Eleanor of Aquitaine: Lord and Lady*, ed. B. Wheeler and J. C. Parsons (New York, 2002), pp. 1–54.

albeit some false – all of which are equally applicable to Saint-Denis. Eventually the monastery of Saint-Martial would even claim to have tombs of some Merovingian dukes in its crypts to join that of Duke Stephen and thereby be even more like Saint-Denis.[47] In addition, in the commentary on the coronation rite, Limoges was said to retain for safekeeping the items used in the ceremony, just as many of the Capetian sacred objects were retained at Saint-Denis.[48]

The question to address at this point is why the churchmen of Limoges were so desirous of fostering the tie with the duke, whereas the nobility of the Limousin seemed constantly at war with the rulers in Poitiers. In addition to patronage, one of the principal reasons was prestige. The pilgrimage to the remains of Martial, Valerie, Stephen *et al.* had brought much wealth to Limoges, especially to the monastery of Saint-Martial. It is truly unfortunate that most of the charters of this house have been destroyed, for they would tell an extraordinary tale. The monastery had amassed a congregation of eighty-four priories by the early thirteenth century in the following dioceses: forty-seven in Limoges, nine in Saintes, eight in Périgueux, five in Bourges, three in Bordeaux, three in Rodez, two in Angoulême, two in Béziers, two in Die, and one each in Clermont, Nevers and Toulouse.[49] Much wealth poured into Limoges, as is evident in the ecclesiastical structures. According to a late twelfth-century chronicler, during the abbacy of Isembert (1174–98) an infirmary was built that was compared by contemporaries to a royal palace.[50] Yet this same wealth drew the rapacious. Henry II's and Eleanor's son Henry, for example, robbed the monastery of a great fortune, which he squandered in battle.[51]

The churchmen of Limoges had hoped for patronage and prestige from their connections with the Plantagenets. Their aspirations were to fade with the death of Richard. The grand hopes were not realized. The great buildings so expensive to build and support became an increasing problem in the thirteenth century. The dream of an Aquitanian center comparable to Saint-Denis proved evanescent and becomes but an interesting footnote for historians of the rise of the national polities, one of those might-have-beens that still offer much insight into the mind and mores of the Middle Ages.

If the value of the new coronation rite to Limoges, especially to the monastery of Saint-Martial, is obvious, what can one say about its utility to the Plantagenets? The central figure is surely Eleanor with her aspirations for her son Richard. Professor Eleanor Greenhill, in an essay in the still useful collection on Eleanor edited by William Kibler nearly thirty years ago, sought to show Eleanor's

47 Lasteyrie, *L'Abbaye*, pp. 37–41.

48 Three very valuable pieces on these parallels and similarities developing between Capetian and Plantagenet burials are in the Wheeler and Parsons collection cited above in n. 46. Together with the piece by Professor Brown already cited from this collection are those of K. Nolan, 'The Queen's Choice: Eleanor of Aquitaine and the Tombs of Fontevraud', pp. 377–405 and C. T. Wood, 'Fontevraud, Dynasticism, and Eleanor of Aquitaine', pp. 407–22.

49 Lasteyrie, *L'Abbaye*, p. 260.

50 'Commemoratio Abbatum Basilice S. Marcialis', in *Chroniques de Saint-Martial de Limoges*, ed. H. Duplès-Agier (Paris, 1874), p. 14: '. . . et honeste domum infirmarie Lemovice ad instar palacii regalis extollens confirmavit'.

51 Warren, *Henry II*, p. 593.

influence in promoting the cult of St Denis when she was married to Louis VII.[52] Greenhill focused on the Pseudo-Turpin and the connection between Santiago de Compostela and the monastery of Saint-Denis. She went on to argue that Geoffrey of Vigeois was the historian at Eleanor's court in Poitiers in the early 1170s who transferred the connection of the Pseudo-Turpin and Charlemagne from Saint-Denis to Saint-Martial as a way of giving additional legitimacy to the Plantagenet dynasty by connecting it to the Carolingians.

Although the role of Geoffrey at Eleanor's court and in such a transference is very much open to question, it is certain that this writer, educated at Saint-Martial and a monk there before being made the prior of the house of Vigeois near Limoges, understood the potential value to Eleanor and Richard of the connection to Saint-Martial through the person of St Valerie. One must ask if Eleanor, beyond the obvious elevation of her duchy to a more prestigious status through the coronation rite within the Plantagenet empire, saw its special value in direct opposition to Saint-Denis and the Capetians. Even if one does not wish to go as far as Greenhill with respect to Eleanor's possible role in promoting the cult of St Denis when she was the queen of France, surely during those fifteen impressionable years of her youth she learned much about the value of identifying kingship with the cult of a national saint.[53] Moreover, a woman whose whole life bore witness to her knowledge and preoccupation with her Aquitanian roots and ducal pedigree would have sought to emphasize the central importance of her lands.[54] Yet the question of whether she actually did take advantage of the opportunity that the cults of St Martial and St Valerie presented, and if so, by how much, is open to debate. As with so much else in the long life of this extraordinary woman, the answer the historian must give is: possibly. Yet the more one reflects on her life and personality, the greater the likelihood that one will answer: very likely.

52 E. Greenhill, 'Eleanor, Abbot Suger, and Saint-Denis', in *Eleanor of Aquitaine: Patron and Politician*, ed. W. K. Kibler (Austin, 1976), pp. 81–113.

53 The donation of a rock crystal vase to Saint-Denis by Eleanor bears witness to this great interest. See G. Beech, 'The Eleanor of Aquitaine Vase', in *Eleanor of Aquitaine*, ed. Wheeler and Parsons, pp. 368–76 and Professor Brown's comments on the vase in 'Eleanor of Aquitaine Reconsidered', in *ibid.*, pp. 19–20.

54 Especially valuable on Eleanor and her Aquitanian heritage are M. Hivergneaux, 'Queen Eleanor and Aquitaine, 1137–1189', in *Eleanor of Aquitaine*, ed. Wheeler and Parsons, pp. 55–76 and J. Martindale, 'Eleanor of Aquitaine', in her *Status, Authority and Regional Power*, no. XI, reprinted from *Richard Coeur de Lion in History and Myth*, ed. J. Nelson, King's College Medieval Studies 7 (London, 1992), pp. 17–50. Jane Martindale's forthcoming book on Eleanor should help to answer with more confidence some of the questions raised in this essay.

The Templar Preceptory of Douzens (Aude) in the Twelfth Century

MALCOLM BARBER

Douzens is situated in the valley of the River Aude, about 20 kilometres east of Carcassonne and not much more than a kilometre south of the river itself. Narbonne and the coast are another 31 km to the east. Just to the south is the constant rumble of the A61, the Autoroute des Deux Mers, which has at least relieved the village of the heavy traffic of the N113. Trapped between the two is the railway line, while north of the Aude is the Canal du Midi. Today Douzens does not rate a mention in Michelin (not 'worth a detour' or even 'interesting') and, admittedly, there is little to see in this rather ordinary village, with its very dark Romanesque church and rather featureless arable surroundings.

Difficult therefore as it is to imagine its twelfth-century character, nevertheless it is evident that this was by no means a backwater, tucked away in some mountain retreat like Montaillou up on the Sault plateau. Just as the autoroute is also designated E80 to signify its importance as a European highway, so too the Romans built the Domitian Way in 118 BC to connect Rome with Spain, which they had conquered fifteen years earlier. This was a major paved route, six metres wide in places, which initially went over the Rhône by means of boats at Tarascon and Beaucaire, but from the second century crossed at Arles, where a bridge was built. Either way it converged on Nîmes, itself a major route centre from nine different directions. The road then went via Montpellier and Béziers to Narbonne, where it split into two, with one branch going directly south across the Pyrenees, the other west to Carcassonne and Toulouse. This westerly branch passed through the territories that came to make up the preceptory at Douzens; it is, indeed, such an obvious route that it has been largely followed by the modern N113. There was, no doubt, some deterioration of the Roman roads in the early Middle Ages, but it should be noted that the Visigoths found both routes convenient as they moved into Aquitaine and Iberia, and that both the Merovingians and the Carolingians made considerable efforts to maintain them.[1] In the twelfth century pilgrimage made other places important – interest in Saint-Gilles, for example, sometimes led pilgrims coming south along the Rhône to bypass Nîmes – but this did not affect the Douzens section along

1 See A. Clément, *Les Chemins à travers les âges en Cévennes et bas Languedoc* (Montpellier, 1984), pp. 89–118.

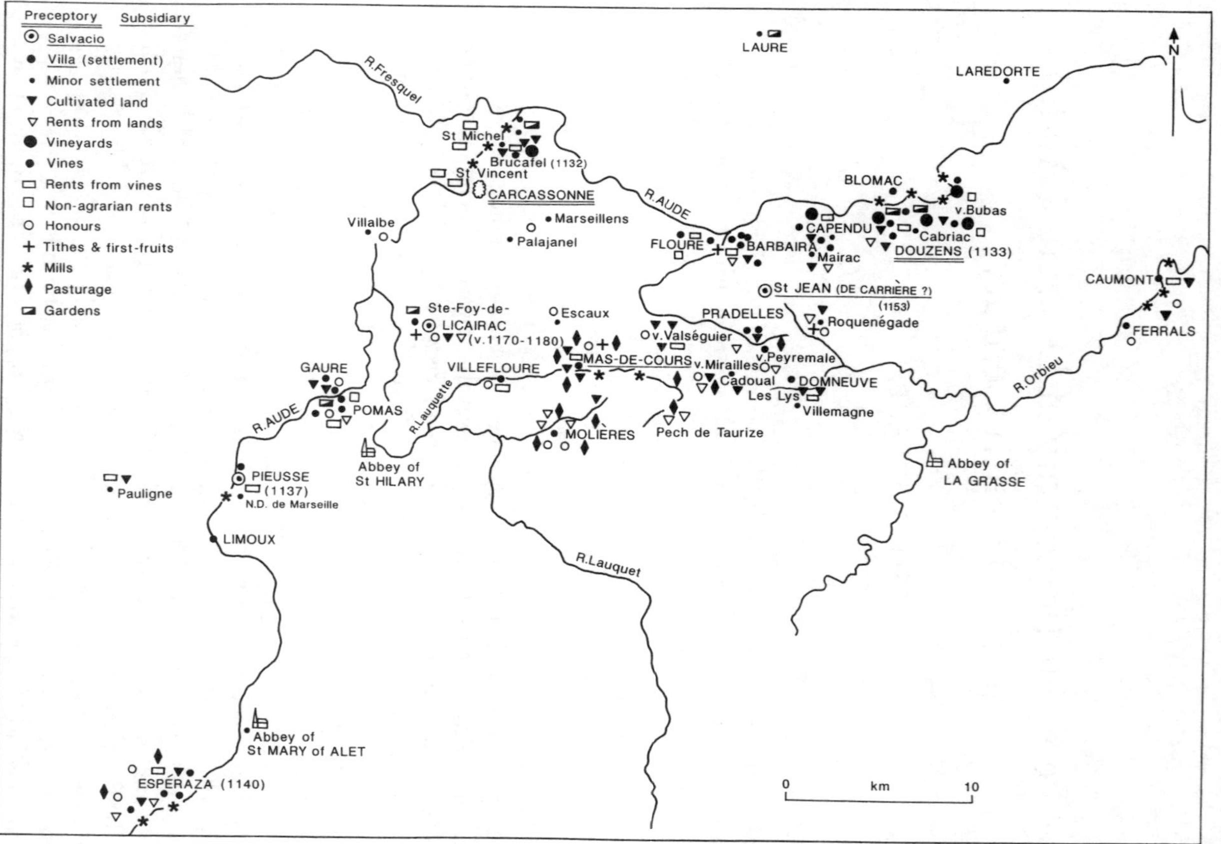

2. Possessions of the Temple in the Region of Douzens (1132–81)
(after *Cartulaire des Templiers de Douzens*, ed. P. Gérard and E. Magnou, Collection de documents inédits sur l'histoire de France 3 (Bibliothèque Nationale: Paris, 1965). Reproduced with kind permission of the authors and publishers.)

which pilgrims could travel to join up with other links to Compostela further to the west.

Hugh of Payns and his co-founders of the Temple had first begun to protect the pilgrim route between Jaffa and Jerusalem in about 1119 and, thanks to some influential contacts, received papal recognition at the Council of Troyes in 1129. The subsequent publicity was reinforced by extensive travel by the Templars in Champagne, Flanders, Picardy and England in the north, and Provence and lower Languedoc in the south, in all of which they acquired donations. In the Aude valley, the Templars received a donation from William Ermengaud (who later joined the Order), possibly at Peyrolles, and two gifts from Roger I, viscount of Carcassonne, and his family, in 1132 and 1133 in the vicinity of Carcassonne.[2] However, the practical foundation of the preceptory of Douzens came in a grant of 11 April 1133, from the families of the lords of Canet and Barbaira, who appear to have been co-seigneurs of what they describe as 'our castle' (*nostrum castrum*) of Douzens. The named members are Bernard of Canet and his wife and son, Aimeric of Barbaira and his wife and four sons, Aimeric's mother Beatrice, and Peter Raymond of Barbaira (presumably a cousin) and his wife and brother-in-law.

> We altogether give to God and the holy knighthood of the Temple of Solomon of Jerusalem and the brothers fighting for God there, into the hand of Hugh Rigaud, *confrater* of their community, this our castle, which we call Douzens, and in all its territories which we have or ought to have, that is the men and women, lands and vineyards, settlements and their appurtenances, gardens and kitchen-gardens, meadows and pasture, woods and thickets, waters and banks, roads and the ways leading to and from them, and the rents, *census*, *usatici* [customary dues], *albergs* and *ademprramenzs*, enclosures and easements [places of communal use], rural and suburban places, which [means] rural and military things; and all that which is in the aforesaid castle and its *villa* [township], and in all of their protected and fortified places . . .

A man called William Mantilinus added a vineyard at Bubas, just to the north-east. In general the grant was made for the conventional reasons of the salvation of their deceased parents and other kin and the remission of their sins, but two members of the family went further in offering themselves to the Order. These two were the sons of Aimeric of Barbaira, the eldest, also called Aimeric, and his brother William Chabert, who 'give themselves body and soul in death or life to the Lord God and the knighthood for the remission of our sins; and when we leave the secular life, the *militia* will have our horses and arms, and if we do not have horses and arms, it will have from each of us 100 *solidi* in the money of Carcassonne'.[3]

This small fortified township or village with some adjacent land outside the walls, together with an outlying piece of vineyard, was sufficient to form the

2 *Cartulaires des Templiers de Douzens*, ed. P. Gérard and E. Magnou, Collection de documents inédits sur l'histoire de France 3 (Paris, 1965), C, 1, A, 171, 115 [hereafter cited as *Douzens*].

3 *Douzens*, A, 1. See, too, D. Selwood, *Knights of the Cloister: Templars and Hospitallers in Central-Southern Occitania c.1100–c.1300* (Woodbridge, 1999), pp. 61–7.

core of the Templar house. Laurent Macé has shown that the pre-Templar settlement consisted of a wall and a ditch, which enclosed a tower and at least four houses, together with other habitations to the south and west of the wall. During the early 1140s the Templars rebuilt part of the tower so that they could provide more suitable accommodation for the brothers, and they extended the enceinte to include the church of St Vincent to the north-east and the houses that had formerly been outside the walls. From the mid-1150s further settlement developed south of the road, creating a faubourg, which continued to expand during the first half of the following century.[4] The house had its own preceptor by 1141, when Peter of Roveria is described as *magister*; thereafter ten men held the position up to and including Bernard of Mairac in 1179.[5] Three subsidiary houses were established at Brucafel, just to the north of Carcassonne, at Mas-des-Cours in a steep-sided mountain valley on the upper reaches of the River Lauquette, and at Saint-Jean-de-Carrière (no longer extant), perhaps about six kilometres to the south-west of Douzens on the north side of Mont Alaric. The first two were endowed by 1133 and 1135 and the third by 1153, although named preceptors do not appear until 1158, 1162 and 1169 respectively.[6] These men would have been responsible to the preceptor at Douzens, while he in turn would have looked to the regional command, initially in the person of the peripatetic Hugh Rigaud, who received the earliest donations in the 1130s, but from c.1150 to the preceptor or master of Carcassonne and the Razès.[7]

Although the order received castles at Soure in Portugal and at Grañera in the county of Barcelona between 1128 and 1130, and the following year was designated one of the three beneficiaries of the will of Alfonso I of Aragon, it is probable that Douzens was the Order's first recognizable preceptory in the West. In the early 1130s there were no 'mother houses' from which a troop of monks could be sent to establish a new colony; nor indeed was there any charismatic individual around whom a new group might coalesce. No powerful patron appeared: the highest-ranked noble donors are the Trencavel viscounts of Béziers and Carcassonne, and the most important prelate involved was Raymond II, bishop of Carcassonne. Finally, the Order itself was a new type of entity for which there was no spiritual or organizational precedent; only the embryonic structure of the

4 L. Macé, 'Morphogenèse villageoise et aménagement seigneurial: l'exemple de Douzens (Aude)', *Archéologie Médiévale* 28 (1998), 149–60, especially Figures 1 and 2.

5 *Douzens*, A, 11. See pp. xxxvii–xli for a full list. Arnold of Sournies is the first individual to be named as actually holding 'the house of Douzens', A, 17, in 1153.

6 *Douzens*, A, 115, B, 1–5, A, 87; A, 133, B, 21, A, 90. See pp. xxii, xxxvii–xli. This subdivision made economic as well as organizational sense, as potential donors were often stimulated to make a grant to a house established in their immediate vicinity. On this, see C. B. Bouchard, *Holy Entrepreneurs: Cistercians, Knights, and Economic Exchange in Twelfth-Century Burgundy* (Ithaca and London, 1991), p. 172.

7 *Douzens*, A, 17, 27. In 1153 Pons of *Leuntiano* is described as custodian of the honour of the Temple in the Carcassès, and in 1167 Peter of St John has the title of 'preceptor of the honour which the brothers of the knighthood of the Temple of Jerusalem have and hold in the episcopate of Carcassonne and the Razès'. See also E. Léonard, *Introduction au Cartulaire Manuscrit du Temple (1150–1317) constitué par le Marquis d'Albon* (Paris, 1930), p. 56.

Hospitallers pointed the way towards a provincial structure centred on headquarters in Jerusalem.[8] The preceptory at Douzens was truly built from scratch.[9]

An analysis of the cartularies of Douzens gives an idea of how this was achieved. There are three cartularies, together with the collection of what the editors call 'isolated acts', making a total of 331 documents. As the editors point out, these documents have been grouped topographically rather than chronologically. Cartulaire A is the most important, containing 207 documents, encompassing material relevant to the property of Douzens itself, the houses of Brucafel and Saint-Jean-de-Carrière, and the possessions in the upper valley of the Aude, including those at Gaure and Espéraza. Cartulaire B has 88 documents and is concerned with the other subsidiary house of Mas-des-Cours which, because of its position in the mountains, appears to have been regarded as different in character from the other holdings. Cartulaire C has only 11 documents, dated between November 1129 and April 1134, all of which relate to Hugh Rigaud, and the editors plausibly suggest that this small collection was assembled at his behest, and is not, therefore, strictly speaking, part of the cartularies of Douzens as such.

Allowing for duplicates, dispute settlements, a survey of the vineyards held at Douzens, transactions that did not involve Douzens, and acts to which the Templars were not a party, there are 287 charters between November 1129 and January 1183. These break down into eighty-two gifts, 102 gifts with conditions, twenty-six exchanges, seventy-one purchases, and six grants or leases by the Templars themselves to other parties. By 'gifts with conditions' are meant transactions in which the donor receives at least some material benefit in return for his or her gift, even though it would not be equivalent in value. Some of these certainly fall into the category of 'countergifts', defined by Constance Bouchard in a Cistercian context as 'an expression of the monks' goodwill', but in others there appears to be a greater material element than this ritualized exchange implies, suggesting that the 'inducement' might be a more appropriate description.[10] Exchanges are usually defined as such by the parties involved and include no clause denoting any spiritual motivation. Straightforward gifts (which may themselves have not been free of pressure of one kind or another) make up just under 29 per cent of the total.

As might be expected, the preceptory was founded upon such gifts: the first modest purchase that can be securely dated was not made until September 1138, when the Templars added another vineyard to their holdings at Bubas, acquired from Raymond Mantilinus, and presumably contiguous with those they had already received as gifts from him in 1135 and from his relative, William, in 1133.[11] However, once this base had been established, the Templars were able to

8 See J. Riley-Smith, 'The Origins of the Commandery in the Temple and the Hospital', in *La Commanderie, institution des ordres militaires dans l'Occident médiéval*, ed. A. Luttrell and L. Pressouyre (Paris, 2002), pp. 9–18.

9 Moreover, once established, it endured, for it still existed at the time of the trial in 1307: Léonard, *Introduction*, p. 57.

10 Bouchard, *Holy Entrepreneurs*, pp. 92–3. A countergift at Douzens seems to be that in which the Templar reciprocation is described as *de caritate*, for example, A, 55 (1150).

11 *Douzens*, A, 73, 21.

undertake the more active role presaged by the consolidation of the vineyards in 1138: taking the year 1156 as the median point, the proportion of transactions from that date encompassing gifts with conditions, purchases, exchanges, and Templar grants and leases, comes to 66 per cent.[12] Even so, the gift element remained central, since gifts and conditional gifts together constituted 64 per cent of all transactions, while purchases were mostly on a modest scale,[13] emphasizing the importance of providing flexible forms of association with the Order. Less predictably, the numbers of unconditional gifts before and after 1156 are almost the same, which suggests that the Order continued to attract donors, and that, contrary to the findings of Constance Bouchard for the Cistercians in Burgundy, in this region potential land for donations was not used up in the first ten to twenty years after the foundation of the house.[14]

The rivers hold the key to this development, most importantly the Aude, both above and below Carcassonne, but to a lesser extent the Lauquette and the Bretonne, both of which flow into the Aude (although the Lauquette does so by means of the Lauquet), and the Orbieu, which also eventually meets the Aude, but at a point closer to Narbonne. With few exceptions, the patrimony of these houses extended along these rivers or on the slopes above them. Arable cultivation of wheat, barley, and what is called 'blad', apparently a mixture of wheat, barley and beans, was closely linked to the acquisition and development of water-mills, mostly used for grinding corn, although there was some limited capacity for fulling as well. Within the period covered by the cartularies, the Templars established or acquired fifteen mill complexes, mainly on the Aude, at Espéraza, 36 km upstream from Carcassonne, Pieusse and Brucafel, and below Carcassonne, at Blomac and Douzens. In addition, there were two mills in the upper valley of the Lauquette at Mas-des-Cours, and three on the Orbieu at Ferrals and Caumont. The mill ponds or reservoirs were also used for keeping fish, especially eels. References to cabbages, pears and figs are indicators of the types of vegetables and fruit produced in the many gardens mentioned in the charters, some of which must have been irrigated,[15] while the chalk terraces along the right bank of the Aude on Mont Alaric were used for vines and probably for olives.[16] Vines were equally important at Carcassonne, Gaure and Espéraza in the upper Aude valley, and at Pradelles along the River Bretonne. Higher in the mountains, at Mas-des-Cours and Molières, pasture predominated; many of the charters concerned with this area are intended to regulate the use of that pasture and the control of the cattle and sheep that grazed on it apparently unfenced. None of this was viable without human labour, and many grants included peasants and their families who came with the land in various degrees of dependency.

12 This compares with 71% for Burgundian Cistercian houses: Bouchard, *Holy Entrepreneurs*, p. 66.

13 *Douzens*, p. xxiv. Most sales to the Temple were 20 *solidi* or less.

14 Bouchard, *Holy Entrepreneurs*, p. 172.

15 *Douzens*, A, 112, 94, 128. There is, however, only one reference to irrigation in the cartularies, A, 44.

16 *Douzens*, A, 58. In 1143 the Templars granted a garden to Arnold Raymond of Fontcouverte for which he was obliged to render a *sextaria* of oil. Rather unexpectedly, this is the only reference to such production on any Templar property in the cartularies.

Judging by the attention paid to them by the Templars, the mills were both vital to the agrarian economy and extremely profitable. Indeed, research on English mills has shown that those of 'high value' were located on a major river or in the vicinity of a population centre; the same holds true for mills on the Aude and near Carcassonne.[17] Concessions made to the Templars for their operations at Douzens and Blomac show that the first mills had already been built or acquired by 1141, possibly even before rights to the relevant land and water had been fully established.[18] Mills were part of a complex that would usually include the water-wheels themselves, several buildings housing the mill-stones, spindle and gearing, habitation for the millers and their families, and grain storage barns, as well as a series of constructions on the river itself, most importantly the dam and the sluices controlling the leats or channels. There was often more than one mill on each site or even within the same building.[19] The acquisition of all the necessary rights, free of encumbrances, could be a difficult process, and there are signs of conflict in some of the Douzens charters as the Templars brought pressure upon those with claims to the desired stretches of the river and its banks.[20] Even then others might retain jurisdictional and financial rights, as in 1152, when the Templars purchased mills on the Aude at Douzens, but were required to pay the *census* previously rendered by the donors. In this case the Templars were at the fourth level of a hierarchy extending to the main overlord, the prior of the house of St Michael of Nahuze on Mont Alaric. Conflicting rights were not the only problem, as this same document shows. The Templars were not required to pay the *census* if the mills were destroyed by flood or if there had been any appreciable water loss for any reason other than negligence.[21] Although the Templars were primarily interested in flour milling, they were also involved with fulling. In 1148 this extended their activity into the valley of the Orbieu at Caumont, where they were given some terraces through which the river passed, together with some existing buildings. If what are called *molendini draperii* were built there, the donors made the condition that the Templars would prepare their own cloth free of charge.[22]

17 See R. Holt, *The Mills of Medieval England* (Oxford, 1988), pp. 12–13.

18 *Douzens*, A, 12, 13, 42. A possible example of pre-emption in 1141 can be seen in the charter by which Peter of Auriac and his wife gave the Templars a dam (*paxeria*) to work their mills 'which you have already constructed on the River Aude': A, 61.

19 *Douzens*, pp. xxix–xxxii. Although no physical remains are extant, Laurent Macé has convincingly plotted the probable sites of the mills of Douzens, Blomac and Caumont, and suggested a detailed plan of the layout of the complex at Brucafel: 'L'Utilisation des ressources hydrauliques par les Templiers de la Commanderie de Douzens, XIIe siècle (Aude)', *Archéologie du Midi Médiéval* 12 (1994), 99–113 (pp. 106–8 and Figs. 2–4). For the technology of mills, see Holt, *Mills*, pp. 117–44. The charters do not indicate whether the wheels were vertical or horizontal, but the former were characteristic of ventures by lords, institutions or corsortia, since the capital investment needed was too great for individual peasants.

20 *Douzens*, A, 50, 54.

21 *Douzens*, A, 2. See also A, 118. The irregular water-flow of both the Aude and the Orbieu determined that the mills had to be built on the banks. Water was then diverted by means of canals. On the much smaller Lauquette it is possible that the mills could have been built in the river itself: see Macé, 'L'Utilisation', p. 106.

22 *Douzens*, A, 140. In a European context, this is an early example. Although the earliest reference is in Normandy in 1087, there is no other identification before 1145: Holt, *Mills*, p. 153.

In these cases the Templars were exploiting the mills directly, but they were also interested in gaining a share of the profits in mills operated by others. In 1166 the Templars granted Arnold of Carcassonne and three business associates facilities for the construction of up to six mills on the Aude within the territory controlled by their house at Brucafel. In return they received an annual *census* of 20 *sextaria* of wheat and 20 of barley, together with free grinding of 4 *sextaria* of blad each week and half of the fish produced from the ponds. The whole operation, including the sumpter animals travelling to and from the complex, remained under Templar protection, so that the Order retained overall lordship.[23] Similarly, at Douzens in 1153 they ceded land within their own milling complex at Arrapesac to four men – two sets of brothers – to build a fulling mill, for an annual charge of 14 *solidi* of Melgueil, dividing the channels with them and granting them fish from their side.[24] The Templars also invested in the equipment needed. In 1147 Berengar of Prat granted them a fifth share in 'the *moleria* which I have with my brothers in the district of St Germain, in a place called *Rocha Rubia*'. He retained the right to cut mill-stones for any mills he might build on the River Aude.[25] This looks like a family business, which was both a quarry and a yard for cutting wheels.

The exploitation of the vineyards was a similar combination of direct cultivation, leasing and capital investment. As has been seen, the Templars' first interest in vineyards began with the acquisitions from William and Raymond Mantilinus in the 1130s, where they were clearly attempting to consolidate relatively small pieces. Their investment in vineyards, however, took a variety of forms. In 1163 the Templars at Brucafel leased land to a certain Guilbert 'in order to plant vines'; once established he was obliged to deliver a quarter of the vintage to the house at Brucafel, as well as making an annual, presumably symbolic payment, of one *denarius* of what is called *vinogolia*, a type of tax paid in the form of wine.[26] Four years later in the same district the Templars granted William and Peter Bels land that had once belonged to their grandparents but had since been donated to the Order, so that they could establish a vineyard. In return they paid 6 *solidi* of Melgueil and the usual *acapte* taxes, but this time they owed half the vintage. As with milling, nature might thwart them. 'If, indeed, you will not be able to hold the vines in that honour at a profit, you should hold the land for ploughing [*ad bene laborandum*], for which you will faithfully give an eighth of the *sextaria* or sheaves to the aforesaid brothers.' [27]

This combination of activities was evidently profitable, since the Templars had cash available not only for investment and purchase, but also to take over lands encumbered with mortgages and pledges, which the owners presumably decided they had no realistic chance of paying off. As early as July 1133, they redeemed a sum of 200 *solidi* of Melgueil on the honour given to them in Douzens by Bernard of Canet and his family, which made up part of their original patrimony. In return Bernard temporarily transferred land mortgaged to him for the same sum, which the Templars would hold until they had recovered their

23 *Douzens*, A, 118.

24 *Douzens*, A, 17.

25 *Douzens*, A, 60.

26 *Douzens*, A, 133.

27 *Douzens*, A, 120.

outlay.[28] Forty years later they were still gaining donations in this way: in 1173 Pons of Molières granted them some peasant dependants, a *census* payment and some woodland, while the Templars freed his honour from a pledge of 50 *solidi* of Melgueil.[29] Undoubtedly the buying out of small-scale pledges by cash-rich institutions played an important part in stimulating the twelfth-century land market, but the Templars were capable of taking over much greater debts as well. In 1147, when Roger I Trencavel needed money to go on crusade, they disengaged his grant of the village of Campagne from a debt of 3,000 *solidi* of Urgel.[30] Most of these financial transactions involved rural property, but the increasing tempo of the rural economy was of course connected to urban growth as well. On several occasions the Templars took on lands in what is described as the *burgus* or *suburbium* of St Vincent of Carcassonne, which was expanding to the west between the walls of the city and the River Aude. A grant of Dias and her husband, Pons Calvert, in 1150, is typical. They gave four plots (*locales*) for building houses. Although this was presented as a gift, it still attracted a *census* of 4 *solidi* of Urgel and an *acapte* of 20 *solidi*. Indeed, it was evidently anticipated that the Templars, rather than building themselves, would lease these to a developer, from whom they would take *census* and *acapte*, since they undertook to share the *acapte* with Dias if this occurred.[31] This type of transaction was clearly more attractive to the Templars than colonization, much practised by the Hospitallers. Only one document, dated January 1168, records them taking on a piece of land 'for breaking up [*ad rumpendum*]'. This they received from Peter of Aragon, prior of St Stephen, at Mas-des-Cours, 'in order that you break up that land and you work it and you give from all its fruits a half of the dues [from the newly cleared lands] and all the tithe and first–fruits to me and my successors in sheaves in the same field or in grain if we will wish it . . .'[32]

For these preceptories to function the Order had to fulfil a number of important roles in local society. The major attraction is expressed in the gift of Douzens itself in 1133. The families of Canet and Barbaira made this for 'the salvation and absolution of the souls of our fathers and mothers and relations and for the remission of our and their sins'. The formulaic nature of this declaration, repeated in the same words or with only slight variants in 95 other charters, and clearly

28 *Douzens*, A, 36. See also D, 15 *bis*, in which Roger of Cabriac's donation to the Templars consisted of a whole series of small pledges owed to him.

29 *Douzens*, B, 74. See also A, 173, B, 75.

30 *Douzens*, D, 4. See G. Constable, 'The Financing of the Crusades in the Twelfth Century', in *Outremer: Studies in the History of the Crusading Kingdom of Jerusalem presented to Joshua Prawer*, ed. B. Z. Kedar, H. E. Mayer and R. C. Smail (Jerusalem, 1982), pp. 64–88 (p. 88), for the importance of the crusades as a solvent in the contemporary land market.

31 *Douzens*, A, 147. See also A, 150, 161, 162, 163, 164. The growth of the city can be seen from 1133, as can be seen by the grant of building land in the suburb of St Michael under the Toulouse gate by Viscount Roger of Béziers: A, 115.

32 *Douzens*, B, 26. Cf. Bouchard, *Holy Entrepreneurs*, pp. 99–103, where she shows that even when monks 'sought solitude' (which the Templars did not) they nevertheless 'practiced a diversified agriculture' in which uncultivated land was hardly the predominant feature. See also G. Constable, *The Reformation of the Twelfth Century* (Cambridge, 1996), p. 120, on the topos of 'wilderness and solitude'. It is likely that in the Templars' case a need for immediate revenues underlay this approach (Douzens, p. xxvii), perhaps because of recurrent crises in the Holy Land.

drafted by the scribes responsible for drawing up the documents, nevertheless does not undermine the potency of this desire, nor the willingness to make material sacrifices in the hope of achieving it. As Jacques Le Goff expresses it, medieval men 'not only cleared new land in this world, they created a new space and time in the next', so that every Christian 'focused his attention on the time of his death'.[33] It was this focus that, above all else, ensured the foundation and expansion of a house like Douzens. Some donors required more bespoke phrasing. Peter Raymond of Barbaira, one of the donors of 1133, eventually entered the house twenty years later, when he made further grants, 'for so many and such great unjust acts, as I have committed many times'. Some wanted their wishes more fully articulated. Laureta, making her gift in 1133/4, did so 'fearing a future day of Judgement when my Redeemer will be seated on his throne of majesty and bring retribution to each of us as he will have conducted himself, for the redemption of my soul and those of my kin that we can, by the mercy of redemption, avoid the punishments of the future'.[34] In 1133, Roger of Béziers and other members of the Trencavel family hoped, in addition, that God would guide them in this life so that the desired outcome would become more attainable: 'that Omnipotent God in his mercy should make us and our posterity live in good perseverance, and that after the course of this life should deign to receive us in a good end'.[35] Finally, implicit in all these, but quite explicit in the very early grant of William Ermengaud and his family in 1130, is the fervent hope 'that Omnipotent God aid and protect us and our kin from the host of the Devil'.[36] There is no doubt that the sculpture to be found on local Romanesque chapels as much as the tympana of the great pilgrimage churches communicated very directly to these people.

The belief, expressed in so many of these charters, that the donors might merit the love of God and thus attain eternal life, stemmed from the conviction that the Order to which they were donating their goods must itself be the recipient of God's approval. Several donors made their grants to the knights fighting for God in Jerusalem, although only the distinctive phrasing of Laureta's charter in 1133 describes them explicitly as those 'who combat the Saracens who are striving to destroy the law of God and God's faithful'.[37] Moreover, only two of the donors did so on the occasion of their actual departure for the East. In 1134 William Peter, described as 'about to go to Jerusalem', made arrangements for the maintenance of his family and the disposal of his goods. The Temple was to receive an estate at Douzens, 'should I remain in Jerusalem, dead or for any other reason'.[38] The other grant was on a much grander scale, for it was made by Roger I Trencavel, viscount of Carcassonne, at the time of his departure from Agde

33 J. Le Goff, *The Medieval Imagination*, trans. A. Goldhammer (Chicago and London, 1989), p. 13.

34 *Douzens*, A, 40.

35 *Douzens*, A, 171.

36 *Douzens*, C, 1.

37 In 1160, 'Isarn, son of Laureta, *servus* of the knighthood of the Temple of Jerusalem' made an agreement with his cousin about property he had inherited from his mother and uncle. As there are only two references to 'Laureta' in the cartularies, it seems probable that this is the same person and that, although she had not been able to enter the Order herself, her son had done so: *Douzens*, B, 46.

38 *Douzens*, A, 45.

(Hérault) on the Second Crusade in July 1147. Most importantly, he gave them the complete village of Campagne-sur-Aude, situated on both sides of the river, about 19 km upstream from Limoux beyond Espéraza. It was, he said, given 'with all its inhabitants and progeny' and with everything that appertained to it, including its mills and fisheries. He waived all jurisdiction in the village and granted its inhabitants exemption from military service. Within Carcassonne itself he gave the Templars the right to their own oven, although they were only to 'cook their own bread and not that of other men'. The grant was accompanied by sweeping tax exemptions: on all the viscount's lands the Templars 'should not give market-dues nor *usaticum* nor water or land tolls'.[39] Here genuine piety and economic interest merged for, as has been seen, before the Templars could enjoy the benefits of the viscount's generosity they had to find 3,000 *solidi* of Urgel to redeem the village from the mortgagee, Bernard Sesmon of Alberdun.

However, even though there are few examples of donors actually intending to travel to the Holy Land, the Order was able to capitalize on the evident admiration of its role by providing a variety of means of association. The most obvious way was to enter, either directly or as a *confrater*, which seems to have meant promises of obedience and future entrance.[40] In either case, this invariably meant a donation of some kind, and from the 1160s at least, sharp minds among the canon lawyers were describing such entry gifts as simoniacal. All Orders nevertheless followed this practice, but in 1213 Innocent III singled out the Templars for criticism on this ground, causing consternation among the leadership.[41] This is not surprising for, without these arrangements, the Order could not have flourished as it did in the twelfth century. At Douzens several of these recruits were, like Raymond of Albas in 1169, 'placed in illness' and were in the process of making their final dispositions.[42] Those who were not, often made provision for joining at some unspecified time in the future. In 1169, for example, a man called Guilbert granted the Order his person and property, promising to make an annual payment of 12 *solidi* of Urgel, 'while I wish to live in the secular life', but 'if I wish to live according to your life, you should receive me, living or dead, with all my rights as a brother'.[43] Arnold of Gaure combined the two, for in 1145 he 'was placed in illness and returned my body to the service of God for all time . . .' However, he must have recovered, since it was not until 1150 that he actually entered what is described as 'your confraternity', finally fulfilling a promise he had first made as long ago as 1137.[44] The ultimate aim of all these men was burial in Templar ground. In 1166, William Corda and his nephew, Raymond, agreed

39 *Douzens*, D, 4.

40 The terms *confrater*, *confratria* and *confraternitas* do not seem to have been used with any precision at this period, since they are sometimes applied to individuals or groups of brothers who are clearly fully professed Templars and not simply associates: for example, A, 1, 191, C, 8. Thus, there remains some ambiguity about their meaning.

41 See J. H. Lynch, *Simoniacal Entry into Religious Life from 1000 to 1260* (Columbus, Ohio, 1976), pp. xi–xvi, 190–2.

42 *Douzens*, A, 8. See also A, 74, D, 17.

43 *Douzens*, A, 159.

44 *Douzens*, A, 119, 173, 181. At least it must be assumed that this meant entrance, as he made arrangements for his two stepsons to be looked after by the Order at the same time (see below).

to pay an annual *census* of 12 *denarii* (apparently the going rate in the 1160s) and to bequeath all their property to the Temple. 'And when death comes to us, each will be received with all his things into the house of the knights [and] is to be buried honourably in the cemetery of the same house.'[45] This cemetery, enclosed within the *villa*, was central to the whole community, ensuring that the dead as much as the living remained part of that society.[46]

Sometimes material needs had a very direct bearing. This could be at a very basic level: in 1167, Peter of Escau gave his person and property in Mas-des-Cours, 'and while I live you will provide me with victuals and clothing as one of your brothers'.[47] It seems probable that he intended to enter the house, although in practice his position was not very different from that of two brothers, Bernard Alaric and Pons, who, two years later, 'recognizing that for a long time we have been receiving sustenance from the goods of the Temple', placed their persons and property under the Order's protection and promised an annual payment of 12 *solidi* of Melgueil. Whichever of the two outlived the other would, in addition, give a measure of wheat and a measure of barley for the soul of the deceased.[48] In 1172, Berengar *Comte*, already holding an 'honour' from the Temple, was concerned to make provision for his old age, although at the time his wife and children were still alive. In return for his grant the brothers would give him 'victuals and clothing always when you wish to receive them for the love of God'.[49]

Other arrangements were more complex. In 1151 Bernard Sesmon of Alberdun gave the very large sum of 1,000 *solidi* of Melgueil in return for which the Templars conceded the honour of Espéraza to him. This was almost the most remote of the holdings of Douzens, for it was about 16 km upriver from Limoux, and it may have suited the preceptor to farm out its administration. It was not simply a business arrangement, however, since Bernard clearly intended to join the Order in the future.

> When I shall have turned my life to the holy militia I shall render myself and make provision with the advice of the brothers for the cure of my soul; and if it should happen that I should die while in a secular occupation, the brothers shall receive me and take my body to be buried in an appropriate place and make me a participant in their alms and benefits.[50]

In 1172, Raymond of Rieux seems to have promised himself to the house because he was in debt:

> I give myself to God and the knighthood, that you might receive me into the above-mentioned house, with my horses and arms; in this agreement that you should give me as long as I remain in secular life 10 *sextaria* of blad, 6 of barley and 4 of wheat from the standing crop; and after my death or when I leave

45 *Douzens*, A, 158.
46 See P. J. Geary, *Living with the Dead in the Middle Ages* (Ithaca and London, 1994), pp. 1–2.
47 *Douzens*, B, 20.
48 *Douzens*, A, 157.
49 *Douzens*, A, 92.
50 *Douzens*, A, 199. Here the Templars regained part of the sum paid to this man when they redeemed Campagne-sur-Aude in 1147.

secular life, the honour and blad will all be for the militia. And it is true that you have freed the honour from a pledge of 165 *solidi* of Melgueil.[51]

The Order also made provision for donors' relatives, both of the previous generation and of the next. In 1137 Séguier and his wife gave the subsidiary house of Saint-Jean-de-Carrière a measure of land on a vineyard in return for 4 *solidi* of Urgel and the promise of 'one service (*ministerium*) per annum in memory of my father'.[52] At the large preceptory of Reims in Champagne the Templars kept an extensive obituary list, which they had taken over from the local church of La Trinité and then continually updated.[53] No such list survives for Douzens, and indeed may never have been thought necessary given the numbers involved, but the principle was the same.

Remembrance of deceased fathers was relatively straightforward; arrangements for children, actual or potential, however, was more complicated. According to the Latin Rule, established at Troyes in 1129, 'although the rule of the Holy Fathers allows boys to be in the congregation, we do not recommend you to encumber yourselves with them'. Parents or relatives wishing to dedicate a boy to the Temple therefore 'should raise him to the age when he is capable of fighting like a man' before placing him in the Order.[54] This is an unambiguous prohibition on the taking of oblates, yet, as has been seen, the very existence of local houses depended upon interaction with the society in which they were established. At Douzens they avoided taking boys as future fighting knights, which would have contravened the Rule, but they did nevertheless undertake responsibility for children as part of their arrangements with adults. Thus, when Arnold of Gaure at last entered the Order in 1150, he still had guardianship of two boys, his stepchildren, 'whom I give and put aside to the brothers, so that they may have victuals and clothing, while in accordance with the sense and wish of the brothers they may wish justly to have them'.[55] No mention is made of the mother, who must be presumed dead, although it is interesting to note that Arnold must have married her long after his initial promise to enter the Temple, originally made in 1137, if the boys were still under-age in 1150. Even then his final entrance into the religious life may have been precipitated by circumstances, since the 'honour' that he granted to the Templars was heavily mortgaged by this time, an encumbrance from which it was freed by the Order. Even childless couples needed to take possible future offspring into account if they did not intend to live celibately or actually enter the religious life, which explains the conditions laid down by William Paul in establishing the terms of the dowry of his wife, Audiard, in 1141. If Audiard outlived him, then she should retain these properties, which thereafter would pass to any children that they might

51 *Douzens*, B, 75.

52 *Douzens*, A, 110.

53 *Obituaire de la Commanderie du Temple de Reims*, ed. E. de Barthélemy, Collection des documents inédits 4 (Paris, 1882), pp. 313–32.

54 *Regula pauperum commilitonum Christi Templique Salomonici*, ed. S. Cerrini, Corpus Christianorum Continuatio Mediaeualis (forthcoming), clause 59. Cf. Constable, *Reformation*, pp. 100–1, on a similar attitude in the new reformed orders.

55 *Douzens*, A, 173.

have had. However, 'after our death, if then we have not produced any children, the aforesaid donation will revert to the knighthood of the Temple of Solomon and its ministers'.[56]

This entrenchment in the local economy and society was not, of course, achieved without a certain amount of friction, both in relation to other institutions and to individuals. However, recorded conflict is not frequent: only thirteen out of the total of 331 documents preserved by the knights at Douzens are overtly connected with settlement dispute, although several others might at least imply pressure exercised by the Templars on particular individuals. There were three important abbeys established on the key rivers, St Mary of Alet on the upper Aude, St Hilary on the Lauquet, and Lagrasse on the Orbieu, while the Hospitallers had their own commandery at Carcassonne. Only St Hilary and the Hospitallers came into conflict with the Templars of Douzens, and even then in single disputes half a century apart. Both matters were minor: in 1133 the abbot of St Hilary claimed that a man and his family living at Pomas who had been granted to the Temple were in fact dependants of the abbey, while in 1183 the Hospitallers disputed the possession of an estate at Brucafel. Both matters were settled by arbitration, the abbot conceding possession of the man and his family, while the property at Brucafel was split between the two orders, of which the Temple received two-thirds.[57] Local churches could also be sensitive about their rights. In 1162 arbitrators had to settle the differences between Peter of Aragon, *prévôt* of the church of St Stephen at Mas-des-Cours, and the Templars, by dividing the tithes, restraining trespass on woods and cultivated lands by the Templars' cattle, and setting down prescribed times of the year when the clergy could celebrate the offices in the church of St Mary at Mas.[58]

Disputes with individuals sometimes had more edge, especially as the settlements usually favoured the institution. A good example is that of Peter Sachet who, after complaining about the knights of the Temple 'concerning the destruction of the castle of Douzens and concerning the mills and concerning the dam which they have built on the River Aude', as well as 'concerning the honour of William Ermengaud and Raymond Ermengaud which they have taken away from me', was obliged in 1141 to capitulate completely, acknowledging that he had 'complained about them unjustly and without reason'. In return the Templars conceded him the lifetime use of a garden, which would revert to the Order at his death.[59] Here perhaps was the kernel of the matter, for his father had apparently granted the disputed honour to the Temple in the first place, and it is not unusual to find relatives attempting to reverse what they perceived to have been over-generosity by their relatives, especially in a region such as this where shared possession was common.[60] Indeed, sometimes the individual himself seems to have regretted the gift. In 1162, Pons Roger of Villalier recognized that he had, a short while ago (*dudum*), given the Order an allod at Caumont on the Orbieu,

56 *Douzens*, A, 78.
57 *Douzens*, A, 185, C, 6, A, 167.
58 *Douzens*, B, 8.
59 *Douzens*, A, 11. See also A, 2.
60 For example, see *Douzens*, A, 20, Richa in 1167.

and that henceforth he would not 'infringe this gift'. The explanation is to be found at the end of the charter: 'I recognize that now for my needs (*meis necessitatibus*), humbly condescending, you give to me for charity two *sextaria* of wheat and one *sextarius* of barley.'[61]

Other disputes arose from clashing interests, inevitable once the Templars began to use their donations to generate income. Control over mills and their adjacent stretches of water was one such issue. On 3 November 1152, a man called Caniot and his family dropped their claim to the weir and leat of the mills at Arrapesac on the Aude, a significant concession in the light of the grant of the previous 8 October by Raymond of Blomac and his brothers of rights on the river at the same place so that the Templars could construct milling facilities there. In return they received 12 *solidi* of Melgueil in alms.[62] In the case of the Blomac brothers there is no mention of a dispute, but in view of the need for them to go to arbitration over the possession of a field at Blomac in 1157,[63] it seems quite likely that the previous grant of river rights had not been entirely voluntary. The Templars' development of these mills remained contentious. In 1160 Raymond of Artiguas sought judgement on the possession of land above the mill at Arrapesac. He was obliged to grant the Temple allodial possession, although, 'for the love of God and at the prayers of our friends and neighbours', they granted occupation to his son during his lifetime in return for a share of the crops.[64]

These charters yield an immense amount of information about the symbiosis between a religious house and its social environment. Equally, and more broadly, they present at least a partial picture of the predominant social ties in and around this part of the middle reaches of the Aude valley. In keeping with accepted views of medieval society there is certainly a network of dependence, but it is almost impossible to fit into conventional constructs, for its variety is almost infinite and its shape quite indeterminate.[65] The most important figures are the members of the Trencavel family, viscounts of Béziers and Carcassonne, and lords of regional importance, strong enough to exploit their dual relationships with both the counts of Barcelona and of Toulouse. However, there is no sign here of either of the latter powers; the predominant currencies of Melgueil, Urgel and Narbonne suggest that they had little political influence in the region and, indeed, emphasize the characteristic political fragmentation of lower Languedoc.[66] Thus Roger I was the single biggest donor to Douzens, granting two complete communities at

61 *Douzens*, A, 143. See also B, 77, the case of Arnold of Villelaur who, having sold his honour at Peyrende to the Templars, withheld the *carta hereditaris*, which they should have received with it. His motives can only be conjectured, but he may have wished to withdraw from the sale.

62 *Douzens*, A, 50, 54.

63 *Douzens*, A, 56.

64 *Douzens*, A, 26.

65 Cf. L. M. Paterson, *The World of the Troubadours: Medieval Occitan Society, c.1100–c.1300* (Cambridge, 1993), pp. 10–36.

66 See M. Castaing-Sicard, *Monnaies féodales et circulation monétaire en Languedoc (Xe–XIIe siècles)* (Toulouse, 1961), pp. 8–10. However, Castaing-Sicard shows that such fragmentation did not mean economic chaos. All the currencies were based on the *denarius* and, within each sub-region, a limited number came to predominate. In the area of Douzens that of Melgueil was clearly the most important: pp. 29–30. It is notable that this currency was stable between 1130 and 1175, coinciding with the period of the foundation and expansion of the preceptory.

Brucafel in 1133 and Campagne-sur-Aude in 1147, as well as extensive financial immunities. The second of his donations, made on the eve of his departure on crusade, was a great occasion with ten Templars present, the largest number listed in any of the charters, where the figure is seldom more than three or four.[67] The superior social status of this family was emphasized in 1167, when Ermengarde, viscountess of Narbonne, appointed the arbiters in a dispute between two members of the same family over a donation to the Temple.[68]

However, the typical donors were the local nobility and knights;[69] the same social milieu that enabled Catharism to flourish also provided aid and support to the military orders.[70] Co-lordship was common and, indeed, provided the basis of the preceptory when the Canet and Barbaira families jointly donated the walled settlement of Douzens.[71] It was not, however, always necessary for co-seigneurs to act together, even when they are designated *pariarii*.[72] Gifts to the Temple at Molières and in the woods of Ourtigne, situated in the narrow valley of the Lauquette in the mountains south of the Audoise plain, took place in five different grants over a period of six years between 1163 and 1169. All the donors were members of the family of the lords of Villar: in three cases they held a sixth each and in a fourth, an eighth. In the fifth case, Isalguier of Clermont, son of William Raymond of Villar, stated explicitly that the honour he was donating 'is mine without any part belonging to another man'.[73] Some sense of the horizontal ties within local aristocratic society can be gained from the testament of Peter Raymond of Barbaira, about to enter the Temple in 1153. He was concerned to make provision for his son and two daughters. Berengar, 'my youngest and greatly loved son', was under-age, so he created a kind of board of trustees to look after his affairs. This contained six named individuals, five of whom were laymen and one of whom was the vicar of Carcassonne, and 'all others of the knighthood of Barbaira, and others from the least to the greatest of the proven men of Barbaira', a list that suggests a kind of knightly confraternity. Two others were to act as *baillis*, administering Berengar's rights and property,

67 It is not possible to estimate numbers of Templars in the house, since transactions are almost invariably conducted by the most important Templars present and there are no lists of Templar witnesses.

68 *Douzens*, A, 20.

69 Cf. Bouchard, *Holy Entrepreneurs*, pp. 21–2.

70 See M. Barber, *The Cathars: Dualist Heretics in Languedoc in the High Middle Ages* (London, 2000), pp. 34–43. However, there were few identifiable Cathar sympathizers here on the eve of the Albigensian Crusade in 1209. Among the families who had contributed to Douzens and its subsidiaries, only that at Laure, in the Minervois to the north, can be shown to have had a house of *perfectae* at that time. See M. Roquebert, *L'Epopée Cathare, 1198–1212: L'invasion* (Toulouse, 1970), pp. 525–37. The crusade itself must have passed by on its way along the Aude valley from Béziers to Carcassonne, but the only expedition into this region was a brief diversion to Montlaur (about 7 km to the south of Douzens) to put down a rebellion in the spring of 1210.

71 *Douzens*, A, 1. See also other co-seigneuries, A, 58, 61, 62, B, 78. Such common ownership was not unique to Languedoc. Similar arrangements were made in Burgundy: see Bouchard, *Holy Entrepreneurs*, pp. 180–1.

72 Defined by Niermeyer as co-partners to a non-partitioned estate: *Mediae Latinitatis Lexicon Minus* (Leiden, 1976), p. 764.

73 *Douzens*, B, 42, 43, 44, 45, 54.

'until he may be such an age that he might be able to rule and ask for all these rights'.[74]

Such men held their property in various ways, most commonly in the form of an *honor* or an *alodium*, terms given twenty-six and sixteen meanings respectively in Niermeyer's *Lexicon*. The editors of the cartularies consider the references to these to be too numerous to list in the index. Less commonly, they held a *feudum* (*fevum*, *fevus*, *feu*) mentioned in thirty documents, a word that escapes with only fourteen entries in Niermeyer. All three indicate the holding of property of some kind, usually with associated rights, both jurisdictional and financial, and often settled with families in various states of dependence. All three could be held from another individual or institution, although there is evidently a distinction between allods and fiefs.[75] The former is sometimes described as a free allod (*per francum et liberum alodium*),[76] which suggests that an allod cannot invariably mean free of any encumbrance as it has sometimes been defined. On the other hand, fiefs were always held from someone else. Men could of course hold some property as allods and some as fiefs, so it is not possible to draw any social distinctions here. Nevertheless, there was a lesser class of knights existing below the level of the lords who first endowed the Temple; thus, the two references in donations by William Peter of Villargel in 1133–35 to 'those fiefs which the knights (*milites*) held from me',[77] while many of the gifts to Douzens are of quite small pieces of land or parts of vineyards.[78]

Proprietors were not exclusively male nor were they all Christians. In 1160 Poncia Raina and her daughter, Guarsenda, gave themselves and 'all the honour we have in the *villa* of Douzens and its district'. They promised to give 3 *solidi* of Melgueil each Christmas for the rest to their lives for holding the honour from the Temple, 'and after our deaths, if there do not survive any legitimate children from my daughter, Guarsenda, all the honour will remain with and revert to you; if a legitimate child of Guarsenda does survive, he will be your man and have and hold this honour and pay the above *usaticum*'.[79] Equally Jewish proprietors were an integral part of the web of landholding: in 1173 four Jewish co-seigneurs confirmed a gift of a vineyard by Aladaidis, daughter of the late Amiel Carbonel, who had held it from them. The Templars would continue to do so, rendering a quarter of the products as he had done and bringing it to their houses in Carcassonne.[80]

Milites, even if relatively poor were, however, freemen. This was not the case for those people granted to the Temple as part of the packages of property and rights that characterize many grants, although once again there is considerable variation in social, economic and legal status. Thus, in 1165, Raymond Hugh of Aiguesvives, granted 'one of my men, William, namely the *parator*, and all his posterity with everything both movable and immovable that he has and holds at

74 *Douzens*, A, 6.
75 *Douzens*, A, 175 (*alodes et feuvos*), B, 57 (*feudos*, *alodios*).
76 *Douzens*, A 115, D, 4. See also p. xxiv.
77 *Douzens*, A, 38, C, 4.
78 For example, the grants of the Mantilini family (see above).
79 *Douzens*, A, 10.
80 *Douzens*, D, 13. See also A, 148, *in honore Bonysach judei*, and A, 133, *in honore judaico*.

present and, while he lives, that he will acquire. . . .' Although this was for the remission of the sins of himself and his relatives, he nevertheless received a sum of 120 *solidi* of Melgueil 'from the alms of the Temple'.[81] It is difficult to determine whether occupational surnames reflect reality, but the sum involved is considerable. A point of comparison is the sale of mills and their associated buildings on the Aude in 1152, for which the Templars paid 400 *solidi* of Melgueil.[82] This suggests that William had valuable skills, probably as a cloth finisher as the name implies, and this, in turn, would explain why he had property and might be expected to acquire more. There is no such ambiguity about the grant by Bernard of Canet of 'William, clerk [*clericus*], the son of one of my men called Arnold of Beiracho' in 1148. This was also the occasion of his manumission, that he 'be free [*liber*] and a freeman [*francum*], and discharged from all yoke of servitude in perpetuity'. That William was regarded as both having some kind of clerical status and as being unfree is quite clear from the fact that the gift was made 'into the hand of Pons, bishop of Carcassonne', and received by Bernard, chaplain of Saint-Jean-de-Carrière.[83] These examples show that although there was a legal barrier between the free and the unfree,[84] social and economic lines were more permeable. The example of Pons Mirabel in 1167 reinforces this impression. At that time Hugh Inard and his sister, Guarsenda, and her husband, Arnold Geoffrey, granted Pons and his children to the Temple, while at the same time freeing them from servitude. However, a curious coda was attached: 'which exemption and freedom of the aforesaid persons we make under such condition, that Peter, son of Pons Mirabel, leads as wife Aladaidis, our aforesaid sister'.[85]

The Templars, however, held not only properties and men, but churches as well. They were granted the right to their own priests and oratories in 1145, on the grounds that 'it is not fitting, and indeed is almost fatal to the souls of religious brothers, to mingle with the crowds of men and to meet women on the occasion of going to church'.[86] Given the continuing existence of proprietary churches (papal reform notwithstanding) and the close communal links between the Templar preceptories and the local community, such a separation seems unlikely. Thus, in 1153, the lords of Barbaira and Canet gave the Order the church at Saint-Jean-de-Carrière and all the buildings appertaining to it, acts confirmed by Pons, bishop of Carcassonne. At the same time a special area of jurisdiction was established around it. 'Within the boundaries named above, namely those designated by crosses, no man or men, woman or women, no cattle

81 *Douzens*, A, 31.

82 *Douzens*, A, 2. See also A, 67 for the sale of what is described as a 'very small' piece of land for 6 *solidi* of Melgueil.

83 *Douzens*, A, 101. Bernard seems to have been prior of a small community at St-Jean-de-Carrière. See Constable, *Reformation*, p. 95, on the entry of serfs into religious houses and on the ordination of serfs.

84 The Templars sometimes underlined this legal servitude, as in A, 160, 52.

85 *Douzens*, A, 27. On the ambiguities of status involved in these transactions, see pp. xxxv–xxxvi.

86 The bull *Militia Dei*, in *Papsturkunden für Templer und Johanniter*, ed. R. Hiestand, Vorarbeiten zum Oriens Pontificius 1: Abhandlungen des Akademie der Wissenschaften in Göttingen 77 (Göttingen, 1972), no. 10, pp. 216–17.

or sheep, no horses or foals, no pack or sumpter horses, no other material of any man on any occasion or summons, shall be reclaimed, except for a thief or thieves.'[87] By this date Raymond Ermengaud, a brother of one of the donors and one of the original founders of the house of Douzens in 1133, had become a Templar himself, and was one of those receiving the gift of the church. Raymond, Pons's predecessor as bishop, had made his own contribution to the Templars' patrimony when, in 1138, he and the canons of the cathedral of Saint-Nazaire at Carcassonne had granted the tithes from the livestock and gardens of the church of St Mary at Mas-des-Cours, while expressing the hope that 'they and their successors may be lawful and faithful friends of St Mary and the clerics living there and the clerics of St Stephen'.[88]

The twelfth-century cartularies of Douzens provide the raw material for an examination of the means by which a new religious house could establish itself within local society. That the house belonged to a unique Order, that of the Temple, a community without previous ideological or organizational models, makes the documents particularly pertinent, as they reflect the ways in which the Templars both engaged with contemporary social and economic changes and at the same time adapted to traditional spiritual needs. Thus, in the first instance, the cartularies show how the Templars, starting with nothing, created a material base that made the preceptory a viable concern, and how, in the second, this ultimately rested upon the medieval conviction that institutions such as this were the most effective means by which a good end might be achieved and, it was hoped, ultimately salvation obtained. In Patrick Geary's striking phrase: unlike western society today, in the medieval world the dead were not banished from society. 'Death marked a transition, a change in status, not an end.'[89]

87 *Douzens*, A, 87. The use of crosses as markers to designate a *salvacio*, or place of security, extending some distance from the church itself, was characteristic of the area. It was particularly valuable where a church and the small community around it were relatively isolated, as was probably the case here. See P. Duparc, 'Le Cimetière séjour des vivants (IXe–XIIe siècle)', *Bulletin Philologique et Historique* (1964), 498.

88 *Douzens*, B, 9. There were, however, later disputes with St Stephen's, apparently resolved in 1162: B, 8, see above.

89 Geary, *Living with the Dead*, pp. 1–2.

Events and Opinions: Norman and English Views of Aquitaine, c.1152–c.1204

JOHN GILLINGHAM

My intention here is to consider what historians writing in Latin in England and in Normandy in the period between Eleanor's marriage to Henry II in 1152 and her death in 1204 knew about her homeland, the duchy of Aquitaine. As Jane Martindale has pointed out, twentieth-century historians writing in English tended to give the impression that twelfth-century Aquitaine was generally in a state of internal chaos, 'an under-developed region awaiting efficient government and rational exploitation of its economic resources by some colonial power'.[1] But do these modern views reflect the views of twelfth-century English and Norman historians? Did contemporaries already look upon Aquitaine as a turbulent and disorderly realm crying out for the smack of firm government? In this chapter I shall rely chiefly, though not entirely, upon the writings of nine authors: five monks and four secular clerks. The monks are three Benedictines, Robert of Torigni, Gervase of Canterbury and Richard of Devizes; an Augustinian canon, William of Newburgh; and a Cistercian, Ralph of Coggeshall. The secular clerks are Roger of Howden, Walter Map, Gerald de Barri and Ralph Diceto.[2] Of these nine, eight wrote in England and for English audiences. The only Norman among them was Robert of Torigni, but his approach to Aquitaine was, I shall argue, to have a significant influence upon chroniclers writing in England. He helped to establish two themes that were to have a substantial impact on the northern view of Aquitaine: traitors in Poitou, heretics in Gascony.

1 J. Martindale, 'Eleanor of Aquitaine', in *Richard Coeur de Lion in History and Myth*, ed. J. L. Nelson, King's College Medieval Studies 7 (London, 1992), pp. 17–50 (pp. 24–6), citing the views of F. M. Powicke and W. L. Warren; reprinted in J. Martindale, *Status, Authority and Regional Power: Aquitaine and France, 9th to 12th Centuries* (Aldershot, 1997), no. XI.

2 Other historical works that might have figured here, but which have little or nothing to say about Aquitaine after 1152, are the chronicles of Ralph Niger, the *Historia Pontificalis* of John of Salisbury (which in the only extant – incomplete – manuscript breaks off at the start of 1152), and the *Draco Normannicus* (despite a few verses on Henry and Eleanor's marriage and the Toulouse problem).

*

I begin with one of the stories told by Gerald in *The Journey through Wales:*

> A powerful seigneur (*dominator*) held prisoner in his castle a man whom he had blinded and castrated. Over time this prisoner was able to commit to memory all the passage-ways of the castle and the steps which led up to the towers. One day he seized the lord's child, his only son and heir, and dragged him to the top of one of the towers. There he stood, outlined against the sky, threatening to throw the boy over the battlements. A great clamour arose and everyone screamed in anguish. The boy's father came running; no one's distress was greater than his. He made every offer he could think of in an attempt to obtain the release of his son. The prisoner said that he would not free the boy until the father had cut off his own testicles. The father begged and pleaded but all in vain. In the end he pretended to agree, and had himself hit an almighty blow on the lower part of his body while everyone present howled in grief. The blind man asked him where he felt most pain, and he replied that it was in his loins. When the blind man made as though to throw the boy over, he had himself struck a second blow, and this time he said the worst pain was in his heart. Still the prisoner did not believe him, and dragged the boy to the very edge of the parapet. The third time, to save his son, the father really did cut off his testicles, and shouted out that it was his teeth that hurt the most. 'Now I believe you', said the blind man, 'and I am avenged'. With that he hurled himself and the boy over the battlements; both were dashed to pieces on the spot.

To save his son's soul, continues Gerald, the lord built a monastery at the place where the two died. 'It is still there, at Châteauroux, today. They call it the Scene of Sorrows (*De Doloribus*).'[3] This same story, or one very like it, was evidently well known to Ralph Diceto, dean of St Paul's.[4] The date at which Gerald told the story matters. He wrote the *Itinerarium* c.1191, in the middle of the period (c.1185–c.1194) that he spent in royal service; indeed he dedicated it to Richard I's chancellor, William Longchamp.

The great lordship of Châteauroux had first come to the notice of northern chroniclers (Roger of Howden, Robert of Torigni, Diceto) in 1177 when Henry II insisted he should have custody of the heiress, Denise of Déols. According to Robert of Torigni, 'some say that it is worth as much as the revenues of the whole of Normandy'.[5] Its central role in the confrontations between Philip Augustus

3 *Itinerarium Kambrie*, I.11, in Gerald of Wales, *Opera*, ed. J. S. Brewer, J. F. Dimock and G. F. Warner, RS 21, 8 vols. (London, 1861–91), VI, 84–5, where a footnote implies that the identification was made only in one manuscript, and that a sixteenth-century one. However, Dimock did not know of the early thirteenth-century manuscript, London, British Library, Additional 34762, where the relevant passage with the words *apud castellum Radulfi* is on fol. 137r. My translation is based on that by L. Thorpe in Gerald of Wales, *The Journey through Wales/The Description of Wales* (Harmondsworth, 1978), pp. 142–3.

4 Twice Ralph noted that the name was derived *a doloribus*: Ralph Diceto, *Opera Historica*, ed. W. Stubbs, RS 68, 2 vols. (London, 1876), I, 425 and II, 49. It may be no more than coincidence that the two English authors to refer to these events had both studied at Paris. For later comment on the story, see Grillon des Chapelles, *Esquisses biographiques du Département de l'Indre*, 3 vols. (Paris, 1862), I, 173.

5 Robert of Torigni, *Chronicle*, in *Chronicles of the Reigns of Stephen, Henry II, and Richard I*, ed. R. Howlett, RS 82, 4 vols. (London, 1884–89), IV, 274.

and the Angevins meant that by the late 1180s there was no place in Aquitaine that was more headline news than Châteauroux.[6] In words written in 1189 Gerald expressed his view of Aquitaine as *terra indomita*, a turbulent, disorderly and lawless land inhabited by a *gens indomita* – or at any rate it had been until taken in hand by Duke Richard (*hic leo noster*).[7] On what did he base this judgement? No doubt it suited his book to highlight the lawlessness of Aquitaine in order to magnify Richard's achievement;[8] nonetheless it seems likely that stories such as this one were the straw out of which he made his bricks.

By the 1190s conventional opinion in England was that Aquitaine was indeed ungovernable. In Diceto's view, the death of the Young King at Martel in the Turenne meant that he died 'among barbarous peoples (*populos satis barbaros*)'.[9] Indeed even in the Muslim world, at the court of Saladin, people had heard about the rebellious Aquitanians. There Saladin's brother, Safadin, praised King Richard for 'having overcome those tyrants whom none of his ancestors had been able to subdue (*tirannos provincie avis et atavis indomabiles*)'.[10] This at least was the fancy with which the Winchester Benedictine, Richard of Devizes, writing in 1193, entertained his readers. At the Capetian court William the Breton expressed the view that Poitevins could not be trusted.[11] As Martin Aurell has recently put it, 'C'est de façon unanime qu'à la fin du XIIe siècle, les chroniqueurs français ou anglo-normands présentent l'Aquitaine et sa noblesse sous les traits de l'insoumission, de l'hostilité à la royauté.'[12] At the end of the twelfth century, certainly, but was this how people had always thought of Aquitaine? Or did late twelfth-century events mean that this tradition was being invented, or reinvented?

Marcus Bull has drawn attention to the consequences of the dearth of historical writing from southern France. We do not have, he points out, 'the sort of material that often permits detailed and nuanced reconstructions of events'. Hence 'scholars are often driven to argue in terms of endemic and persistent conditions – for instance, political fragmentation, weak feudal ties, under-resourced princely power – as in some sense givens that suffice to explain why

6 The struggle for Châteauroux meant that the events of 1187–89 within and outside its walls were reported by Howden, Diceto, Gervase, Gerald de Barri, William of Newburgh and Coggeshall, as well as by Rigord of Saint-Denis and William the Breton.

7 Gerald praised Richard for bringing order to a disorderly people, establishing law where all was lawless, beating down obstacles, levelling all that was rough, and restoring the ancient bounds and rights of Aquitaine (*terram hactenus indomitam..tanta virtute rexit et domuit .. longe plenius et tranquillius solito pacificaret . . . In formam igitur informia redigens, in normam enormia quaeque reducens, fortia confundens et aspera complanans, antiquos Aquitanie terminos et jura reformavit . . . gentis indomitae reprimeret audaciam*). This is from the second recension of *Topographia Hibernica*, ed. J. F. Dimock, in Gerald, *Opera*, V, 195–6.

8 M. Aurell, *L'Empire des Plantagenêt* (Paris, 2003), p. 207. I know of no evidence that Gerald ever visited Aquitaine. At the date at which he told this story, Paris and Chinon were probably the furthest he had travelled from Manorbier.

9 Diceto, II, 19.

10 Richard of Devizes, *Chronicle*, ed. and trans. J. T. Appleby (London, 1963), p. 76.

11 *Oeuvres de Rigord et de Guillaume le Breton, historiens de Philippe-Auguste*, ed. H. F. Delaborde, 2 vols. (Paris, 1882–85), I, 210.

12 Aurell, *L'Empire des Plantagenêt*, p. 206.

warfare was widespread'.[13] But as Geoffrey Koziol has recently emphasized, power was a fragile commodity everywhere in France, even in the supposedly strongest principalities such as Normandy, Anjou and Flanders. If the kings of France had troubles with their counts and castellans, so too did 'every territorial prince'. Every ruler, even the strongest, was affected by what was virtually a life cycle of political change: 'hard times in the early years, stability in the middle years, restive jockeying for position before an impending death at the end'. [14] It is far from clear that the political structures of Aquitaine were unusually weak. Indeed, Jean Dunbabin has recently paired eleventh-century Aquitaine with eleventh-century Normandy as two regions where 'power was less fragmented' than elsewhere.[15]

In this context the chronology of historical writing is important. In Henry II's reign, very little by way of contemporary history was written in England until the 1180s. Indeed, it is tempting to suggest that when Henry came to the throne of England in 1154 one of his first achievements was to put a stop to the writing of contemporary history that had flourished so much in the second quarter of the twelfth century.[16] Evidently the acquisition of Aquitaine and the arrival of Eleanor at the Angevin court had not acted as a stimulus to historical writing. Given the absence of any tradition of historical writing at the princely courts of south and south-west France this is hardly surprising. Henry was undoubtedly interested in supporting history written in French, notably the histories of Wace and Benoît de Saint Maur, but these works turned out to be the history of his ancestors, not a history of his own times. Moreover he seems to have been uninterested in Latin history in any form – doubtless to the disappointment of would-be historians who knew that the young Henry had been unusually well-educated and may well have hoped that, in consequence, a learned prince would lend them some serious support. It was not to be.[17]

Not until the early 1170s did Roger of Howden take up his pen and even then, so far as Latin prose is concerned – setting aside the Becket biographers – his remained an isolated voice until the 1180s. In the 1180s Walter Map began to put together his remarkable ragbag *De Nugis Curialium* and Diceto began to compose his *Ymagines Historiarum*, followed later in that decade by Gervase of

13 M. G. Bull, *The Miracles of Our Lady of Rocamadour: Analysis and Translation* (Woodbridge, 1999), p. 80.

14 G. Koziol, 'Political Culture', in *France in the Central Middle Ages 900–1200*, ed. M. G. Bull (Oxford, 2002), pp. 55–8.

15 J. Dunbabin, *France in the Making, 843–1180*, 2nd edn (Oxford, 2000), p. xxi.

16 Henry of Huntingdon's *Historia Anglorum* came to an end with 1154. It may be that it was only illness or death (he died c.1157) that prevented Henry from writing the new book for a new king that he promised, but there is nonetheless a pattern here. The Peterborough Chronicle also ended with 1154, and so did the work generally known as the *Gesta Stephani* – although in the one surviving manuscript its title is *Historia Anglorum*. See *Gesta Stephani*, ed. and trans. K. R. Potter and R. H. C. Davis (Oxford, 1976), p. xii. If, as suspected, Robert, bishop of Bath, wrote it, then we have an author who lived until 1166 but who composed no *Gesta Henrici*.

17 Thus when in the 1190s Roger of Howden needed information to fill the gap between 1148 (the end of the *Historia post obitum Bedae*) and his own starting point in 1170, he had to go outside England to Scotland, and to the Melrose Annals – which have something to say about the 1159 Toulouse expedition in which King Malcolm participated, but nothing else on Aquitaine.

Canterbury. The first version of Gerald de Barri's first major work, the *Topographia Hibernica*, was completed in 1188. In the 1190s all five authors continued to write new works or tinker with their old ones and were joined by Richard of Devizes, Ralph of Coggeshall and William of Newburgh. It was this unprecedented burst of creativity that has led to the last two decades of the twelfth century being described as 'a golden age of historical writing in England'.[18] In Normandy the pattern was entirely different. Here Robert of Torigni, abbot of Mont-Saint-Michel, pressed determinedly on with the history he had begun even before Henry II came to the throne. After his death in 1186 no one in Normandy continued his work apart from an anonymous annalist at Jumièges.[19]

This chronology is important. A product of the schools of Paris such as John of Salisbury may have liked to scoff at the schools of Poitiers and might indeed have picked up other anti-Poitevin views in the Capetian capital. In a letter written in 1166 to John of Canterbury, bishop of Poitiers, he referred to *speciales Aquitanorum consuetudines et inaudita iura*.[20] But this probably referred to ecclesiastical customs he did not like rather than to political turbulence. Indeed, I think it unlikely that anyone living in England in the 1150s and 1160s after the recent experience of the events of Stephen's reign would have thought that Aquitaine was peculiarly lawless. But in England there was no one chronicling events in the later 1150s and 1160s. Robert of Torigni referred to Henry suppressing a rebellion 'by certain people' in Aquitaine in 1154, capturing Thouars in 1158 and Castillon-sur-Agen in 1161 'to the wonder and terror of Gascons', but it was only with the Lusignan revolt of 1168 that he gave episodes of this sort more than a cursory mention.[21] In consequence the events of 1154, 1158 and 1161 seem to have made no impression on the minds of any of Robert's known English readers. Nor indeed did they impinge on Geoffrey of Vigeois; the Limousin chronicler recorded no revolt against Henry II before 1168.[22] Moreover, although the leading barons of Poitou and the Angoumois participated in the great rebellion of 1173–74, the threat to Henry II's power was much more serious in Normandy and England than it was in Aquitaine.[23] All this changed in the second half of

18 A. Gransden, *Historical Writing in England, c.550–c.1307* (London, 1974), p. 219.

19 When the Jumièges annals mention Poitevins or Gascony, as occasionally in the entries between 1173 and 1214, their tone is neutral: *Annales de l'Abbaye Royale de Saint-Pierre de Jumièges*, ed. J. Laporte (Rouen, 1954), pp. 69, 79, 85, 87, 99.

20 *The Letters of John of Salisbury. Volume Two: The Later Letters (1163–80)*, ed. W. J. Millor and C. N. L. Brooke (Oxford, 1979), no. 177, p. 178. Cf. the reference to *urbs garrula et ventosa* – probably Poitiers – in a letter to Ralph Niger, *ibid.*, no. 182, p. 206; also *levitatem gentis*, meaning Poitevins, in *Johannis Saresberiensis Episcopi Carnotensis Policratici*, I.13, ed. C. C. J. Webb, 2 vols. (Oxford, 1909), I, 57.

21 Torigni, pp. 179, 198, 211, 235–8.

22 Geoffrey of Vigeois, Bk 1 c. 66. I cite Geoffrey in this way to facilitate reference to a badly needed future edition of his *Chronica* as well as to those in P. Labbe, *Novae Bibliothecae Manuscriptorum Librorum*, 2 vols. (Paris, 1657), vol. II and *RHGF*, vols. 12 and 18. Although Geoffrey wrote in the early 1180s, his history, written, as he put it in his preface, 'to the honour of God and in praise of my country' – by which he meant not Aquitaine but the Limousin – stretched back to the time of his birth (c.1140) and beyond.

23 The lists of rebels given by Roger of Howden name comparatively few from northern Aquitaine when compared with the numbers from England and Normandy: *Gesta Regis Henrici Secundi*, ed.

Henry's reign. In this period England, Normandy and (until early 1189) Anjou remained at peace, while in parts of Aquitaine King Henry II and Duke Richard were more or less permanently engaged in war. Whereas in the years prior to 1174, Henry II occasionally took what from a local point of view might be seen as bullying action in Aquitaine, after 1175 he and Richard did so very frequently.[24] In consequence rebellion, especially in the Limousin and the Angoumois, became much more common, and so also did war in Aquitaine's frontier regions – Quercy, the Toulousain and Berry – against the count of Toulouse and the king of France. Whereas the principal theatre of the first dynastic crisis 1173–74 was in England and Normandy, the second, that of 1183, was in the Limousin. As a consequence of the active policy undertaken from 1175 onwards by Duke Richard at his father's command, Aquitaine became a visibly more turbulent place.[25] It may have been this, rather than repetition of older slurs, that led to the creation of the late twelfth-century stereotype.

Of course as members of a French-speaking Latin-writing cultural elite, English chroniclers might have been aware of an older northern French or Frankish hostility to the south.[26] There is some sign of this awareness in the writings of earlier Anglo-Norman historians, but chiefly where the Gascons are concerned. In the *Gesta Pontificum* William of Malmesbury alluded to the *Guasconica ferocitas* of the monks of La Réole responsible for the killing of Abbo of Fleury. In his *Gesta Regum* William showed himself to be fascinated by the character of Duke William IX, but when writing about him did not feel moved to generalize about Poitevins or Aquitanians. Indeed, for some of his stories about necromancy and wonders in Italy one of William's sources was an old

W. Stubbs, RS 49, 2 vols. (London, 1867), I, 46–7, while, so far as we can tell, the southern part of the duchy, including the Limousin, seems to have been untouched by the revolt of 1173–74: Vigeois, Bk 1 c. 67; J. Gillingham, *Richard I* (London, 1999), p. 47.

24 'By 1180 . . . Henry's and Richard's lordship relied more blatantly on force than their predecessors.' From now on it was undoubtedly 'a land which unsympathetic English chroniclers regarded as plagued by turbulent barons': Dunbabin, *France in the Making*, pp. 343 and 345. See also R. V. Turner and R. R. Heiser, *The Reign of Richard Lionheart* (Harlow, 2000), pp. 31–3 and 62–71.

25 Aurell has calculated that there was a rebellion in Aquitaine every three and a half years throughout Henry II's reign: *L'Empire des Plantagenêt*, p. 209. The statistic can be elaborated and refined: rebellions in Aquitaine in seven of the first twenty-three years of Henry's rule over Aquitaine (1154, 1158, 1161, 1168–69, 1173, 1174) and in eight of the last fifteen (1175, 1176, 1177, 1178, 1179, 1182, 1183, 1188). Of course, there is no doubt that from 1170, when the detailed narrative of Howden's *Gesta Henrici* begins, we have much more evidence than before. In the Rolls Series edition Torigni covers the period from 1170 to 1185 in 70 pages; the equivalent for Howden is 342 pages. However, I do not think that the greater frequency and seriousness of Aquitanian revolt in the latter part of the reign is just a trick of the evidence.

26 Dudo of Saint-Quentin referred to 'cowardly and mean' Poitevins, though the force of this is diminished somewhat by the fact that the Norman duke in whose mouth this characterization was placed promptly gave his sister in marriage to Count William of Poitou: *History of the Normans*, trans. E. Christiansen (Woodbridge, 1998), p. 69. In Benoît's version of c.1175 it was made explicit that the duke was only joking – 'as friends often do' – and the joke was followed by splendid marriage celebrations: *Chroniques des ducs de Normandie par Benoît*, ed. C. Fahlin (Lund, 1951), ll. 12059–64, 12079–112. I am not aware of any evidence that any Norman or English author knew of Ralph Glaber's criticism of Aquitanian mores, although Glaber was certainly known to a mid-twelfth-century reviser of the *Gesta Consulum Andegavorum*.

Malmesbury monk, *genere Aquitanico*.[27] In the context of a narrative of the crusade of 1101, Orderic Vitalis referred to both Aquitanians and Gascons as 'quarrelsome folk' (*contumaces*), but reserved his main criticism for the *improbi Gascones*.[28]

At this point some observations on terminology may be useful. Although the authors I am considering here used the word 'Poitou' in a fairly consistent fashion and meant by it more or less what we mean by it, the terms 'Aquitaine' and 'Gascony' were used significantly more loosely. 'Aquitaine' could be used 'correctly' to mean the whole duchy, as when William of Newburgh described Aquitaine as 'stretching from the borders of Anjou and Brittany to the Pyrenean mountains which divide Gaul from Spain'.[29] (It may, of course, be significant that William felt he needed to locate Aquitaine in this way.) At other times it seems to imply just the lands south of Poitou, as when Robert of Torigni wrote of a rebellion of 'the greater part of the Poitevins and Aquitanians' in 1168.[30] Coggeshall (while consistently referring to Aquitaine as a county) also distinguished Poitevins and Aquitanians.[31] On one occasion Gervase of Canterbury adopted the same terminology when referring to Eleanor's land as Aquitaine and Poitou, yet then twice, in the manner of Orderic, wrote of 'Aquitaine and Gascony' as though for him Aquitaine meant just the northern part.[32] This was Gerald de Barri's usage at the end of the 1180s. 'Today', he wrote 'all Gascony and Aquitaine enjoy the same rule as Britain.'[33]

If Aquitaine was treated as a movable province, at least no one had any doubt that Gascony lay in the south. Yet here too there was a zone of uncertainty. Just how far did Gascony extend? Was, or was not, the Toulousain within its borders? No doubt Eleanor's claim to Toulouse muddied the waters here. According to Herbert of Bosham, when Henry II's army was *in partibus Tolosanis* in 1159 they were 'beyond Gascony', *ultra Guasconiam*.[34] Yet when William of Newburgh described the same campaign, we are told that Henry led an army *in partes Gasconie* and that *Gasconiae fines ingressus est*. Diceto not only wrote of Gascony

[27] *De Gestis Pontificum Anglorum*, ed. N. E. S. A. Hamilton, RS 52 (London, 1870), p. 249; William of Malmesbury, *Gesta Regum Anglorum*, ed. R. A. B. Mynors, R. M. Thomson and M. Winterbottom, 2 vols. (Oxford, 1998–99), I, 288. As Thomson points out, William must have had an Aquitanian source for his material on Raymond IV of Saint-Gilles, perhaps the elderly monk: *ibid.*, II, 345. The other widely read English historian of William's generation, the far more insular Henry of Huntingdon, made no mention of the duchy of Aquitaine, or of Poitevins or Gascons. For him Eleanor was just the unnamed daughter of an unnamed count of Poitou: *Historia Anglorum*, ed. and trans. D. E. Greenway (Oxford, 1996), pp. 756–8.

[28] *The Ecclesiastical History*, ed. and trans. M. Chibnall, 6 vols. (Oxford, 1969–80), V, 330 and 332. Indeed in his eyes Gascony and Aquitaine were two different things; for him the duchy of Aquitaine ended at the Garonne: *ibid.*, V, 280. Even if little read outside Saint-Evroul, Orderic's views no doubt reflect a strand of Norman opinion.

[29] William of Newburgh, *Historia Rerum Anglicarum*, in Howlett (ed.), *Chronicles*, I, 93.

[30] Torigni, p. 235. Under 1169 he wrote 'Pictavia et Wasconia'.

[31] *Chronicon Anglicanum*, ed. J. Stevenson, RS 66 (London, 1875), pp. 13–14, 25, 70, 135–6, 146.

[32] *Historical Works*, ed. W. Stubbs, RS 73, 2 vols. (London, 1879–80), I, 149, 162, 167. Indeed, in one passage Gervase implied that Poitou was outside Gaul: I, 149.

[33] *Topographia Hibernica*, p. 149.

[34] *Materials for the History of Thomas Becket, Archbishop of Canterbury*, ed. J. C. Robertson and J. B. Sheppard, RS 67, 7 vols. (London, 1875–85), III, 175.

as though it extended as far as Toulouse, he also stretched it north of the Dordogne, describing the land of Turenne as 'in Gascony'.[35] According to the early thirteenth-century author of the Margam Annals, Toulouse was *metropolis Gasconiae*.[36] As Nicholas Vincent has pointed out, there was 'a fair degree of ignorance' and 'a lack of precise terminology that would permit a distinction between the various regions of Aquitaine and the south'.[37] What matters here is that however widely or narrowly these authors drew the boundaries of Gascony, by having the Gascons within Aquitaine, they were allowing themselves to inherit centuries of Frankish historical writing in which the evil and perfidious ways of this people were prominent. *Perfidia vasconica* in the words of Einhard's Life of Charlemagne – words that were quoted by Ralph Niger writing in the 1190s.[38] Moreover, given the high profile of Toulouse in the early history of Catharism in the south of France, the notion of a wider Gascony embracing Toulouse was one that had implications. Its inhabitants were in grave danger of being branded not only as perfidious but as adherents of a false faith. Indeed, in 1178 the threat of heresy moved Abbot Henry of Clairvaux to write about 'the shit of Gascony', a phrase taken up twenty years later by none other than Pope Innocent III.[39] All a far cry from the recent *Country Life* description of Gascony as 'the new Gloucestershire'.[40]

Where could later twelfth-century English historians find out about events in the duchy in the years after Henry's marriage to Eleanor? Ralph Diceto's list of 'the famous men who wrote history' – his words – begins with Trogus Pompeius and ends with Ralph, dean of London. The penultimate name in the list is 'Robert abbot of Mont-Saint-Michel in Normandy who took his chronicle up to 1167'. [41] It has long been known that, as well as Diceto, the Waverley and Osney annalists and, most influentially, Roger of Wendover and Matthew Paris also read and used Torigni. In my view the name of William of Newburgh should be added to this list. As the only contemporary chronicler of events in the later 1150s and 1160s, Robert was to have a significant impact upon historical writing in England, not the least of which was his version of events in Aquitaine.

For example, in his entry for the year 1168 Robert used the phrase *dolo*

35 Newburgh, *Historia*, I, 121 and 123; Diceto, II, 19 and 55. Gerald's usage is less clear. In one passage we are told that Duke Richard entered *Gasconiae fines* in force, did well, then invaded *Tholose fines* and was about to attack the noble city of Toulouse, to which his mother had a claim, when envoys from Philip Augustus asked him to desist: *De Principis Instructione*, in *Opera*, VIII, 245–6. The ambiguity of the word *fines* adds to the uncertainty here.

36 *Annales Monastici*, ed. H. R. Luard, RS 36, 5 vols. (London, 1864–69), I, 32.

37 N. Vincent, 'England and the Albigensian Crusade', in *England and Europe in the Reign of Henry III (1216–1272)*, ed. B. K. U. Weiler and I. W. Rowlands (Aldershot, 2002), pp. 67–97 (p. 70).

38 *Chronica*, ed. R. Anstruther (London, 1851), p. 148. I am not aware of any evidence that the *Pilgrims' Book of Compostela*, with its praise of Poitevins and humorously insulting treatment of Gascons, was known in either England or Normandy. I have had the considerable benefit of being able to read the typescript of a forthcoming paper by Guilhem Pépin, 'Les Aquitains et les Gascons au haut Moyen Age: genèse et affirmation des deux peuples'.

39 'Tolosanos et faeces Vasconiae', in *PL* CCIV, col. 218, no. 3; cf. Innocent III's letter of 1198, *PL* CCXIV, col. 71, no. 81.

40 As cited in *Private Eye*, no. 1079, May 2003.

41 Diceto, I, 20–4. In fact it is clear that he used Torigni up until at least 1171.

Pictavensium. Such phrases were to resonate through early thirteenth-century English history. As Nicholas Vincent noted, 'by the 1230s Poitou and Poitevins had became bywords for duplicity and the senseless waste of resources'.[42] According to Coggeshall, in 1205 John had assembled forces at Portsmouth ready to return to the Continent, but was prevented from doing so after it had been powerfully argued that it was not safe to trust to 'the treachery and fickleness of the Poitevins who have always been accustomed to hatch plots against their ruler' (*dolositati et levitati Pictavorum qui semper erga principes suos aliquid doli machinari consueverant*). According to Roger of Wendover and Matthew Paris, in 1214 John suffered as a result of the 'customary treachery of the Poitevins' (*solita Pictavensium proditio*).[43] When Torigni employed the phrase *dolo Pictavensium*, it was with explicit reference to the killing of Earl Patrick of Salisbury, commander of the king's forces in Poitou, the most shocking incident in the 1168 revolt. Roger of Howden, writing in the 1190s, represented Earl Patrick as a pilgrim returning from Compostela.[44] According to the *History of William Marshal*, the earl had been killed 'from behind by a traitorous assassin'. William himself had been wounded in the same attack – naturally only because he too had been unfairly attacked from behind – and the author knew what lessons to draw. 'Our story leaves us in no doubt that the men of Poitou were always in revolt against their lords.'[45] Who was it whose arguments prevented John leaving in 1205? William Marshal. But the killing of Earl Patrick was also the most hotly disputed part of the revolt. The Poitevins themselves, as reported in a letter written by John of Salisbury, said that King Henry's army attacked them while peace talks were going on, and that it was while they were defending themselves that Earl Patrick was killed.[46]

Where then did Abbot Robert get his information and opinions from? The sequence of entries for 1161 is revealing.

> After making a truce with King Louis VII, Henry advanced into Aquitaine, and took vigorous action there; for example he besieged Castillon-sur-Agen, a fortress strongly defended by nature and artifice, and within a week, on 10 August, he captured it – to the admiration and terror of the Gascons. At Domfront Queen Eleanor gave birth to a daughter, who was baptized by Cardinal Henry, the papal legate, and was named Eleanor after her mother. Among those to act as sponsors at her baptism were Achard, bishop of Avranches, and Robert, abbot of Mont-Saint-Michel.[47]

42 N. Vincent, *Peter des Roches: An Alien in English Politics 1205–1238* (Cambridge, 1996), p. 28.

43 Coggeshall, pp. 152–5. For this and other allusions to Poitevin treachery by the St Albans chroniclers see Matthew Paris, *Chronica Majora*, ed. H. R. Luard, RS 57, 7 vols. (London, 1872–83), II, 452, 577, III, 84; Matthew Paris, *Historia Anglorum*, ed. F. J. Madden, RS 44, 3 vols. (London, 1866–69), II, 150.

44 Torigni, p. 236; Roger of Howden, *Chronica*, ed. W. Stubbs, RS 51, 4 vols. (London, 1868–71), I, 273–4. On Howden's mistake, see Aurell, *L'Empire*, p. 335 n.59

45 *History of William Marshal. Volume 1*, ed. A. J. Holden, S. Gregory and D. Crouch (London, 2002), ll. 1577–9, 1625–8, 1694–1705.

46 *Letters of John of Salisbury*, no. 272, p. 564.

47 Torigni, p. 211.

On at least one occasion Robert attended the court in Poitou.[48] It was presumably on occasions such as this and the baptism of Eleanor that Abbot Robert picked up both the information and, more importantly, the spin put on that information. When, under the year 1177, he reported that Henry bought the county of La Marche for 6,000 marks, he added a revealing touch: 'it was worth, said King Henry, 20,000 marks'.[49] Robert was very close to the royal family, and was writing a history he intended to present to them. As the Rolls Series editor, Howlett, observed, 'We can see that throughout the work his pen is controlled by a design long cherished though not carried out until 1184 of presenting a copy of his book to the king.'[50] He was, in effect, an official historian – or, at least, he wanted to be. In his account of the hostilities between Henry II and 'the greater part of the Poitevins and Aquitanians' in 1168 he referred to the actions of the rebels as 'madness'. His strongly royalist point of view means that he saw royal action against a king's enemies as 'peace making'. He wrote, for example, that in August 1169 Henry II returned to Normandy 'having pacified almost the whole of Poitou and Wasconia'.[51] Not everyone saw things in this way. John of Salisbury and Gervase of Canterbury did not. According to Gervase, the Poitevin rebels had been resisting the loss of their liberties, and no sooner had Henry II come to terms with them than he broke his word.[52]

Although it did not have quite the resonance of Poitevin treachery, in late twelfth-century English writing the idea of heresy in Gascony was a troubling one, and this too goes back to Robert of Torigni. In his entry for 1152 he observed that the pernicious teaching of the heretic Henry had taken an especially strong hold in Gascony until a young girl from that province was inspired by God to preach the Catholic faith so wisely and well that she brought back to the Church many of those who had been seduced.[53] This whole paragraph was taken over verbatim by Ralph Diceto, though he placed it in 1151.[54] It may also have been Torigni's influence that lay behind the otherwise puzzling assertion made by William of Newburgh in Book II chapter 13 of his history, that the founder of the heresy that reached England in 1165 came from Gascony (*ex Gasconia incerto auctore*). It has been suggested that William conjured this unknown *auctor* in Gascony 'out of the air'.[55] This conforms to the twentieth-century orthodoxy

48 He witnessed a grant to the men of Pontorson given at Surgères in 1167/8: N. Vincent, 'King Henry II and the Poitevins', in *La Cour Plantagenêt 1154–1204*, ed. M. Aurell (Poitiers, 2000), pp. 103–35 (p. 113).

49 Torigni, pp. 274–5.

50 A note in the Mont-Saint-Michel manuscript records the abbot's eventual success: 'Robertus abbas fecit historiam continentem res gestas Romanorum, Francorum Anglorum usque ad presens tempus, continentem scilicet annos usque ad annum 1184 quem librum praesentavit karissimo domino suo Henrico regi Anglorum': Torigni, pp. xx and lx.

51 Torigni, pp. 235–8, 242.

52 Gervase, I, 205 and 211. Gervase's chronicle, it should be noted, remained for centuries unread outside his own house.

53 Torigni, p. 168. This was presumably Henry of Lausanne.

54 Diceto, I, 295.

55 P. Biller, 'William of Newburgh and the Cathar Mission to England', in *Life and Thought in the Northern Church, c.1100–c.1700: Essays in Honour of Claire Cross*, ed. D. Wood, Studies in Church History Subsidia 12 (Woodbridge, 1999), pp. 11–30 (p. 20).

that William's history of his own times was almost entirely an independent creation. In my view, however, William read every history he could get his hands on, and this included Torigni.[56]

Other features of William's treatment of the heretics who came to England are intriguing. As Biller notes, he sandwiched his account of their arrival and of their fate between his account of the renewal of peace after the 1159 Toulouse campaign (chapter 12) and the 1163 Council of Tours (chapter 14). In chapter 15 he cited verbatim the canons of the 1163 Council of Tours, one of which stated that heresy emerged in Toulouse and then spread from there to Gascony (*in partibus Tolosae damnanda haeresis dudum emersit, que more cancri paulatim se ad vicina loca diffundens, per Gasconiam et alias provincias quamplurimos jam infecit*). In fact the Council of Oxford that condemned the heretics who had been arrested in England had not taken place between 1159 and 1163 but rather later, in 1165. By placing his narrative where he did, and by dating these events only vaguely as occurring 'in those days', William effectively associated what he saw as the first heresy to threaten England since the days of Pelagianism not only with Gascony, but also with Toulouse.[57] Moreover the effect of another remarkable feature of William's history – the longest and most detailed of all surviving accounts of the murder of Raymond Trencavel at Béziers and of the subsequent revenge massacre of the townspeople by Raymond's son – is to reinforce this perception of the south of France, especially since he chose to place his narrative of incidents that had actually occurred in 1167 and 1169 in Book II chapter 11, that is to say immediately after his account of the 1159 Toulouse campaign in chapter 10. What had stimulated a Yorkshire historian's curiosity about savage events that occurred so far away? Perhaps once again the fact that he found them mentioned by Robert of Torigni. Indeed, he and Torigni – and Diceto – all made the same mistake, calling the murdered Trencavel William instead of Raymond.[58] This, of course, does not explain how William apparently came to know so much more about these events than had Torigni or Diceto; conceivably contacts with a newly appointed, and astonishingly well-informed, bishop of Durham, or with someone on the bishop's staff, may explain this (see below p. 70). However this may be, it seems clear that the thread of William's history is being driven not by chronological order but by a sequence of ideas. Occitania, the breeding ground of heresy and the scene of shocking bloodshed, was being represented as an alarmingly dangerous part of the world.

56 J. Gillingham, 'Two Yorkshire Historians Compared: Roger of Howden and William of Newburgh', *Haskins Society Journal* 12 (2002/2003), 15–37 (p. 24). In addition to the points made there it should be noted that the one case of heresy on the Continent that William dealt with explicitly, that of Eudo of Stella (Newburgh, I, 60–4), was also mentioned by Abbot Robert: Torigni, pp. 156–7. This is just one example of several that suggest that Newburgh was adapting Torigni rather than Diceto.

57 R. I. Moore, 'Les Albigeois d'après les chroniques angevines', a paper given at the Colloque International du Centre d'Etudes Cathares, Carcassonne, October 2002 (forthcoming). I am particularly grateful to Bob Moore for bibliographical advice and thought-provoking discussion.

58 Torigni, p. 243; Diceto, I, 346. The dean of St Paul's placed the murder in 1171. His previous item, also borrowed from Torigni, and taken from the latter's entry for 1171, presumably explains how he came to make this mistake.

What was known in Normandy and England about the history of Aquitaine between the Carolingian conquest and Eleanor's marriages? Probably not much, if anything. Even Diceto, the most self-consciously learned of twelfth-century English historians, clearly knew very little. He compiled a number of annotated lists. This includes lists of the emperors, of the kings of France, of the kings of Britain, the dukes of Normandy, the counts of Anjou and the counts of Flanders.[59] But there is no list of the counts of Poitou or of dukes of Aquitaine. One of the most celebrated features of Ralph's history is his system of *signa*, symbols placed in the margins as an aid to ready reference. Among the twelve *signa* are a crown for the kings of the English, a sword for the dukes of the Normans and a spear for the counts of the Angevins. But he had no symbol for the dukes of the Aquitanians.

Despite this Diceto was clearly curious about Aquitaine. Near the beginning of his *Ymagines Historiarum* he inserted a long passage describing the duchy and its inhabitants. It begins:

> Aquitaine overflows with riches of many kinds, excelling other parts of the western world to such an extent that historians consider it to be one of the most fortunate and flourishing (*felicior et fecundior*) of the provinces of Gaul. Its fields are fertile, its vineyards productive and its forests teem with wildlife. From the Pyrenees northwards the entire countryside is irrigated by the River Garonne and other streams; indeed it is from these life-giving waters [*aquae*] that the province takes its name.

It then continues with uncomplimentary allusions to the reputation of its inhabitants for smooth and slippery language and for being all too appreciative of fine cooking, before launching into an elaborate description of Poitevin cuisine.[60]

How might the dean of St Paul's have come by this information? One possibility might be through his contacts with two Englishman who held high office in the church of Poitou: Richard of Ilchester, archdeacon of Poitiers and treasurer of Saint-Hilaire, and John des Bellesmains of Canterbury, bishop of Poitiers.[61] Although Richard of Ilchester was a member of the royal household, it seems likely that he was at times detached from it in order to carry out tasks in the region in which he held such important posts. Indeed, he was called 'Richard the Poitevin' in a Glastonbury survey drawn up soon after 1171.[62] But given that he became bishop of Winchester in 1173 and that Ralph did not write up his history until the 1180s, John of Canterbury, bishop of Poitiers (1162–81) and archbishop of Lyons (1181–93), is a more likely source. John remained in touch with

59 Printed by Stubbs under the title *Opuscula*: Diceto, II, 213–75.

60 Diceto, I, 293–4.

61 *Ibid.*, pp. 318–20.

62 He may, for instance, have summoned the army of Aquitaine in 1164 to oppose a threat to Auvergne by Louis VII: *The Correspondence of Thomas Becket*, ed. and trans. A. Duggan, 2 vols. (Oxford, 2000), I, 106 (though see editor's note of caution); *Letters of John of Salisbury*, no. 182 implies that Richard was in Poitiers in 1166; *Surveys of the Estates of Glastonbury Abbey c.1135–1201*, ed. N. E. Stacy (Oxford, 2001), p. 75. For his career, see C. Duggan, 'Richard of Ilchester, Royal Servant and Bishop', *Transactions of the Royal Historical Society*, 5th ser. 16 (1966), 1–21.

friends in England. Diceto's *Abbreviationes* begins with an exchange of letters between Ralph and Archbishop John; William of Newburgh includes a scene in which John is shown talking about Anglo-French politics while on a visit to England.[63]

Other potential informants are much harder to identify. Many English and Normans must have participated in the great Toulouse campaign of 1159 and Thomas Becket himself may have talked to William fitz Stephen and Herbert of Bosham, but when they wrote their Lives they had other concerns in mind.[64] Whenever the royal court was in Aquitaine, litigants such as Richard of Anesty and seekers after patronage or political and military aid such as Diarmait Mac Murchada were likely to be drawn to the south. A snapshot of what this could have meant at any one moment in time is provided by reports of the way a number of delegations were halted on their way to the king's court by the unexpected news of Richard I's death. Bishop Hugh of Lincoln had got as far as Saint-Nicolas near Angers; a canon and a clerk of St David's had entered Aquitaine but returned at once to Chinon; others on the way included a monk from Christ Church, Canterbury, and a group of Hereford cathedral clergy, Walter Map among them.[65] The potential of this information stream should not, however, be overestimated. Nicholas Vincent has calculated that Henry II spent less than 15 per cent of his reign south of the Loire. More telling still in this context is his count of only 25 charters issued at locations within Aquitaine out of a total of more than 3,000 known to have been granted by Henry II.[66]

A few other Englishmen stayed for longer, either going to school in Poitiers as Jordan Fantosme and Ralph Niger may have done,[67] or obtaining high office as did Isaac, abbot of L'Étoile (near Chauvigny) 1147–c.69, and William,

63 Diceto, I, 5–6. Diceto's account of the defeat of Count Vulgrin of Angoulême's Brabançons in 1176 may well have come from the bishop of Poitiers (on this, see Gillingham, *Richard I*, p. 54 n.7), as may also the story, that he alone among English historians has, about the election of the dean of Poitiers as bishop of Limoges: Diceto, II, 4–5. According to Newburgh, John told English ecclesiastics that King Philip was more financially oppressive than King Richard: *Historia Rerum Anglicarum*, II, 421–2.

64 J. Martindale, 'An Unfinished Business: Angevin Politics and the Siege of Toulouse, 1159', in *Anglo-Norman Studes XXIII: Proceedings of the Battle Conference 2000*, ed. J. Gillingham (Woodbridge, 2001), pp. 115–54.

65 Adam of Eynsham, *Magna Vita Sancti Hugonis*, ed. and trans. D. L. Douie and H. Farmer, 2 vols. (Edinburgh, 1962), II, 130–2; Gerald de Barri, *De rebus a Se Gestis*, in *Opera*, I, 153; Gervase, I, 593–4, on which see J. Gillingham, *Richard Coeur de Lion* (London, 1994), pp. 169–70, repr. from *Speculum* 54 (1979).

66 Vincent, 'King Henry and the Poitevins', pp. 110 and 126. Richard, out of the approximately 86 months (July 1189–July 1190, March 1194–March 1199) of his reign that he was not on crusade or in prison in Germany, spent roughly ten and a half months in Aquitaine, i.e. 12–13%, a little less than his father; and John, from April 1199 until the end of 1202, i.e. while he still held on to virtually the whole of his inheritance, spent even less, about 8%: J. Gillingham, *The Angevin Empire*, 2nd edn (London, 2001), p. 73. See also the calculations made by J. C. Holt, 'The Writs of Henry II', in *The History of English Law: Centenary Essays on 'Pollock and Maitland'*, *Proceedings of the British Academy* 89 (1996), 47–64.

67 Fantosme may have studied with Bishop Gilbert de la Porrée (1142–54): M. Strickland, 'Arms and the Men: War, Loyalty and Lordship in Jordan Fantosme's Chronicle', in *Medieval Knighthood IV: Papers from the Fifth Strawberry Hill Conference 1990*, ed. C. Harper-Bill and R. Harvey (Woodbridge, 1992), pp. 187–220 (pp. 216–18).

archbishop of Bordeaux (1173–87). But there is no surviving evidence of any of them keeping friends in England informed about events in Aquitaine.[68] Although the Yorkshire landowner, Robert of Turnham, may well have provided Roger of Howden with information based upon his experience as seneschal of Anjou (1195–99), the chronicler died too soon to benefit in a similar way from Robert's time as seneschal of Poitou. Coggeshall warmly praised Robert's courageous defence of King John's cause against Philip Augustus and rebel Poitevins in 1204–05, but there is nothing to indicate he had insider information here.[69]

As well as northern visitors to Aquitaine, we should obviously also consider how much English and Norman chroniclers might have been told by Poitevins or Gascons. Coggeshall's account of Richard I's death at Chalus in April 1199 seems to have been based on what he had been told by Milo, abbot of Le Pin; his account of John in 1204 hoping to raise troops in Gascony might derive, perhaps via a meeting at the king's court, from Elie de Malemort, archbishop of Bordeaux, then in England.[70] It seems clear that the arrival of Philip of Poitou, bishop of Durham (1196–1208), in the north of England lay behind some of the material in both Roger of Howden's chronicle and William of Newburgh's *Historia*. Indeed, William's uniquely clear overall strategic understanding of European politics in the 1190s may well derive ultimately from Bishop Philip, King Richard's most confidential clerk.[71] But the input of Philip of Poitou and of Milo of Le Pin into English historical writing dates from very late in the period under consideration, from the late 1190s.[72] Moreover this input could only be of short duration, partly as a result of John's loss of continental territories including much of Poitou and partly because historical writing in England dwindled rapidly in quantity and quality in the early 1200s. By 1203 Newburgh, Howden, Diceto, Devizes and Map were all either dead or had ceased to write; not until the second half of John's reign did the anonymous Barnwell chronicler take up his pen. It had been a short-lived golden age.

68 *Correspondence of Becket*, I, 104. For Isaac's problems with Hugh de Chauvigny, see Aurell, *L'Empire des Plantagenêt*, p. 210. I am grateful to Frédéric Boutoulle for advice on Archbishop William.

69 Coggeshall, pp.146 and 152. Cf. 'Pictavenses duces regi Francorum Philippo resistentes, in multis praevaluerunt, regis Anglorum Johannis partes defendentes', *Annales de Jumièges*, p. 87.

70 Coggeshall, pp. 94–8, 146–7. On Milo, see Gillingham, *Richard Coeur de Lion*, pp. 163–4. Le Pin was close to the ducal castle of Montreuil-Bonnin, 14 km from Poitiers.

71 On Philip of Poitou and Robert of Turnham as sources for Roger, see D. Corner, 'The Earliest Surviving Manuscripts of Roger of Howden's "Chronica" ', *EHR* 98 (1983), 309–10; J. Gillingham, 'Historians without Hindsight: Coggeshall, Diceto and Howden on the Early Years of John's Reign', in *King John: New Interpretations*, ed. S. D. Church (Woodbridge, 1999), pp. 1–26 (pp. 16–21). On Philip of Poitou and Newburgh, J. Gillingham, 'Royal Newsletters, Forgeries and English Historians: Some Links between Court and History in the Reign of Richard I', in *La Cour Plantagenêt*, ed. Aurell, pp. 171–86 (p. 184); *idem*, 'William of Newburgh and Emperor Henry VI', in *Auxilia Historica: Festschrift für Peter Acht*, ed. W. Koch *et al.* (Munich, 2001), pp. 51–71.

72 Until Richard's reign few Poitevins came to England. For the rare possible exceptions, Eleanor's uncle Ralph de Faye, granted the barony of Bramley (Surrey), and Saldebreuil, constable in Poitou, see Vincent, 'King Henry and the Poitevins', pp. 122–4. On the 1190s, see the discussion by R. R. Heiser, 'The Royal Familiares of Richard I', *Medieval Prosopography* 10 (1989), 25–50.

As by far the most assiduous chronicler of the years from 1170 to 1201, the king's clerk, Roger of Howden, has provided modern historians with more information about events within Aquitaine than any other chronicler. And not only modern historians. Diceto and Gervase of Canterbury knew the *Gesta Henrici* (in the version going up to September 1177) and William of Newburgh relied heavily on the *Chronica*. At times Howden's two historical works, the *Gesta Regis* and the *Chronica*, are in effect court diaries such is the detail with which they report the king's movements.[73] In April 1176, for example, Howden was surely at the Easter court at Winchester when Duke Richard came in person to ask his father for more assistance against rebels. This would explain why he was able to list some of them: Vulgrin of Angoulême and his brothers, Aimar of Limoges, the viscount of Turenne, Eschivard of Chabanais and Will de Mastac.[74] Occasionally he may have travelled with the court when the king went to Aquitaine – the pilgrimage to Rocamadour and the campaign into Berry in 1170 are possible examples.[75] He may well have been at the great court at Limoges in 1173 when the count of Toulouse did homage, and when Henry II first learned of the conspiracy within his own family. But Roger reports so little about the 1174 campaigns in Poitou by which Henry II brought Richard to submission that it seems likely that he was then elsewhere, almost certainly in the king's service still, but detached in order to perform some mission away from court.[76]

However that may be, he was undoubtedly able to use his position as a royal clerk to get his hands on copies of government records such as the charter recording Audemar of La Marche's sale of his county to Henry II at Grandmont in December 1177, a document that he reproduced *verbatim*.[77] His account of Henry's instructions to Richard in 1175 clearly reflects the language of the writs with which the young duke must have been provided. His task was to slight some of the castles of former Poitevin rebels and reduce others to the state they were in before the war; all baillis throughout Poitou were to supply him with everything he needed, and put all their armed forces at his disposal.[78] It is striking just how much information Howden has on Aquitaine for the period from the summer of 1175 to Whitsun 1179 – most likely derived from a series of written reports that Richard sent his father. Howden's narrative of Richard's actions in these years is very much an official one.[79] In these concise narratives the duke punishes those

73 Already Stubbs had reckoned that the author of the *Gesta*, although he could not name him, must have been 'a member of the king's court': *Gesta*, I, xiv–xvi, lvii, On the basis of evidence accumulated over the last 50 years the author has been identified as Roger of Howden. See D. M. Stenton, 'Roger of Howden and Benedict', *EHR* 68 (1953), 574–82; D. Corner, 'The *Gesta Regis Henrici Secundi* and *Chronica* of Roger, Parson of Howden', *Bulletin of the Institute of Historical Research* 56 (1983), 126–44.

74 *Gesta*, I, 114–15.

75 *Ibid*., pp. 7 and 10–11. See E. Mason, ' "Rocamadour in Quercy above all Other Churches": The Healing of Henry II', in *The Church and Healing*, ed. W. J. Shiels, Studies in Church History 19 (Oxford, 1982), pp. 39–54.

76 His only explicit references to himself in the whole of his work relate to two such missions in 1174 and 1175, *Gesta*, I, 80 and 91–2.

77 *Gesta*, I, 197, and repeated with the purchase sum corrected in *Chronica*, II, 147–8.

78 *Gesta*, I, 81.

79 *Ibid*., pp. 101, 120–1, 131–2, 212–13. Just occasionally Howden's own words may break through,

who break the peace or who rob pilgrims. We get no sense of events from the point of view of his opponents.

Howden's story of events in Aquitaine after Whitsun 1179 could not be more different. He says nothing about the rest of that year, and nothing about 1180 and 1181. Does this mean that Richard had stopped sending reports to his father? Or was Howden himself no longer so much at court, and so less well placed to see and make copies of any such reports that may have come in? The case of 1181 is especially significant because Henry II visited the duchy at the beginning of that year, yet Roger seems not to know.[80] Similarly Howden has virtually nothing about Henry II in Aquitaine in 1182.[81] Indeed, after 1179 he rarely had more information about events in Aquitaine than other English or Norman historians. This was partly because he was less often at court.[82] By the 1190s it was also because, as a result of a new government practice, other chroniclers were almost as likely as he was to receive official reports such as that in which in 1194 Richard I announced his capture of Taillebourg and Angoulême.[83] But there are two exceptions to this generalization about Roger's post-1179 coverage of Aquitaine. The first is his narrative of the dramatic events in the Limousin during the great dynastic crisis of 1183. This is very different from the laconic reports of Richard's successes between 1175 and 1179. This time he does give some sense of rebel grievances, and his narrative at times reads like an eyewitness account (see Appendix). The second is his version of Richard's 1188 campaign against Toulouse, and his detailed account of Richard's justification for that war. This probably derives from information supplied by John Cumin, archbishop of Dublin, clearly an acquaintance of Roger's, if not indeed a friend, and on this occasion Richard's envoy to his father.[84]

A royal clerk who certainly at least twice accompanied the king's court to Aquitaine was Walter Map. He tells us that he had the responsibility for looking after Peter, archbishop of Tarentaise, when the latter attended the king's court at

as when he asserted that it was *pravo usus consilio* (*Ibid.*, p. 121) that the Young King withdrew his help from his brother.

80 The visit is reported only by Vigeois, Bk 1 c. 72.

81 Under 1182 Howden reported that Henry advanced into Poitou to campaign against his enemies, but returned in haste to Normandy when he heard of the arrival of his daughter and Henry the Lion: *Gesta*, I, 288. When in the 1190s Howden rewrote his entry for 1182, he omitted the journey into Poitou altogether, thus adding to the impression that in his eyes the king's business in Poitou had been both hurried and marginal. In fact we know from Geoffrey of Vigeois that Henry was in Aquitaine for at least two months, and perhaps for significantly longer: Vigeois, Bk 2 c. 2.

82 For the argument that Howden was at court much less frequently after September 1177 than he had been earlier in the 1170s, J. Gillingham, 'The Travels of Roger of Howden and his Views of the Irish, Scots and Welsh', in *Anglo-Norman Studies XX: Proceedings of the Battle Conference in Dublin 1997*, ed. C. Harper-Bill (Woodbridge, 1998), pp. 151–69, repr. in J. Gillingham, *The English in the Twelfth Century* (Woodbridge, 2000), pp. 69–91.

83 *Chronica*, III, 256–7. Diceto also saw a copy of this report addressed to Hubert Walter, and clearly intended for wider circulation: Diceto, II, 118–19. On the new practice of Richard I's government, see Gillingham, 'Royal Newsletters'.

84 *Gesta*, II, 34–6, 40. A 'Rogerus de Hoveton' witnessed a charter in favour of John Cumin, archbishop of Dublin, granted by Count John, as lord of Ireland, in G. MacNiocaill, 'The Charters of John, Lord of Ireland, to the See of Dublin', *Repertorium Novum* 3 (1961–4), 290–1.

Limoges for eleven days in 1173. He was there again in 1183 when he saw the Young King swearing false oaths to his father – 'again and again, as I witnessed myself' – and he saw Henry II's humiliation when forced to abandon the siege of Limoges, disband his army and withdraw northwards.[85] Map also implies that he saw Henry II's troops punishing the *principes Lemovicis* for their refusal to give the king his *iustas pensiones et servicia debita*.[86]

The fact that Howden, Map and Gerald de Barri were all attached to Henry II's court had important consequences for their view of Aquitaine. In this period, as Nicholas Vincent has demonstrated, routine government and administration of the duchy was supervised first by Eleanor and then by Richard.[87] The king himself only went south of the Loire when there was trouble or when huge opportunities opened up, as in 1177 when Henry took custody of the heiress to Châteauroux and bought the county of La Marche. Although modern historians have tended to write in positive terms about such actions, seeing them as strengthening 'public' authority, the usual consequence of grabbing such opportunities was to destabilize the region – much as Quercy had been destabilized when seized by Henry's forces in 1159.[88] This meant that the king-centred history written by these authors was a history of instability, of rebellion and war. The Aquitaine that the royal clerks knew and which they wrote about was inland, turbulent Aquitaine.[89] The other Aquitaine of the Atlantic seaboard, of the wine trade and of salt production, was one that passed them by.[90]

In recent years it has been widely noted that later twelfth-century English historians showed a remarkable interest in the early development of heresy in Occitania. Peter Biller, Monique Zerner, Jean-Louis Biget, Nicholas Vincent and Bob Moore have all drawn attention to this phenomenon.[91] Roger of Howden, Ralph Diceto, Gervase of Canterbury, Walter Map and William of Newburgh all wrote about pre-1179 heretical activity in the south of France. This undoubtedly contrasts with the lack of interest in heresy shown by Orderic

[85] Walter Map, *De Nugis Curialium*, ed. and trans. M. R. James, C. N. L. Brooke and R. A. B. Mynors (Oxford, 1983), pp. 134, 280–2. He tells us that he wrote his commentary on the dramatic events of the siege of Limoges while at Saumur in the month that the Young King died, i.e. June 1183.

[86] Map, *De Nugis*, pp. li and 96. This may have been later in 1183 when Henry, in destructive mood, returned to the region after his son's death (*Gesta*, I, 303) or it might have been in 1177. 1173, a date mooted as a possibility by the editors, is unlikely.

[87] Vincent, 'King Henry and the Poitevins', pp. 117–19.

[88] Bull, *The Miracles of Our Lady*, pp. 78–9. Cheyette has described W. L. Warren's attitude to the paid troops whom the king used to enforce his will in these regions as one 'so royalist that he almost succeeds in turning these cutthroats into London bobbies': *Ermengard of Narbonne and the World of the Troubadours* (Ithaca, 2001), p. 425 n. 22.

[89] Moreover the one south-western shrine English and Norman chroniclers wrote about, Rocamadour, also lay in the more turbulent borderlands. We are indebted to Robert of Torigni's interest in saints' cults and relics for a Norman view of the mountainous and difficult landscsape in which it lay: Torigni, p. 248; Bull, *The Miracles of Our Lady*, pp. 71–4.

[90] Except, of course, when the wine fleet sank (Torigni, p. 275).

[91] Biller, 'William of Newburgh', pp. 12–14; M. Zerner, *Inventer l'hérésie: discours polémiques et pouvoirs avant l'inquisition* (Nice, 1998), p. 135; J.-L. Biget, 'Les Albigeois: remarques sur une dénomination', in Zerner, *Inventer l'hérésie*, pp. 219–56 (pp. 232–3, 240–1); Moore, 'Les Albigeois'.

Vitalis, William of Malmesbury and Henry of Huntingdon.[92] It can plausibly be argued that this new interest was a natural response to a new situation: a combination of the fact that heresy had come to England in 1165 and that the king's dominions now included both Gascony and a claim to Toulouse. On the other hand, as Bob Moore has emphasized, the readiness of English historians to write about heretics in the south of France in the years before the Lateran Council of 1179 stands in marked contrast to the silence of historians who lived much closer to the troubled regions. It has indeed been argued by Biget, Moore and Vincent that 'the rhetoric against heresy served as a rallying cry to those who already had a vested interest in pursuing the Plantagenet war against Toulouse'. Biget suggested that as early as 1163 Henry II's enthusiasm for the council of Tours was in part the king finding other ways, by labelling Toulouse as the well-spring of heresy, of getting at Count Raymond after the setback of 1159.[93] This charge is certainly implicit in the letter, traditionally dated 1173, in which Pons, archbishop of Narbonne, urged Louis VII to do something about the heresy 'in our diocese' and in the next breath warned him that Henry *sua callida et subdola simulatione* would invade his kingdom *sub occasione Tolose*.[94]

It may well be that this is what lay behind the anti-heresy mission that was sent to Toulouse in the autumn of 1178 under the aegis of Kings Henry II and Louis VII. According to Roger of Howden, the two kings' first thought had been for both of them to go there with an armed force, but they eventually decided to send a high-powered preaching mission instead. It was to be headed by a papal legate, Cardinal Peter of St Chrysogonus, the archbishops of Bourges and Narbonne, Bishops Reginald of Bath and John of Poitiers, Abbot Henry of Clairvaux, the count of Toulouse, Raymond of Châteauneuf and the viscount of Turenne.[95] The *Gesta Henrici* is the principal source for the events of the mission. Nearly all the details that Roger of Howden gives in his narrative can be deduced from the texts of two letters that he included, one letter written by Abbot Henry of Clairvaux, and one by Cardinal Peter, but not all can.[96] These additional details suggest that either Roger went there himself or he had an informant who did – perhaps a member of the staff of one of Henry II's two bishops. If the information came via Bishop John, it is, however, slightly odd that Howden, despite his continuing worry about heresy, received no more information from that

92 M. Chibnall, *The World of Orderic Vitalis* (Oxford, 1984), pp. 163–5. None of them mentioned Henry of Lausanne, despite the fact that his long and chequered career included a confrontation with Hildebert of Le Mans in 1116.

93 Vincent, 'England and the Albigensian Crusade', p. 68; Biget, 'Les Albigeois', pp. 232–3. Diceto emphasized that all the bishops of England were there, save only three – Winchester, Lincoln, Bath – excused on grounds of ill-health: Diceto, I, 310. This was remarkably enthusiastic attendance and presumably reflects the impression Henry II intended to give. See W. L. Warren, *Henry II* (London, 1973), pp. 451–2.

94 *RHGF* XVI, 159–60. I am very grateful to M. Biget for confirming that no one so far has seen good reason to question the dating of the package of letters to which this one belongs.

95 *Gesta*, I, 198–9.

96 *Ibid.*, pp. 202–6, 214–20. The most recent discussion of the letters, as dated by Y. Congar, 'Henri de Marcy, abbé de Clairvaux, cardinal-évêque d'Albano et légat pontifical', *Analecta Monastica*, Studia Anselmiana 43 (1958), 1–70 (pp. 10–23) are Cheyette, *Ermengard*, pp. 314–18 and B. M. Kienzle, *Cistercians, Heresy and Crusade in Occitania, 1145–1229* (New York, 2001), pp. 112–27.

source, since John, promoted archbishop of Lyons, was to remain active against heresy in the 1180s and 1190s. It is perhaps more plausible that at the Lateran Council of 1179 Howden met someone who had been to Toulouse the year before.[97]

But the simplest explanation of Roger's additional information on the 1178 Toulouse mission is that he was part of it himself. It would be extraordinary if Henry II had not sent some of his own clerks to accompany – and keep an eye on – his two bishops. The king himself stayed in England during the autumn of 1178.[98] If Howden was either at court or residing in his parsonage at Howden (Yorkshire), it is curious that he found nothing to report about the king's activities between 6 August and December. Moreover we know that at some point in time he obtained a long documentary record of a meeting held at Lombers (south of Albi) in 1165. Here the beliefs of a group of *boni homines* were examined and condemned as heretical by a panel of high-ranking ecclesiastics and lay people. In the form in which Roger gives it – in the later *Chronica* only, not the *Gesta Henrici* – the document is undated. It could have been as late as 1200 or 1201 that he had it copied into his *Chronica* under the year 1176, together with a rubric: 'in this year the Arian heresy which had polluted almost the whole province of Toulouse was condemned in the presence of archbishops and bishops and the other honourable and religious men named below'.[99] No other chronicler writing anywhere in Europe even so much as mentions the Lombers meeting, let alone shows any knowledge of this record of it. It is hard to see where Howden can have obtained his abridged copy, possibly already in undated form, of a document relating to a meeting at a small and virtually unknown place in Occitania unless at some point he had been in the region himself. In this case 1178 would be the most likely date.[100] He may well have been one of the unnamed 'many others' whom he says the two kings chose to add to the mission. In 1178 he would no doubt have known that the meeting at Lombers had taken place a dozen or so years earlier and hence was not suitable for adding to the chronicle, the *Gesta Henrici*, on which he was working then, since its starting-point was Christmas 1169.

Whether or not Roger himself was one of them, it is to my mind unthinkable that Henry II did not send royal clerks on the mission to Toulouse. It is noticeable that although, according to Howden, the archbishops of Bourges and Narbonne were among the high-ranking churchmen chosen to go, they are not mentioned in the letters written by Cardinal Peter and Henry of Clairvaux. To

97 As the canon referring to Cathars, *publicani* or Paterini *in Wasconia, Albegesio et partibus Tolosanis et aliis locis* makes plain, the threat of heresy was on the Lateran Council's agenda. The canons were cited in full by William of Newburgh, I, 206–23; by Roger of Howden, *Gesta*, I, 222–38; and by Gervase, I, 278–92.

98 I owe much to Judith Everard's kindness in sending me a copy of her new itinerary of Henry II.

99 *Chronica*, II, 105–17. The fact that it is the last item under 1176 suggests that it was entered as an afterthought in the space he habitually left blank at the end of his narrative of each year's events.

100 Vaissete apparently saw a version of the Lombers document, bearing the date 1165, in a manuscript belonging to the Inquisition of Carcassonne: *HGL*, VII, 1; cf. Biget, 'Les albigeois', p. 233. Cheyette also links Howden's copy of the document with the mission of 1177–78, suggesting that he probably got it from the bishop of Bath or someone in his company: *Ermengard*, p. 427 n.30.

judge from this evidence, it appears that proceedings were conducted only by the letter writers themselves and by the bishops of Bath and Poitiers – King Henry's bishops. At about this time Henry II was making sure that the abbot of Clairvaux was beholden to him. He promised to contribute to the cost of a lead roof at Clairvaux, in return receiving from Abbot Henry the gift of one of St Bernard's fingers. The abbot told King Henry that at the Cistercian general chapter he had made sure that the assembled abbots knew of the king's generosity, and that while in Gascony and Toulouse he had taken every opportunity, both private and public, to speak in glowing terms of 'your majesty's magnificent virtue'.[101] It looks as though, whatever the original intentions may have been, the anti-heresy campaign of 1178 had become much more Henry II's business than Louis VII's.[102] It may be significant, as Moore has pointed out, that Cardinal Peter had originally gone to France as papal legate in order to put pressure on Henry II to fulfil his promise to marry Richard to Louis VII's daughter Alice. Did his enthusiasm for the anti-heresy campaign usefully divert the legate's attention from this highly embarrassing demand?[103]

By 1181 Louis VII was dead and the new young king of France was in no position to make life awkward for Henry II. In this year the former Abbot Henry, now cardinal-bishop of Albano, once again accompanied by John des Bellesmains, now archbishop of Lyons, led a new drive against heretics under the protection of Roger, viscount of Béziers, a man who had provoked Abbot Henry's wrath in 1178.[104] This involved military operations against Roger's castle of Lavaur as well as more preaching. No English or Norman chronicler reports the 'pre-crusade' of 1181. This is all the more remarkable since Henry of Albano was present when the two kings, Henry of England and Philip of France, conferred with Count Philip of Flanders near Senlis in April 1182. Although both Diceto and Howden were interested in the conference, and Howden in the developing career of the former abbot of Clairvaux, it looks as though neither received a report of what the cardinal had done in 1181.[105] The 'pre-crusade' does, however, figure in the chronicles of Geoffrey of Vigeois, Robert of Auxerre and William de Puylaurens as well as Geoffrey of Auxerre's commentary on Revelation.[106] Yet these same sources say not a word about the mission of 1178. The mission of 1178 evidently made little impression in the south, yet it figured largely in Roger of Howden, and was known to Robert of Torigni as well as, it would seem, to Gervase of

101 *PL* CCIV, cols. 219–20, letters 5 and 6.

102 This would be ironic if we can trust the evidence of a letter from Abbot Henry to Louis VII, thanking him for persuading the king of England to get involved: *RHGF* XVI, 165–6.

103 *Gesta*, I, 180–1; Gervase, I, 271. Gervase of Canterbury's account of this is immediately preceded by the text of an undated letter that purports to have been sent by Raymond of Toulouse to the Cistercian General Chapter, admitting that the threat of heresy was greater than he could cope with, and asking for advice and help from them and from the king of France: Gervase, I, 269–71. Suspicions concerning the genuineness of the letter have been raised by Moore and Lobrichon; see Moore, 'Les albigeois'. It is certainly curious that the letter to the General Chapter should surface only in so Benedictine a chronicle as Gervase's.

104 For Roger of Béziers in 1178, see Howden, *Gesta*, I, 219–20.

105 Diceto, II, 10; *Gesta*, I, 238, 285–6, II, 51, 55–6.

106 'Roberti canonici S. Mariani Autissiodorensis Chronicon', *MGH SS*, XXVI, 245; Vigeois, Bk I c. 72; Guillaume de Puylaurens, *Chronique*, ed. J. Duvernoy (Paris, 1976), p. 28.

Canterbury and to the author of the 1178 entry in the Winchester Annals.[107] People writing in England and Normandy evidently knew about heresy in the south only when publicizing it suited Henry II's political interests – as it did in 1177–78, and did not in 1181.

It has sometimes been suggested that, with the exception of the borderlands of Quercy and the Agenais,[108] heresy made few inroads into the Angevin Empire itself.[109] This is not what some contemporaries believed. A canon promulgated at the 1179 Lateran Council, and cited by Howden, Gervase and William of Newburgh, named Gascony first of the places where heresy was rife: *in Wasconia, Albegesio et partibus Tolosanis et aliis locis*. According to Roger of Howden, there were very many heretics (*publicani.. perplurimi*) in Henry II's lands. Although this comment is placed in his *Chronica* under the year 1182, it looks like a later addition to his entry for the year and was probably not written until 1200 or 1201 when Roger was becoming more preoccupied with religious and spiritual matters.[110] According to Walter Map, writing in the 1180s or 1190s, although the cat-kissing heretics were unknown in Normandy and Brittany, 'there are many in Anjou and now there are masses of them in Aquitaine and Burgundy'.[111] In 1198 Pope Innocent III wrote of the plague of heresy *in partibus Vasconie ac circumpositis terris*. This was in a letter addressed to the archbishop of Auch, in which the pope said that his information on the matter came from the archbishop and from many others.[112] Robert of Auxerre was to claim that Alexander III sent Cardinal Henry on his 1181 expedition because while in many places there were secret heretics, in Gascony they went around openly.[113] Indeed, according to Geoffrey of Auxerre's commentary on Revelation, the cardinal had been appointed papal legate in Aquitaine.[114] Recently Nicholas Vincent has discussed 'the explanations offered for the failure of heresy to spread from Languedoc', concluded that none of them is 'wholly satisfactory' and pointed out that 'we know nothing of heresy in the

107 'Haeresis Publicanorum emersa est in Gallia': *Annales Monastici*, II, 61.

108 Abbot Robert referred to the heretics who appeared at Toulouse in 1178 as *Agennenses*: Torigni, 279. So too did Hervé de Bourgdieu, cited by Biget, 'Les albigeois', p. 232 n. 6.

109 In part this reflects the demonstration by Guy Lobrichon that the letter once thought to prove the existence of heresy in mid-twelfth-century Périgord had actually been written c.1000, 'The Chiaroscuro of Heresy: Early Eleventh-Century Aquitaine as Seen from Auxerre', in *The Peace of God: Social Violence and Religious Response around the Year 1000*, ed. T. Head and R. Landes (Ithaca, 1992), pp. 80–103 (pp. 81–6).

110 *Chronica*, II, 272–3. Howden's comment on the number of heretics comes in a story about Walter, servant of Eustace de Flay, hearing a voice from heaven with instructions for King Henry, and a warning that if he ignored God's word he and his sons would die. Soon afterwards, noted Howden, two of his sons, Henry and Geoffrey, did indeed die. Eustace de Flay plays a prominent part in the chronicle only in 1200 and 1201, and this story is the last entry for the year 1182.

111 Map, *De Nugis*, pp. 118–20.

112 *PL* CCIV, col. 71, no. 81. According to Innocent, it might be necessary to call upon princes and people to use the material sword against those polluted with this shit (*hac faece*).

113 'heresis execranda, quae Christi abnegat sacramenta, per id tempus clam quidem pluribus in locis irrepserat, sed palam in Guasconia maxime populos occuparet': 'Roberti Chronicon', p. 245. Presumably the wording of the 1179 heresy canon, 'iam non occulto sicut alibi . . . sed errorem suum publice manifestent', had some influence on Robert's train of thought.

114 Cited by Kienzle, *Cistercians, Heresy*, p. 133 n. 99.

Plantagenet south, because we have few records of its persecution'.[115] Certainly there are no records indicating that any of the Angevin kings took any measures against heretics in their own French dominions. Indeed, the whole point of the story told by Howden under the year 1182 was to criticize Henry II for refusing to allow heretics to be burned in his dominions 'as they were in many places throughout the kingdom of France'.[116] After dealing with the heretics in England in 1165–66, Henry II's zeal against their like on the Continent was confined to those who lived in the lands of the count of Toulouse.

On the whole the evidence suggests that Henry II allowed anxieties about heresy in the south to be whipped up by enthusiasts such as Henry of Clairvaux and John of Poitiers at times when it suited his own political purposes to put pressure on the count of Toulouse and the lords of the Toulousain. Then the wayward people of Toulouse could be presented as in need of being disciplined by a good son of the Church – much as in 1171–72 Henry proclaimed that he had gone into Ireland in order to bring good Christian order and decency into a disreputable island. In consequence, as Vincent has put it, 'the inhabitants of Languedoc were demonised and dehumanised by the chroniclers of the Plantagenet court'.[117] Vagueness about just where the frontiers lay added to the likelihood that the inhabitants of Eleanor's duchy would be tarred with the same brush. Anxieties of this kind once roused in the minds of men such as Roger of Howden, Walter Map, William of Newburgh and Peter of Blois did not go away.[118]

The rhetoric of heresy was reinforced by the rhetoric of pacification, of peace-making, as – especially after 1175 – Duke Richard, at his father's command, overturned traditional networks of power within the duchy of Aquitaine, above all in the Limousin, Angoumois and Gascony. Walter Map, for all that he was a royal clerk, took a cynical view of the activities of King Henry's peace-making armies. In his words, 'the king brought in an army and ordered it to ravage everything. Some men enjoyed this. What we are doing, they claimed, is not robbery or violence, we are bringing *pax et obedientia*.'[119] But authors whose writings circulated much more widely than the single manuscript of *De nugis curialium*, authors such as Roger of Howden, Gerald de Barri in the *Topographia Hibernica* (his most popular work) and Robert of Torigni, all adopted the preferred language of a government that claimed to bring peace and order. Those who resisted were the turbulent and the untrustworthy. It was out of this series of events, the campaign

115 Vincent, 'England and the Albigensian Crusade', pp. 70–1.

116 *Chronica*, II, 273.

117 Vincent, 'England and the Albigensian Crusade', p. 70.

118 See Biller, 'William of Newburgh', pp. 25–6 for Peter of Blois' concern. In a letter prefacing his *Tractatus de Fide*, Peter asserts that *in Italia, Gotia Provincia et in magna parte Hispanie* the Catholic faith is being undermined by the cancerous plague of heresy: *The Later Letters of Peter of Blois*, ed. E. Revell (Oxford, 1993), no. 77, p. 326. So far as I know there is no evidence that Peter ever visited Aquitaine. I am grateful to John Cotts for his advice on this point. The early thirteenth-century Margam annalist who in effect placed the Périgord heresy letter under the year 1163 (*Annales Monastici*, I, 15) was mistaken, but presumably the mistake reflects his concern.

119 Map, *De Nugis*, p. 96.

against the heresy of Toulouse and the driving up of ducal power after 1175, that the stereotypical view of Eleanor's duchy was established.

Appendix

Roger of Howden on 1183

There are distinct oddities about Howden's version of the crisis of 1183. His account of the year begins, as we would expect, with the Christmas 1182 court held at Caen, and it follows the sequence of events – though without dating them – until the moment when Henry II went to Limoges in support of Richard. The narrative then switches to events that took place in the papal curia at Velletri, an episode in a long-drawn-out dispute over the bishopric of St Andrews, ending with mention of a papal mandate commanding King William of Scotland to accept the papal decision. Howden then returns to Henry II and the king's order, issued as Easter approached (*appropinquante sollemnitate Paschali*), to arrest all those who had been against him in 1173–74, an order that when transmitted to England was carried out by the judges.[120] At this point Howden provides a recapitulation of the beginnings of the dynastic crisis, and indeed emphasizes what he was doing by inserting a rubric: *Causa discordiae inter regem et filios suos*.[121] Having taken the story to the point – Henry II's arrival at Limoges – that he had already reached once before, he continues with an exceptionally well-informed narrative of events in and around Limoges in the spring of 1183, ending with the Young King's plundering of the shrine of St Martial. Howden tells the story in vivid detail, supplying the names of little-known members of the king's household, and taking up nearly four pages in the printed edition of the *Gesta Regis Henrici*.[122] When in court diary mode he tends to give frequent and precise dates. In this passage too, however, there are no exact dates for any of the incidents recounted.

Between 1 January 1183 and 11 June 1183 (the date of the Young King's death) Howden gives only one precise date. He tells us that on 26 May the archbishop of Canterbury and the bishops of Bayeux, Evreux, Lisieux, Sées and Rochester *in communi plebis audientia* at St Stephen's, Caen, on Henry II's orders solemnly excommunicated all, except the Young King, who impeded the making of peace between the king and his sons.[123] This precise and concrete detail suggests that either Roger of Howden had a documentary record of the excommunication or he himself was there. But if at Caen on 26 May, then could he have been in the Limousin earlier that year? The answer, I believe, is yes. The item before the excommunication runs as follows:

> The lord king the father sent his envoys to England to the church of Lincoln, for the election of a bishop. So it was that, meeting at the king's command, the clerks of Lincoln chose a bishop, and did so unanimously; their choice was

120 *Gesta*, I, 291–4.

121 *Ibid.*, pp. 294–5.

122 *Ibid.*, pp. 296–9. The testimony of Geoffrey of Vigeois, Bk II, cc. 13–14, enables us to date the plundering of Saint-Martial to Lent 1183.

123 *Gesta*, I, 300.

> Master Walter of Coutances, clerk and *familiaris* of the lord king. When this was announced to the king [*regi*: not surprisingly Stubbs suspected that a word was missing here and that it should be *regi filio*], he replied that he would not permit anyone to be a bishop in his kingdom who was chosen without his consent and desire; he forbade his consecration and appealed on this matter to the lord pope.[124]

As it stands, this entry tells us that envoys travelled from the Limousin to Lincoln, and then returned to the king's court (place unspecified); even if we accept Stubbs's emendation, a messenger would still have gone to Henry II informing him of the election of his trusted *familiaris*.[125] Howden's narrative then moves from the Caen excommunication to the Young King's illness and death at Martel in the viscounty of Turenne on 11 June, and to Henry II's reaction to the news, including an emotional address, given in direct speech, to his entourage telling them that they should rejoice over his son's death even if he could not.[126]

This is a remarkable account, in parts very detailed, but also leaving much out.[127] It does not tell us what Henry II, or the Young King, or Richard, or Geoffrey or the Aquitanian rebels did between Easter (17 April) and 11 June. It leaves out what Walter Map tells us, that Henry II was forced to abandon the siege of Limoges. Nor does it tell us what Philip of France, Alfonso of Aragon, Hugh of Burgundy and Raymond of Toulouse were doing. For, as Geoffrey of Vigeois makes plain, 'neighbouring princes were marching into Aquitaine in order to play their part in what was rapidly developing into a showdown on the scale of 1173–74'.[128] If Roger had been in the Limousin, it is very hard to imagine him saying not a word about any of this. Moreover, as we have seen, Howden interweaves his main theme with information relating to the St Andrews dispute and the election to Lincoln. As it happens, these items of business are precisely ones that long concerned Howden: the affairs of the Scottish church, and ecclesiastical elections.[129] Up to a point then it is anything but surprising that he should include this material. But how can we explain *both* what he includes and what he leaves out?

A neat way – all too neat, some may say – of explaining the oddities of the narrative would be to see it as another illustration of his work as in large part a journal of his travels. That is, he was the envoy sent from the Limousin to

124 *Ibid*., p. 299.

125 When Howden abbreviated his account of Walter's election to the see of Lincoln, he simply said that 'the lord king gave the bishopric to his clerk': *Chronica*, II, 281.

126 *Gesta*, I, 300–2.

127 When, in the 1190s, Howden revised his *Gesta*, he simplified the narrative by leaving the sub-themes – the St Andrew's dispute and the Lincoln election – out (to be dealt with concisely after the story of the crisis had been told), but did little to fill in the gaps. The only change of substance was in allowing the Young King to repent of his sins and make a good death: *Chronica*, II, 278–9. He added the detail that before falling ill, the Young King had plundered the shrine of Rocamadour. Henry II's speech was suppressed, but the message stood.

128 Gillingham, *Richard I*, p. 74.

129 Gillingham, *The English*, pp. 71, 76–83, 89; A. A. M. Duncan, 'Roger of Howden and Scotland', in *Church, Chronicle and Learning in Medieval and Early Renaissance Scotland*, ed. B. E. Crawford (Edinburgh, 1999), pp. 135–59.

Lincoln, also carrying with him to the ministers in England the king's orders to arrest those whom he suspected of disloyalty. In that case Roger would have left the Limousin before Easter (*appropinquante sollemnitate Paschali*), i.e. before 17 April, at a time when the last item of local news would have been the Young King's plundering of Saint-Martial. Howden himself had not been at court during the early months of 1183, but had – as on several other occasions – gone to the papal curia on the business of the Scottish church, which was also, of course, after 1175 and the treaty of York, the business of the king of England. Having given the king his report on the way the St Andrews dispute had been handled at Velletri, he was sent on to England. Before leaving he would have heard the court gossip about the treachery of the Young King and Geoffrey, about how they deceived their father and about how close the latter came to being killed. Being gossip, it contained vivid detail but carried no dates. After having witnessed the election of Walter of Coutances – according to Diceto, the election took place on 8 May in the presence of envoys from king and archbishop[130] – he presumably returned to the Continent, was at Caen on 26 May, and then went on to the king's court to report what had been done and, perhaps, to witness Henry's response to the news of his son's death. All this is conjecture, but I can see no better way of explaining what is in, and what is not in, Howden's account of the crisis of 1183.

130 Diceto, II, 14.

Occitan Literature and the Holy Land

LINDA M. PATERSON

The original impulse behind this chapter was an idea that there was an 'Antioch connection' with Occitan literature. That the Second Crusade, scene of the infamous visit of Louis VII and Eleanor of Aquitaine to Antioch, provoked poetic responses among the generation of troubadours that included Jaufre Rudel, Marcabru and Cercamon, is well known. Investigations into the famous *lavador* song in which Marcabru extolled the merits of the Reconquista over the failed Second Crusade suggested that Marcabru was in touch with events in northern Syria prior to the death of Raymond of Antioch in 1149, namely the disappearance in action at Edessa in 1146 of Baldwin of Marash.[1] The battle of Antioch had also been the subject of what may have been the earliest, and was certainly a very substantial, example of vernacular historiography in a romance language, probably at the instigation of the first western ruler of Antioch, Bohemond of Taranto. And despite the enormous production of crusading epics in the vernacular, Raymond of Antioch is the only Frankish ruler known to have promoted such literature while in Outremer. So my initial question was, what was the place of the Antioch connection with Occitania in the cultural developments of the time? This led me to attempt an overview of the troubadours' links not only with Antioch but with the Holy Land and the eastern crusades as a whole. In this chapter I want to explore these through the production of firstly *chansons de geste* and secondly troubadour lyrics. I shall be looking at responses in the Occitanian West to the eastern crusades, literary production in the East (whether by Occitan authors or for an Occitan patron), evidence of cultural exchange between Occitans and non-Occitans, and (briefly) Occitan conceptualizations of the Holy Land.

The first Occitan literary response to the crusading movement, and in particular its astonishing victory at Antioch, was a substantial and highly innovatory one. This was quite possibly the earliest, and certainly a massively weighty, example of vernacular historiography in a romance language. Our record of it is indirect but reliable. According to the Limousin chronicler Geoffrey of Vigeois, a knight named Gregory Bechada with some knowledge of Latin wrote a massive volume

1 L. Paterson, 'Syria, Poitou and the *Reconquista* (or: Tales of the Undead): who was the Count in Marcabru's *Vers del lavador?*', in *The Second Crusade*, ed. J. P. Phillips and M. Hoch (Manchester, 2001), pp. 133–49.

over a period of twelve years, narrating events of the First Crusade. It was commissioned by the local bishop Eustorgius (1106–37), and produced with advice from one Gaubert the Norman. Bechada's lord was Gouffier of Lastours, who achieved renown for outstanding deeds during the First Crusade, and who was also Geoffrey of Vigeois's great-grand-uncle. To make himself comprehensible to lay people Bechada wrote in the vernacular and in popular metre. While his narrative could have been commissioned at any time during Eustorgius' episcopacy, it seems most likely to have been prompted by Bohemond's pilgrimage to Saint-Léonard-de-Noblat in Lent 1106 during a recruitment drive to drum up support for Antioch, which was in a fragile situation after Bohemond's three-year period of captivity. As Carol Sweetenham's research has shown, Saint-Léonard, some twenty kilometres east of Limoges and fifty kilometres north-east of Lastours, was one of his first ports of call. To quote her words,

> Saint Leonard had been famous since the early eleventh century as the patron of prisoners, and the church was reportedly full of fetters and chains. Bohemond claimed to ascribe his safe release to this saint, and this provided a particular pretext for the destination of his pilgrimage, though the sources show that his trip was at least as much designed to publicize Antioch's need for help and in the process to raise his own profile.

Orderic Vitalis comments that he regularly regaled clerics and lay people with accounts of his crusading exploits. If Bohemond's trip was indeed what prompted the commissioning of Bechada's work, and if we take at face value Geoffrey's report that it took twelve years to write, Bechada was the first to produce a work of vernacular historiography in a romance language, pre-dating the earliest Anglo-Norman texts by some two decades, and continental French by nearly a century.[2]

Bechada's text is partially preserved, in two forms. The more important is a manuscript fragment now in Madrid, a late twelfth-century reworking of Bechada's original, preserving many of its features. The fragment describes the most extraordinary success of the western crusading movement, the battle of Antioch. It highlights the role of Occitan knights, particularly Bechada's lord Gouffier of Lastours, as well as Southern Norman knights, especially Bohemond. It formed part of what was known as the *Canso d'Antioca*, which provided the model for the later *Song of the Albigensian Crusade*. It contains some eyewitness testimony, and represents an independent if limited source for events of the First Crusade. Secondarily, there are traces of Bechada's text in the late thirteenth-century compilation, the *Gran Conquista de Ultramar*, which preserves not only passages translated verbatim from the text as it is found in the Madrid fragment, but other passages with similar features, which are likely to come from what has been lost.

We can conclude from this, firstly, that Antioch loomed large in the minds of some important figures in the Limousin in the early twelfth century, and that stories about the remarkable battle reverberated through to the thirteenth

2 *The 'Canso d'Antioca': An Epic Chronicle of the First Crusade*, ed. and trans. C. Sweetenham and L. Paterson (Aldershot and Burlington, 2003), p. 122.

century, as of course they did also in the North where there was a massively greater production of literature concerning the First Crusade and its aftermath. Secondly, we can probably conclude that the connection with Occitania was made initially through Bohemond and the Southern Normans. And, thirdly, we can cautiously give credit to an Occitan writer for remarkable innovation in vernacular historiography.

When the thirty-four-year-old second son of William IX of Aquitaine, Raymond of Poitiers, became prince of Antioch in 1136, he came from a well-established centre of troubadour culture, where his brother Duke William X of Aquitaine was a patron of troubadours until his death in 1137. Raymond also had Norman connections, having spent some years at the court of Henry I. According to William of Tyre, writing between 1163 and 1184, he enjoyed a reputation for an interest in letters, though was himself 'illiteratus' (not a learned man? not trained in the practice of writing Latin?).[3] Hans Eberhard Mayer makes the following statement about his role as a patron of literature:

> As a consequence of Raymond's arrival the Norman elements in Antioch were finally ousted by French influence. One indication of this change is the fact that the *Chanson des Chétifs*, an epic poem in Old French, was written at Raymond's court shortly before 1149. It was based largely on memories of the 1101 crusade, the crusade which failed. This remains as the only surviving piece of evidence for the contribution to vernacular poetry which was made by the crusader states.[4]

The *Chanson des Chétifs* as it has survived is not the poem composed for Raymond, but is a late twelfth- or early thirteenth-century reworking by Graindor de Douai, who integrated it into what is known as the 'First Crusade Cycle' consisting of the *Chanson d'Antioche*, the *Chétifs* and the *Chanson de Jérusalem*. The *Chétifs* consists of three fantastical episodes. The first describes how Richard of Chaumont, one of Corbaran's Christian captives, fights a judicial duel on his behalf in return for the freedom of all the Christian prisoners; the second how Baldwin of Beauvais kills the dragon Sathanas who has just eaten his brother Ernoul alive; and the third how Harpin of Bourges helps to rescue Corbaran's nephew from assorted wild animals and a band of robbers.[5] There is also an introductory section before at the beginning of the *Antioche*, which lists various knights who will be later known as the 'chétifs' or captives and explains

3 '[L]itteratorum, licet illitteratus esset, cultor', in William of Tyre, *Chronicon*, ed. R. B. C. Huygens, Corpus Christianorum Continuatio Mediaeualis 63, 2 vols. (Turnhout, 1986), I, 8–9, 14, 21; for 'illitteratus', see M. T. Clanchy, *From Memory to Written Record*, 2nd edn (Oxford, 1993), pp. 224–52, and J. Martindale, ' "Cavalaria et Orgueill": Duke William IX of Aquitaine and the Historian', in *The Ideals and Practice of Medieval Knighthood II: Papers from the Third Strawberry Hill Conference*, ed. C. Harper-Bill and R. Harvey (Woodbridge, 1988), pp. 87–116 (p. 113).

4 H. E. Mayer, *The Crusades*, trans. J. Gillingham, 2nd edn (Oxford, 1988; German original, Stuttgart, 1965), pp. 85–6. J. S. C. Riley-Smith, in *The Crusades: A Short History* (London, 1987), p. 56, comments on the low educational level in the Holy Land and remarks that the settlers looked to western Europe for their learning and culture.

5 See Myers's analysis on pp. xi–xiii of *The Old French Crusade Cycle*, ed. J. A. Nelson, E. J. Mickel *et al.*, 10 vols. (Tuscaloosa, AL, 1977–96), V: *Les Chétifs*, ed. G. M. Myers (1981).

how they were captured at the battle of Civetot.[6] This is what Graindor says of Raymond's role in the production of the *Chétifs*:

> Segnor, or escoutés, france gens honoree,
> Huimais orés cancon de bien enluminee,
> De mellor ne sai poi[n]t quant [ele] est bien cantee.
> Li boins princes Raimons ki la teste ot colpee,
> Ke Sarrasin ocisent, la pute gens dervee,
> – Anthioce en remest dolante et abosmee,
> La terre fu perdue que Franc ont conquestee,
> (Onques puis par nul home ne fu si grant gardee,)
> Bien doit s'arme estre salve et devant Deu portee –
> Ceste cancons [fist faire] de verités provee.
> Li dus Raimons l'estraist, dont li arme est alee;
> Cil ki le cancon fist en ot bone soldee,
> Canoines fu Saint Piere, de provende donee.
> Tant con li clers verqui fu li cancons gardee,
> Et quant il dut morir et l'arme en fu alee,
> Al Patriarce fu cele cancons livree:
> Si conme Bauduins a la ciere menbree,
> Ki de Bialvais fu nés, cele cité loee,
> Conbati al serpent al trencant de l'espee,
> Por cou que son frere ot l'arme del cors sev[r]ee . . . (ll. 1663–82)

(Now listen, my lords, you noble, honoured people, you will now hear a song shining with goodness. I know no better one when it is sung. Good prince Raymond who had his head cut off, who was murdered by the Saracens (the infidel whores! Antioch was left grieving and downcast, the land was lost that the Franks had conquered, no greater territory has been guarded by any man since, his soul must indeed be saved and carried before God) – he had this song composed, on the basis of proven truth. Duke Raymond, whose soul has flown, had it translated [?]; the man who composed the song was well paid for it; he was a canon of St Peter's, and had a good prebend. As long as the clerk was alive, the song was kept safe, and when he came to die and his soul went away, this song was delivered to the patriarch: [It told] how Baldwin the dearly remembered, who was born in Beauvais, that praised city, fought with the serpent with his sword blade, because his brother had his soul separated from his body . . .)

> Mais ancois vos dirai con Ernols devia;
> Il ala el mesage, mais ainc n'en repaira.
> Li bons princes Raimons, qui ceste estoire ama,
> Fist ceste cancon faire que rien n'i oblia.
> Dex ait merci de l'arme qui l'estorie trova! (ll. 1776–80)

(Now I will tell you how Ernoul went wrong; he took the message, but never came back. Good prince Raymond who liked this story had this song

[6] U. T. Holmes and W. M. McLeod, 'Source Problems of the *Chétifs*: A Crusade *chanson de geste*', *Romanic Review* 28 (1937), 99–108 (p. 102).

composed, for he forgot no part of it. God have mercy on the soul that composed the history!)

This tells us, then, that Raymond liked the story and had the song written by a cleric in order to preserve it. The composer was a canon of Saint Peter's (of Antioch), who was well paid for it: the implication seems to be that his prebend was the reward for his work, rather than that he was already a canon when he wrote it. On his death the song was passed to 'the patriarch', whom Holmes and MacLeod for no clear reason take to be the patriarch of Jerusalem, though it seems more likely that the relevant man was Aimery of Limoges, Latin patriarch of Antioch from 1140 to c.1196.[7] Relations between Raymond and the previous patriarch, Ralph of Domfront (also a southerner) left much to be desired, and Raymond succeeded in deposing him on accusations of immorality, simony and having been elected in an irregular manner; according to William of Tyre, he then imposed his own choice, by a combination of threats and bribes, on the prelates charged with designating a successor. Aimery, who got on well with Raymond, was not a highly educated man but was adept at cultivating literary relations. He seems the obvious recipient of the book.

The text printed by Myers indicates that Raymond 'l'estraist'. This version occurs in only two of the ten manuscripts, the others simply indicating that when the story was brought before Raymond the composer was well rewarded. Old French *estraire* can mean 'to translate', and Myers takes it this way.[8] So it is possible that Raymond had some hand in 'translating' it: either simply that he *had* it translated, or just conceivably that he retold the story as he had heard it in, say, Armenian or Greek, and commissioned the cleric to write it in a polished form in a romance vernacular. All scholars all seem to agree that the *Chétifs* drew heavily on oriental legends and motifs current in Syria, especially those that appear in the Byzantine epic *Digenis Akritas*.[9]

Most assume also that the romance language was French. French was the dominant language in Frankish Outremer, and Raymond spent several years at the court of Henry I. But it it is not impossible that the original romance version was in Occitan, the literary language of the Poitevin court where Raymond was brought up, and presumably the vernacular tongue of patriarch Aimery (and indeed his predecessor).

In the text as printed, the canon is named as the author of the dragon episode only. Suzanne Duparc-Quioc however dismisses the idea that the rest of the

7 *Ibid.*, p. 105; for Ralph and Aimery, see C. Cahen, *La Syrie du Nord à l'époque des croisades* (Paris, 1940), pp. 501–8.

8 See the examples cited in A. Tobler and E. Lommatzsch, *Altfranzösisches Wörterbuch*, 10 vols. to date (Berlin, 1925–), III, 1437, and Myers, *Chétifs*, pp. 145–6 n. 68.

9 A. Hatem, *Les Poèmes épiques des croisades: Genèse – historicité – localisation* (Paris, 1932), pp. 375–94; R. Goossens, 'Les recherches récentes sur l'épopée byzantine', *L'Antiquité Classique* 2 (1933), 449–72; Holmes and McLeod, 'Source Problems', p. 102; S. Duparc-Quioc, *La Chanson d'Antioche*, 2 vols. (Paris, 1976–78) and *Le Cycle de la croisade* (Paris, 1955), p. 83; Cahen, *Syrie*, pp. 569–78; Sweetenham and Paterson, *Canso*, p. 52. Holmes and MacLeod interpret the claim that the song was made from 'verités provee' as meaning that for Graindor, the dragon episode was a legend current in that section of Syria or Cilicia where its place names would localize it ('Source Problems', p. 106).

Chétifs was not part of the story commissioned by Raymond.[10] At any rate there are links, albeit rather tenuous ones, between the *Chétifs* as a whole and the crusade of 1101–02 of which William IX's contingent formed a part: in particular the historical Harpin de Bourges was one of William's companions and was captured by the Saracens at the battle of Ramleh in 1102.

Duparc-Quioc asks whether the *Chétifs* were composed to celebrate the seigneurial dynasty of the dukes of Aquitaine. Given the fantastical nature of the narrative, the fact that the other main protagonists (Richard of Chaumont and Baldwin of Bourges) are northerners, and that there is no mention of the house of Poitou beyond the acknowledgment of Raymond's patronage, this seems unlikely. More probably, Raymond had heard stories in Poitiers about the crusade of 1101 and brought them over to Antioch. Orderic Vitalis relates that after his return from the Holy Land, William IX 'often recited the miseries of his captivity in the presence of kings and magnates and groups of Christians, using rhythmical verses with elegant modulations'.[11]

No satisfactory explanation has ever been proposed for the reference to William's 'captivity': while most of his men were slaughtered by the Turks in the Anatolian marshes and, to quote William of Malmesbury, he himself was 'stripped almost to a state of nature',[12] he is reported to have escaped to Antioch and continued with a pilgrimage to Jerusalem before returning home. Leslie Topsfield sought to explain the reference to 'captivitatis suae' by suggesting that 'captivitatis' might mean 'wretched state', on the assumption that the word gives the Old French 'chétif'.[13] However, given the existence of the *Chanson des Chétifs* where 'chétifs' clearly means 'captives', and given that at least one of its heroes has the same name as one of William's companions who had in reality been a captive, it seems preferable to accept the view of Cahen and Duparc-Quioc that the original plot of the *Chétifs* probably synthesized several different episodes of Christian captivity during the crusade of 1101–02 and that these became conflated with tales of William's adventures.[14] If William's songs were not about his own (non-existent) captivity, there is no reason to doubt that songs there were. Raymond (and no doubt some of his companions) will have heard songs and stories at William's court, and brought them over to Antioch with him, in however garbled a form, where they were stitched together with the oriental elements of the narrative to form the version of the *Chétifs* that Graindor then reworked.

Mayer claimed that the *Chanson des Chétifs*, being written in Old French, is one indication that as a consequence of Raymond's arrival the Norman elements in Antioch were finally ousted by French influence. This is an odd statement given that Normans wrote in Old French; apart from the unquestioned

10 Duparc-Quioc, *Antioche*, II, 126.

11 Orderic Vitalis, *The Ecclesiastical History*, ed. and trans. M. Chibnall, 6 vols. (Oxford 1969–80), V, 342 and n. on p. 343. See Cahen, *Syrie*, pp. 574–5.

12 William of Malmesbury, *Gesta Regum Anglorum*, ed. and trans. R. A. B. Mynors, R. M. Thomson and M. Winterbottom, 2 vols. (Oxford, 1998–99), I, 682–3.

13 Martindale, 'Cavalaria', pp. 112–13; L. Topsfield, *Troubadours and Love* (Cambridge, 1975), p. 261 n. 2.

14 Cahen, *Syrie*, p. 571; Duparc-Quioc, *Antioche*, II, 101 and 126.

assumption about the language of the original, Mayer's suggestion does not square with the Norman elements present in the text. Indeed Duparc-Quioc thought the author was of Norman origin. Richard of Chaumont is referred to as a Norman, and when the 'chétifs' rejoin the Christian army at the beginning of the *Jérusalem* they enquire what has been happening to 'our Norman barons' – their absence corresponding to the length of the real captivity of Richard along with Bohemond.[15] As to the date of 'shortly before 1149', it would of course be fascinating to speculate about whether the *Chétifs* was written for the entertainment of Louis VII and Eleanor when they visited Antioch in 1148, and what such a tale harking back indirectly to a failed crusade might mean, before or after the débâcle of Damascus. However, the only really secure evidence of a *terminus post quem* is Raymond's arrival in Antioch in 1136, though for the reasons I have given, I would place it after Aimery became patriarch in early 1140.[16]

What we can conclude from the *Chétifs*, then, is that Antioch under the rule of Raymond of Poitiers was a place where literature had the potential to thrive, in a cosmopolitan milieu where some oriental stories were absorbed into western ones and eventually transmitted to France. It also seems to have been a place where Norman and Occitan elements continued to interact in epic production. But was the *Chanson des Chétifs* simply an isolated phenomenon? It is possible, though not proven, that the *Chétifs* was the tip of an epic iceberg. Anouar Hatem tried to argue that the whole of the First Crusade Cycle was originally composed at Antioch in 1148 for a Frankish audience. This has not met with general acceptance, but several scholars have seen behind Graindor's reworking a wider vernacular epic tradition concerning events at Antioch and associated with the name of Richard the Pilgrim (who may or may not have existed), one version of which may have been produced at Antioch.[17] Whatever the truth of this may be, after the death of Raymond, there is no more trace of vernacular epic produced in the Holy Land. Epic in the Occitan language produced back in Europe only resurfaces with the extant reworking of Bechada's text in the late twelfth century, perhaps stimulated by the Third Crusade.

In thinking about the place of an 'Antioch connection' with Occitania in the cultural developments of the time, I needed an overview of troubadour lyric responses to the crusades. The first task was to establish a corpus of relevant material. The most comprehensive scholarly work on troubadour crusading lyrics is still Lewent's 'Das altprovenzalische Kreuzlied' published in 1905.[18] Advances in scholarship make some of the details out of date, and Lewent focused on

15 G. Myers, 'Le développement des *Chétifs*: la version fécampoise?', in *Les Épopées de la croisade*, ed. K.-H. Bender (Stuttgart, 1987), pp. 84–90, links the origins of the *Chétifs* with the Norman abbey of Fécamp.

16 Hatem, *Les poèmes*, pp. 392–3, arrives at the same *terminus post quem* by arguing that the author of the *Chétifs* must have written after the *Chrétienté Corbaran* since Corbaran there announces his future conversion and quarrels with his mother, details that appear in the *Chétifs*. This is unconvincing since we do not know which elements were in the original *Chétifs* and which were added by Graindor.

17 Sweetenham and Paterson, *Canso*, pp. 51–78.

18 K. Lewent, 'Das altprovenzalische Kreuzlied', *Romanische Forschungen* 21 (1905), 321–448.

narrowly defined 'crusading songs' rather than 'songs which mention the crusades', although he refers quite extensively to songs of tangential interest and provides indices where these can be followed up.[19] Appendix 1 shows the result of my own efforts to identify a corpus, with indications of overlap with Lewent. I cannot claim completeness. Beyond consulting the secondary literature my 'method' has consisted in checking in the COM[20] for key words that came to my mind as potentially relevant, and following up leads. In identifying relevant texts I have been more inclusive than most since my interest was not 'what was a crusading song' but rather 'what was the scope and nature of troubadour responses to the crusades'. Inevitably there are grey areas of inclusion and exclusion.[21]

To arrive at an overview, and also to provide an accessible way of locating references to particular moments of the crusading movement, it then seemed worthwhile attempting to place all the relevant texts in chronological order, with essential bibliographical details and some indication of the content of each piece. The results are too extensive to include here and can be found on my website (where it can potentially be corrected and updated).[22]

The first conclusion to draw from these data is that they are rather extensive. Elizabeth Siberry remarked that 'only a very small proportion of the troubadours who flourished in Europe in the twelfth and thirteenth centuries made any reference to the crusades'.[23] According to my calculations, they amount to between a sixth and a seventh of the total number of troubadours (ignoring anonyma), of which there are 460 in Pillet and Carstens: that is, 75 to 80, depending on the method of counting. The number of texts in my corpus is 130. The Third Crusade provoked the most extensive reactions among the troubadours. But troubadour responses to the crusading movement as a whole persist from the Second Crusade through to the fourteenth century, with many allusions in the intervening lulls in major crusading expeditions (see Appendix 2).

My second conclusion concerns the troubadours' awareness of geographical

19 Other studies include H. Schindler, *Die Kreuzzüge in der altprovenzalischen und mittelhochdeutschen Lyrik* (Dresden, 1889); P. Hölzle, *Die Kreuzzüge in der Okzitanischen und der Deutschen Lyrik des 12. Jahrhunderts* (Stuttgart, 1980); P. Bec, 'La Chanson de croisade', in *La Lyrique française au moyen âge*, 2 vols. (Paris, 1997–98), I, 150–8; E. Siberry, 'Troubadours, Trouvères, Minnesingers and the Crusades', *Studi Medievali* 29 (1988), 19–43, and *Criticism of Crusading, 1095–1274* (Oxford, 1985); S. Guida, *Canzoni di crociata* (Parma, 1992); *idem*, 'Canzoni di crociata ed opinione pubblica del tempo', in *Medioevo romanzo e orientale: Testi e prospettive storiographiche. Colloquio Internazionale, Verona, 4–6 aprile 1990: Atti*, ed. A. M. Babbi, A. Pioletti, F. Rizzo Nervo and C. Stevanoni (Rubbettino, 1992), pp. 41–52. Guida offers a vehement challenge to Siberry's view that vernacular poets did not reflect public opinion. See also his 'Le canzoni di crociata francesi e provenzali', in *'Militia Christi' e Crociata nei secoli XI–XIII: Atti della undecima Settimana internazionale di studio Mendola, 28 agosto–1 settembre 1989*, Miscellanea del Centro di studi medioevali 13 (Milan, 1992), pp. 403–42.

20 P. T. Ricketts and A. Reed, *Concordance de l'occitan médiéval* (CD-ROM, Turnhout, 2001).

21 Texts relevant to the Reconquista are added, but not the many responses to the Albigensian Crusade, for which see especially E. Ghil, *L'Âge de Parage: Essai sur le poétique et le politique en Occitanie au XIIIe siècle* (New York, 1989), and M. Aurell, *La Vielle et l'épée: Troubadours et politique en Provence au XIIIe siècle* (Paris, 1989).

22 See <www2.warwick.ac.uk/fac/arts/french/about/staff>.

23 Siberry, 'Troubadours', p. 20.

locations and ethnic variety in the East. The COM searches in particular enabled me to try to map the troubadours' mental geography of the Holy Land.[24] These show, I think, that the range of overall awareness of specific locations was quite extensive; that most of the place names correspond to locations at or near the coast, with the exception of Jerusalem (for obvious reasons), Edessa (probably because the Occitan name *Roais* provides a very convenient rhyme word), and Damascus (because of the impact of the disaster of the Second Crusade); and that while the Christians' enemies were most often referred to generically as Saracens or Turks, the troubadours voiced a fearful public awareness of various other groups looming threateningly from the East. It is also clear that Antioch is not mentioned significantly more often than some other locations, and that the connection with Occitania so far explored in this chapter needs to be set in the wider context of the Holy Land as a whole. However, to attempt a comprehensive analysis of the great variety of themes, events and sympathies articulated in this broad corpus is not possible here. They have in any case been analysed in a certain amount of detail by Lewent, Siberry and others.[25] I shall focus instead on the question of what lyrics were produced in the Holy Land, and in what context.

Mayer's contention that the *Chétifs* represents the only surviving piece of evidence for the contribution to vernacular poetry made by the crusader states is almost true, if one excludes Hatem's hypothesis that other epics at the core of the First Crusade Cycle were produced in Outremer, and if one also excludes poetry produced in the Holy Land by poets who were 'just visiting'. I say 'almost true' because there has survived a song from c.1265, between the first and second crusades of Saint Louis, by a Templar in the Holy Land named Ricaut Bonomel (PC 439.1), which laments the pope's abandonment of the crusaders. We know nothing of how this came to be preserved, and can only speculate that it was sent to the West to attempt to arouse support among the laity for the crusading cause.

If there is little evidence of poets among the Frankish settlers, a number of troubadours did go overseas to the Holy Land, and some songs they composed there have survived. Troubadours who journeyed to Outremer include William of Poitou, Jaufre Rudel, Gaucelm Faidit, Peire Vidal, Giraut de Borneil, Peirol, Peire Bremon lo Tort, Pons de Monlaur,[26] Pons de Capduoill if his *vida* is to be believed, and possibly Olivier lo Templier (who may have taken part in James I of Aragon's crusade). Surviving songs are all from the Third Crusade: Peire Vidal's 'Ajostar e lassar' (PC 364.2) and stanza VI of his 'Be.m pac d'ivern e d'estiu' (PC 364.11), Guiraut de Borneil's 'Ben es dreitz, pos en aital port' (PC

[24] *Toponyms*: Suria (Syria, Holy Land) (23); Roais (Edessa, 20); Sur (Tyre, 15); Ierusalem (14); oltramar, oltramarin (14); Acre (7); Jordan, flum (7); Antioca (6); Damiata (5); Domas, Damas (5); Turquia (4); Corrozana (3); Tripol (3); Alap (2); Alexandria (2); Egipte (2); Persa (2); Surians (2); Alsuf (1); Cesaria (1); Cipres (1); Daro (1); Ibelin (1); Mongizart (1); Tabaria (1); Toron (1); Tunis (1). *Pagans*: Turcs (47); Sarrazis (43); paians, paianor (in crusading context, 10); Masmutz (7); Mor (7); Persanz (6); Caninieu (= barbarians from the East, 2); Armenis (1); Colmis (= Kwarismanians, 1); Perses (1); Tartres (1).

[25] See the references in n. 19 above, particularly Guida, 'Le canzoni di crociata francesi'.

[26] For Pons de Monlaur, see F. Pirot, *Recherches sur les connaissances littéraires des troubadours* (Barcelona, 1972), p. 307.

242.24) and 'De chantar / Ab deport' (PC 242.30), and Peirol's 'Pus flum Jordan ai vist e.l monimen' (PC 366.28).

As is well known, troubadours were also in evidence in Greece. Raimbaut de Vaqueiras spent some time there during and after the Fourth Crusade with his patron Boniface of Monferrat, whose court was also visited by Elias Cairel. The songs produced here show Boniface associating himself with the courtly way of life, and (unsurprisingly for the location) also a certain level of cosmopolitan exchange. They include Raimbaut de Vaqueiras' 'Conseil don a l'emperador', 'No m'agrad' iverns ni pascors', and Epic Letter; Elias Cairel's 'Pos cai la fuolha del garric'; and dialogue poems between Raimbaut de Vaqueiras and the French poet Conon de Béthune, and between Elias Cairel and Ysabella.[27] Some linguistic evidence suggests Ysabella may not have been a native Occitan speaker.[28]

Did similar court activities take place in Outremer? The fact that troubadours composed some songs in the East points in this direction. One song was even posted to the Holy Land for performance: Marcabru's deliberately 'refined' and 'courtly' song on love, 'Cortesamen vuoill comensar' (PC 293.15), sent to Jaufre Rudel 'oltramar', criticizing adulterers (perhaps in response to rumours about Eleanor), and allegedly meant to cheer the hearts of the French – no doubt a sarcasm.[29] We shall never know whether it reached them; we can but imagine the potential impact of such a song performed in the presence of Louis, Eleanor and Raymond at the Antiochene court.

Not all songs performed or produced overseas were directed towards crusading goals. Peire Vidal entertained a Frankish audience, apparently at the court of Raymond III of Tripoli, with a song about his alleged love-life (the so-called 'adventure of the kiss'). Expressing homesickness for Provence, where a small field would be preferable to the Palestinian castles of Daron, Toron, or Ibelin, he declared he was forced to become a crusader because of his disgrace with his *domna*.[30] Just as at the court of Boniface of Montferrat in Greece, this Frankish court appears to have welcomed a reaffirmation of the values of *Cortesia* and a form of entertainment that did not automatically give priority to serious religious matters.

While many troubadour songs move comfortably between *Cortesia* and crusade, others reveal a tension between them.[31] Some poets felt constrained to defend the courtly way of life, while others (in a minority) criticized any distraction from the spiritual goals of the crusades. In the West, after the fall of Edessa in

27 PC 392.9a, PC 392.24, Epic Letter (ed. Linskill, p. 303), PC 133.9, PC 392.29, PC 252.1.

28 H. Jaeschke, *Der Trobador Elias Cairel* (Berlin, 1921; repr. Liechtenstein, 1967), poem 7. S. Asperti, 'Contrafacta provenzali di modelli francesi', *Messana* 8 (1991), 5–49 (esp. pp. 44–9), has shown that the period of the Third and Fourth Crusades witnessed an upsurge of imitation of metrical and musical form by troubadours of trouvères and vice versa.

29 *Marcabru: A Critical Edition*, ed. S. Gaunt, R. Harvey and L. Paterson (Woodbridge, 2000), no. XV.

30 PC 364.2; see D'A. S. Avalle, *Peire Vidal, Poésie* (Milan–Naples, 1960), p. 36 (who mistakenly refers to Raymond III as Raymond II), and my website, under 1187 *taq*.

31 For *Cortesia*, see J. Rüdiger, *Aristokraten und Poeten: Die Grammatik einer Mentalität im Tolosanischen Hochmittelalter* (Berlin, 2001).

1144 and the launch of the Second Crusade in 1146, Cercamon defends the value of *fin'amor* in the face of troubadours (such as Marcabru) who try to frighten lovers, husbands and wives into believing that love has a corrupting effect on society:

Per joy d'amor nos devem esbaudir . . .
Ist trobador entre ver e mentir
Afollon drutz e molhers et espos,
E van dizen qu'Amors torn' en biays . . .,

(We ought to rejoice for the joy of love . . . These troubadours alarm lovers, wives, and husbands with half-truths, and go around saying that love is corrupted . . .)

and moves seamlessly to the expiatory value of journeying towards Edessa:

Ara.s pot hom lavar et esclarzir
De gran blasme, silh q'en son encombros;
E s'i es pros, yssira ves Roays,
E gurpira lo segle perilhos . . .[32]

(Now a man who is burdened with great guilt may cleanse and purify himself of this, and if he is brave, he will make his way to Edessa, and abandon the perilous world . . .)

Jaufre Rudel's 'Quan lo rossinhols el foillos' (PC 262.6) concludes in some MSS with the spiritual need to follow Jesus to Bethlehem; whether he composed this before or after he arrived in the East, presumably with the southern contingent of crusaders who landed at Acre in April 1148, is not known. Both of these troubadours implicitly defend the compatibility of love with crusading ideals. Marcabru on the other hand attacks those who take the cross while allowing themselves to be duped by 'lurve':

Ja el no.s senh ab sa ma
cui amors enguanara! (PC 293.7, no. VII, 55–6)

(The man whom love will deceive should never sign himself [with the Cross] [become a Crusader]!)

The final words of the song he sends to Jaufre Rudel 'oltramar' suggests that listening to secular songs may be a sin for crusaders:

Lo vers e.l son voill enviar
a.n Jaufre Rudel oltramar,
e voill que l'aion li Frances
per lor coratges alegrar,
que Dieus lor o pot perdonar,
o sia peccaz o merces. (PC 293.15, no. XV, 37–42)

32 *Il trovatore Cercamon*, ed. V. Tortoreto (Modena, 1981), PC 112.3a, no. VI, ll. 12, 19–21 and 43–5. Marcabru had declared some years earlier that he was regarded as a scaremonger ('espaorit', PC 293.8, no. VIII, l. 18).

(I want to send the *vers* and the melody to Sir Jaufre Rudel, in Outremer, and I want the French to have it, to cheer their hearts, for God can allow them this, whether it is a sin or a good deed.)[33]

And in his famous *lavador* crusading song, he contradicts Cercamon's recommendation of spiritual cleansing in the East to extol the Spanish Reconquista as the better place of spiritual purgation.

This sort of difficulty seems to have existed also at the time of the Third Crusade, both in the West and in Outremer. To judge by Giraut de Borneil's defensiveness, songs of any kind seem to have run up against disapproval as the crusade was in preparation:

De faire chansos
Sol hom dir qu'es faillimens,
Et es bes e chauzimens
C'uns qecx chan
E digu'e mostr' en chantan
Can ric guizardo n'aten,
Cel q'a Deu ser bonamen.[34] (PC 242, 41, no. LXIV, 6–12)

(People tend to say that composing songs is wrong, and yet it is a good and wise thing for every man to sing and tell and show in song how richly God rewards the man who truly serves Him.)

Once in the Holy Land, Giraut defended the courtly way of life against lack of interest and accusations that courtly songs were idle nonsense. He also sought to promote the courtly way of life in the context of the crusade:

Alegrar
Mi voill fort
E son aisi passatz,
E si non sembles fatz,
No camiera.l talan;
Mas tenon s'a masan
Mains bos sonetz qu'eu fatz
Vilan d'avol linatge,
Qu'anc pros hom de paratge,
S'en ben auzir ateis,
De l'escoutar no.s feis
Ni.l plaszer no n'estrais.
E non es ben savais
Cui iois non platz ni chans? (PC 242, 30, no. LXXI, 20–33)

(I wish to achieve great joy and for this reason I have crossed over [to the Holy Land], and, save that I look a fool, I would not change my inclination [to feel joyful]; but churlish men of base lineage consider many of my fine songs as idle

33 Note to ll. 41–2 in *Marcabru*, ed. Gaunt, Harvey and Paterson: 'whether listening to such a secular song is a sin for the crusaders for whom it is intended or not'.

34 Quotations from *The Cansos and Sirventes of the Troubadour Giraut de Borneil*, ed. R. V. Sharman (Cambridge, 1989).

nonsense, though no excellent man of noble birth, if he succeeded in catching their meaning, ever excused himself from listening to them or belittled the pleasure they afforded. And is a man who takes no pleasure in joy and song not thoroughly despicable?)

Per que.s degra.l plus richs plus fort
Esforsar con mais li plagues,
Pos gens garnirs ni bels conres
Ni cortezia ni deportz
No.il notz des que Sains Esperitz
   Hi met razitz,
Ni ia per sos bels garnimens,
Des que sa vid' es avinens,
   Non deu doptar
Que nostre Senher dezenpar
Los genseis tenens ni.ls plus pros,
Si no.ls en tol autra razos. (PC 242, 24, no. LXX, 25–36)

(For this reason, the more rich and powerful a man is, the more effort he should make to be pleasing to God, since fine clothing and splendid banquets, courtly manners and joyful pastimes do him no harm when such pursuits are nurtured by the Holy Spirit. And, provided he leads a correct life, the rich man need not fear, on account of his lavish life style, that God may disinherit those who are most elegantly dressed or most courtly in their conduct, unless they are dispossessed for some other reason.)[35]

So where was Giraut? Are we back in Antioch? The *razo* (commentary) to 'Non puesc sofrir', found in MSS *N2Sg*, relates how Giraut travelled to the Holy Land with King Richard and Viscount Ademar of Limoges, was present at the siege of Acre, and went on to the 'good prince of Antioch' where he was warmly welcomed and where he spent the winter awaiting the spring passage back to the West.[36] The *razo* is wrong in some respects: according to the unpublished research of Ruth Harvey and John Gillingham, Giraut did not accompany Ademar on the Third Crusade, and his journey overseas may have preceded it. However, it is clear from the extracts quoted that Giraut must have been at a court that allowed him to sing courtly songs, even if he did not feel the courtly way of life was entirely up to scratch. The obvious candidates were Antioch and the court of Raymond III of Tripoli. We know Peire Vidal sang at Raymond's court before the latter's death in 1187 (whether in Tripoli itself, or Jerusalem during one of Raymond's regencies, or his wife's lands in Galilee). What of Antioch? The prince of Antioch was Raymond's son Bohemond III. Had Bohemond perpetuated courtly traditions from his family line? Or, if Giraut did indeed turn up at his court some forty years after the Second Crusade and the death of his father when Bohemond was a young boy, did this visiting troubadour present a rather quaint appearance, harking back to a bygone age and providing a little exotic entertainment?

35 The Monk of Montaudon also refers to religious disapproval of composing songs: M. J. Routledge, *Les poésies du Moine de Montaudon* (Montpellier, 1977), PC 305.12, no. XIII, ll. 25–8.
36 PC 242.51, ed. Sharman, no. XXXVII; *BdT*, p. 51.

The euphoric victory at Antioch in 1098 and the need to protect the Christian conquests on which it centred sparked the creation of vernacular epic historiography in the West. The *Canso d'Antioca* reverberated into the thirteenth century in Occitania, France and Spain. Antioch was the most stable and long-lasting of Frankish conquests, and most crusaders who reached the Holy Land found their way to Antioch at some point. So it is no surprise that such records as there are of vernacular literary activity in the Holy Land stem almost exclusively from there, with the court of the count of Tripoli, wherever this was, very much in second place. Continuity from Poitiers to Antioch through Raymond, perhaps supported by the Latin patriarch Aimery from the Limousin (or did he simply have a convenient library?), generated a milieu that was receptive to vernacular poetry in the 1140s and even as late as 1191. It cannot be said that records for such court entertainment are extensive, or comparable with those of court life in the West, though there are a few more of them than is perhaps usually recognized. From the time of the Second Crusade up to the fourteenth century, those who saw the Holy Land solely from their homes in the West may have remembered the First Crusade victory at Antioch, but their concerns moved on with events. The troubadour lyric comments abundantly on particular actors and events throughout this period, offering, as Saverio Guida has so fervently demonstrated, a fertile source of public opinion and mood – anxious, disturbed, frustrated, excited, light-hearted, or cynical.[37]

37 Guida, 'Canzoni di crociata'.

Appendix I

Texts referring to crusades or Holy Land[a]

9.10	Aimeric de Belenoi	La
10.11	Aimeric de Peguilhan	La
10.37	Aim. de Peg. & Elias d'Ussel	
16.11	Albertet	
19.1	Alexandre & Blacasset	
29.8	Arnaut Daniel	
40.1	Austorc d'Aorlhac	Lb
41.1	Austorc de Segret	Lb
53.1	Bernart Alanhan de Narbona	Lb
66.2	Bernart de Rovenac	Lb
66.3	Bernart de Rovenac	Lb
74.11	Bertolome Zorzi	Lb
76.8	Bertran d'Alamanon	Lb
76.9	Bertran d'Alamanon	Lb
76.15	Bertran d'Alamanon	
76.16	Bertran d'Alamanon	
76.19	Bertran d'Alamanon	Lb
80.2	Bertran de Born	
80.3	Bertran de Born	Lb
80.4	Bertran de Born	La
80.9	Bertran de Born	
80.17	Bertran de Born	
80.19	Bertran de Born	
80.30	Bertran de Born	La
80.32	Bertran de Born	Lb
82.12	Bertran Carbonel	Lb
106.5	Cadenet	
107.1	Calega Panza	Lb
112.3a	Cercamon	Lb
119.8	Dalfi d'Alvergne	
124.5	Daude de Pradas	
126.1	Duran sartor de Paernas	
133.9	Elias Cairel	
133.11	Elias Cairel	La
136.3, 167.13, 136.2, 167.3a	Gauc. Faidit & Elias d'Ussel	Lb
154.1	Folquet de Lunel	Lb
155.3	Folquet de Marselha	
155.7	Folquet de Marselha	La
155.15	Folquet de Marselha	La
156.2	Falquet de Romans	Lb
156.11	Falquet de Romans	Lb
156.12	Falquet de Romans	La
167.9	Gaucelm Faidit	La
167.14	Gaucelm Faidit	La
167.15	Gaucelm Faidit	Lb
167.19	Gaucelm Faidit	Lb
167.22	Gaucelm Faidit	Lb
167.36	Gaucelm Faidit	Lb
167.58	Gaucelm Faidit	Lb
168.1a	Gauceran de Saint Leidier	La[b]
173.1a	Gausbert de Poicibot	
174.10	Gavaudan	La
177.1	Gormonda	
184.1	Count of Provence and Arnaut	
189.5	Granet & Bertran	Lb
202.10	Guilhem Ademar	Lb
202.12	Guilhem Ademar	
206.2	Guilhem d'Autpol	
206.4	Guilhem d'Autpol	Lb
210.16	Guillem de Bergueda̋	
216.2	Guilhem Fabre	La
217.1	Guilhem Figueira	La
217.2	Guilhem Figueira	Lb
217.7	Guilhem Figueira	La
217.8	Guilhem Figueira	Lb
223.2	Guillem Magret	Lb
226.2	Guilhem de Mur	Lb
242.6	Giraut de Borneil	La
242.15	Giraut de Borneil	Lb
242.18	Giraut de Borneil	
242.24	Giraut de Borneil	Lb
242.28	Giraut de Borneil	
242.30	Giraut de Borneil	
242.32	Giraut de Borneil	
242.33	Giraut de Borneil	
242.41	Giraut de Borneil	La
242.56	Giraut de Borneil	Lb
242.73	Giraut de Borneil	Lb
242.77	Giraut de Borneil (?)	Lb
243.1	Guiraut de Calanso	Lb
248.17	Guiraut Riquier	Lb
248.48	Guiraut Riquier	La
248.79	Guiraut Riquier	Lb
248.87	Guiraut Riquier	Lb
262.6	Jaufre Rudel	Lb
273.1b	Jordan Bonel	
282.20	Lanfranc Cigala	La
282.23	Lanfranc Cigala	La
289.1	Lunel de Monteg	La
290.1	Luquet Gatelus	
293.1	Marcabru	Lb
293.7	Marcabru	
293.15	Marcabru	Lb

[a] La = texts designated as crusading songs by Lewent. Lb = texts touching on the crusades or Holy Land but not considered by Lewent as crusading songs.

[b] (under PC 234.10)

293.21	Marcabru	Lb
293.35	Marcabru	La
299.1	Matieu de Caerci	Lb
305.11a	Monk of Montaudon (?)	
305.12	Monk of Montaudon	Lb
312.1	Olivier lo Templier	La
323.3	Peire d'Alvernha	
323.5	Bernart de Venzac?	Lb
323.3	Peire d'Alvernha	
323.19	Peire d'Alvernha	
323.22	Anon	La
330.14	Peire Bremon Ricas Novas	Lb
330.20	Peire Bremon Ricas Novas/Gui	
331.1	Peire Bremon lo Tort	
331.2	Peire Bremon lo Tort	
335.12	Peire Cardenal	Lb
335.18	Peire Cardenal	Lb
335.31	Peire Cardenal	Lb
335.51	Peire Cardenal	Lb
335.52	Peire Cardenal	
335.54	Peire Cardenal	Lb
364.2	Peire Vidal	
364.4	Peire Vidal	Lb
364.8	Peire Vidal	Lb
364.11	Peire Vidal	
364.35	Peire Vidal	Lb
364.43	Peire Vidal	Lb
364.45	Peire Vidal	
365.1	Peire del Vilar	
366.28	Peirol	Lb
366.29	Peirol	Lb
375.2	Pons de Capdolh	La
375.8	Pons de Capdolh	La
375.22	Pons de Capdolh	La
389.8	Raimbaut d'Aurenga	
389.27	Raimbaut d'Aurenga	
392.3	Raimbaut de Vaqueiras	La
392.5	Raimbaut de Vaqueiras	
392.9a	Raimbaut de Vaqueiras	La
392.24	Raimbaut de Vaqueiras	Lb
401.1	Raimon Gaucelm de Beziers	La
401.8	Raimon Gaucelm de Beziers	La
427.4	Rostaing Berenguier	Lb
436.2	Albert & Simon Doria	
437.18	Sordel	Lb
439.1	Templier = Ricaut Bonomel	Lb
442.1	Tomier / Palazi	Lb
442.2	Tomier / Palazi	Lb
449.3	Uc de la Bacalaria	
456.1	Uc de Pena	
461.35a	Anon	
461.67a	Anon	
461.122	Anon	
	Raimon de Cornet I	La
	Raimon de Cornet II	Lb
	Lo Paire de Raimon de Cornet	Lb

Reconquista

66.3	Bernart de Rovenac	Lb
80.42	Anon	Lb
155.12	Folquet de Marselha	Lb
155.15	Folquet de Marselha	La
174.10	Gavaudan	La
202.9	Guilhem Ademar	
210.9	Guillem de Berguedà	Lb
225.5	Guilhem Montanhagol	Lb
242.28	Giraut de Borneil	
242.74	Giraut de Borneil	Lb
243.6	Guiraut de Calanso	Lb
245.1	Guiraut del Luc	
248.37	Guiraut Riquier	
293.12a	Marcabru	Lb
293.22	Marcabru	La
293.26	Marcabru	
293.35	Marcabru	La
299.1	Matieu de Caerci	Lb
323.3	Peire d'Alvernha	
323.7	Peire d'Alvernha	Lb
335.18	Peire Cardenal	
364.38	Peire Vidal	Lb
364.36	Peire Vidal	
364.38	Peire Vidal	
406.12	Raimon de Miraval	Lb

Appendix 2

References to Crusades in Troubadour Lyrics

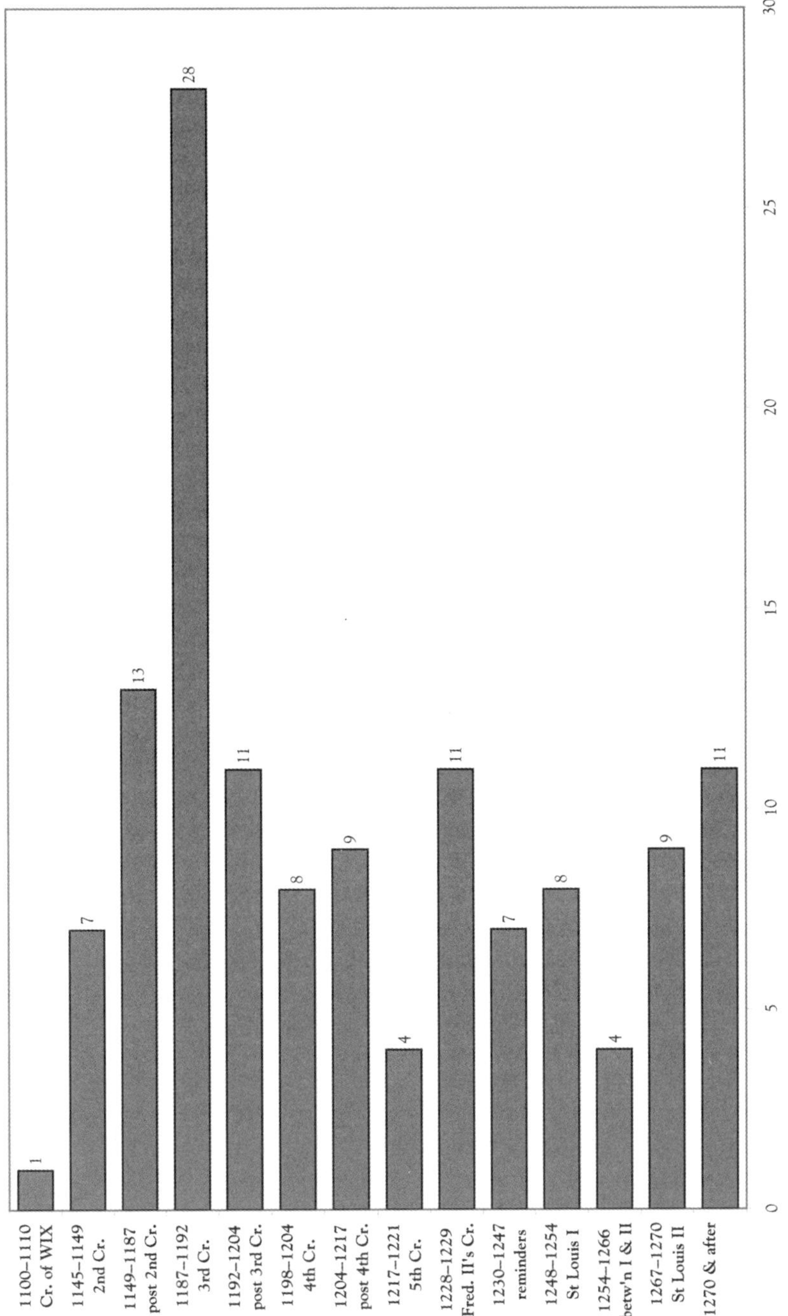

Eleanor of Aquitaine and the Troubadours

RUTH HARVEY

> Huguet mos cortes messatgers
> chantatz ma chanso volonters
> a la reïna dels Normans.[1]

(Huguet, my courtly messenger, sing my song eagerly to the queen of the Normans.)

Despite all that has been claimed for Eleanor's enthusiasm for and patronage of troubadour song, this instruction to his *joglar* at the end of a love-song by Bernart de Ventadorn is acknowledged as the only explicit and apparently secure reference to Eleanor in the troubadour lyric corpus, and even this one, I will suggest, is not entirely straightforward. This chapter asks why this should be so and explores some of the associated issues.

The literary view of Eleanor that long prevailed can be broadly summed up by saying that, as the descendant of notable patrons of poets and the mother of others, she herself also played this role. Although we can identify only one such individual with any certainty, Alfred Jeanroy remarked, we can be sure that 'des troubadours pullulaient autour d'elle'.[2] Since so many of the Occitan troubadours from the middle decades of the twelfth century came from her lands, it was thought that there was a necessary connection between this flowering of vernacular culture and the person of the duchess of Aquitaine.[3] More recently, however, a more measured, cautious note has been sounded by a number of scholars who point out that Eleanor's literary role and importance have surely been overstated, particularly by Rita Lejeune whose erudition and enthusiasm were directed towards a demonstration of the richness and precocity of the Occitan literary tradition and its independence of any northern French influence.[4] It

1 *Bernart von Ventadorn: seine Lieder mit Einleitung und Glossar*, ed. and trans. C. Appel (Halle, 1915), poem 33, ll. 43–5; also *The Songs of Bernart de Ventadorn*, ed. and trans. S. G. Nichols *et al.* (Chapel Hill, 1962).

2 *La Poésie lyrique des troubadours*, 2 vols. (Paris, 1934), I, 151.

3 R. Lejeune, 'Le Rôle littéraire d'Aliénor d'Aquitaine et de sa famille', *CN* 14 (1954), 5–57; also *idem*, 'Le Rôle littéraire de la famille d'Aliénor d'Aquitaine', *CCM* 3 (1960), 319–37.

4 See for example M. Aurell, 'La Cour Plantagênet (1154–1204): entourage, savoir, civilité', in *La Cour Plantagênet (1154–1204)*, ed. M. Aurell (Poitiers, 2000), pp. 9–46; W. Meliga,

remains the case that no detailed reassessment of Eleanor's connections with the Occitan troubadours has yet been produced.[5]

Along with Bernart de Ventadorn, the troubadours repeatedly cited in connection with Eleanor are 'from her lands and from the same period'. According to Lejeune, they knew each other's works, knew each other and treated in their songs such similar themes that one may speak of a single 'school' of poetry and thought. Who were they? Cercamon and Marcabru (Gascons whose careers began at the court of her father); Marcoat and Alegret (Gascon *joglars*); Peire de Valeria (Gascon); Jaufre Rudel, 'prince' of Blaye; Peire d'Alvernhe and Peire Rogier (from the Auvergne); Bernart Marti; Rigaut de Barbezieux (from Saintonge); and Arnaut Guilhem de Marsan (another Gascon).[6]

Since Lejeune's seminal article, critical approaches to the troubadours have developed and diversified considerably, and a different light is shed on the corpus of songs that bear witness to the cultural phenomenon. To give just a couple of examples: the treatment of the same themes and the echoing of similar phrases are no guarantee that the poets concerned formed 'une école poétique déterminée'.[7] Similarly, the 'autobiographical approach', which saw the words of the poets as diary-entries charting their real emotional experiences, has given way to a much more complex view of the relationship between song and social reality, the 'uses of *fin'amor*'. Moreover, more detailed studies of some individual poets have been able to redefine more precisely and plausibly the *Sitz im Leben* of their subjects, whereas the evidential basis for such a contextualization of some others now looks thin and tenuous.

These studies produce, for Lejeune's list of poets, the following results. Nothing in the works of Marcoat, Alegret, Peire de Valeria, Peire Rogier or Bernart Marti[8] indicates any kind of association with Eleanor. The link between Jaufre Rudel and the queen boils down to the fact that they both went on the Second Crusade, Jaufre probably accompanying the count of Toulouse. Rita Lejeune argued passionately that Rigaut de Barbezieux's songs should be dated to c.1140–60, but Saverio Guida's careful and judicious exploration of the *vida*'s information, together with archival documents, supports Varvaro's placing of

'L'Aquitania trobadorica', in *Lo Spazio letterario del Medioevo 2. Il medioevo volgare: I. La produzione del testo, in due tomi*, ed. P. Boitani, M. Mancini and A. Varvaro (Rome, 2001), II, 201–51 (pp. 245–6); S. Gaunt and R. Harvey, 'The Arthurian Tradition in Occitan Literature', in *The Arthur of the French*, ed. G. Burgess and K. Pratt (Cardiff, forthcoming).

5 K. M. Broadhurst, 'Henry II of England and Eleanor of Aquitaine: Patrons of Literature in French?', *Viator* 27 (1996), 53–84, devotes a scant page to the troubadours. My focus is on the known Occitan exponents of the art of *trobar* whose works have survived, rather than obscure *ioculatores*: cf. R. Harvey, '*Joglars* and the Professional Status of the Early Troubadours', *Medium Ævum* 62 (1993), 35–55 (p. 227); Aurell, 'La Cour Plantagenêt', p. 35.

6 Lejeune, 'Rôle littéraire d'Aliénor', p. 19. See the entries in M. de Riquer, *Los Trovadores: historia literaria y textos*, 3 vols. (Barcelona, 1975).

7 See for example J. Gruber, *Die Dialektik des Trobar* (Tübingen, 1983) and M. L. Meneghetti, *Il Pubblico dei trovatori* (Modena, 1984).

8 Probably to be identified with Bernart de Saissac: see A. Roncaglia, 'Due postille alla "galleria letteraria" di Peire d'Alvernia', *Marche Romane* 19 (1969), 71–5.

him towards the end of the twelfth century, where a number of literary features of his work also sit much more easily.[9]

However exaggerated its polarized attitudes of optimism and pessimism for the future, Cercamon's *tenso* with an otherwise unknown Guilhalmi points up the profound uncertainty produced among William X's followers by their lord's death in April 1137, an uncertainty one might suppose to have been accentuated by the fact that, as they present it, the new count was not to be a Poitevin heir but an 'unknown quantity' 'de Fransa'.

> – Maïstre, conte novel
> aurem nos a Pantacosta
> que·us pagara ben e bel.
> – Guilhalmi, fols es qi·eus escota:
> vo·m pagatz d'autrui borcel. (VIII, 50–4)

(Master, we shall have a new count at Whitsun who will pay you well and truly. – Guilhalmi, a man is a fool to listen to you: you are paying me out of someone else's purse.)[10]

This anxiety over a change of lordship is echoed by the words of Marcabru in a poem from the autumn of the same year when, in the context of drumming up support for a Reconquista campaign led by King Alfonso VII of Leon-Castile, his bitter reference to Louis VII strongly suggests that, in his eyes, Poitou and Berry are now subjugated to a foreign lord and foreign customs:

> Mas Franssa Peitau e Beiriu
> aclin' a un sol seignoriu,
> veign' a Dieu sai son fieu servir!
>
> Q'ieu non sai per que princes viu,
> s' a Dieu no vai son fieu servir![11]

(Since France subjects Poitou and Berry to a single jurisdiction, let him come here to God to earn his fief! For I do not know why a prince lives if he does not go to God to earn his fief!)

A new order prevails in Aquitaine, and Cercamon and Marcabru, troubadours in the following of the late duke, then seem to have relocated. Marcabru went to Spain. Cercamon may perhaps have contemplated doing the same, for his lament for the death of his master is sent to Eble, usually identified as Eble de Ventadorn, and in it he addresses

> Gasco cortes, nominatiu,
> perdut aves lo segnoriu:

9 For previous studies, see S. Guida, 'Problemi di datazione e di identificazione di trovatori. I. Rigaut de Berbezilh. II. Sifre e Mir Bernat. III. Guillem Augier', in *Studi Provenzali e Francesi, 86–87*, ed. G. Tavani and L. Rossi, Quaderni Romanica Vulgaria 10–11 (L'Aquila, 1990), pp. 87–126 (pp. 87–108).

10 *Il trovatore Cercamon*, ed. V. Tortoreto (Modena, 1981).

11 *Marcabru: A Critical Edition*, ed. S. Gaunt, R. Harvey and L. Paterson (Woodbridge, 2000), XXII, ll. 55–9.

fer vos deu esser et esqiu,
don Jovenz se clama chaitiu,
qar us no·n troba on s'aiziu[12]
mas qan n'Anfos, q'a joi conquis. (VII, 31–6)

(Famous and courtly Gascons, you have lost your lord: this must be terrible and awful for you, which is why youth declares itself to be wretched, for not one of you can find a place except with Lord Alfonso, who has conquered joy.)

Although scholars have hesitated over the identity of *n'Anfos*, given Cercamon's clear connections with the late William X and the current political tensions between Aquitaine and Toulouse,[13] an identification of this figure with Alfonso of Castile may seem more plausible than with Alfonso of Toulouse.

These poets' references thereafter to Poitevin matters are at best fleeting and always negative. It is likely that Marcabru returned north of the Pyrenees, but he devotes a song (XXXIX) to an allegorical tree rooted in *malvestatz*, which has spread from Spain to overshadow France and Poitou and is characterized by avarice, the absence of joy, the ruination of *joven* and its desertion by justice and fidelity. Furthermore, if these two troubadours' criticisms of a certain woman's inappropriate conduct in Syria (which will be bruited abroad from there as far as *Peitau*) do indeed refer to scandal surrounding Eleanor during the Second Crusade,[14] probably based on gossip from returning crusaders, they do not support a picture of troubadours either in her entourage or 'on her side', as it were.

If Eleanor was accompanied by troubadours when she went to Paris, we cannot trace them;[15] if she attracted poets to her side during her tours of her lands while she was married to Louis, we cannot trace those either. Rather, there seems to have been a sharp break in the association of troubadours with the house of Poitou at the watershed of 1137, and the void of troubadour lyric activity is only filled some fifteen years later, apparently, by Bernart de Ventadorn.

Nearly all that we think we know about Bernart de Ventadorn comes from his own songs. If I go over that evidence again here, it is because aspects of it point up a number of awkward issues involved in attempts to illuminate the relations of Occitan troubadours with known patrons and with Eleanor in particular. The well-known evidence for Bernart de Ventadorn's association with Eleanor I have already quoted, and he apparently visited England – one of only two troubadours to do so – for another of his songs concludes 'this poem has been completed [. . .] far from the Norman land, across the wild, deep sea':[16]

E si·m sui de midons lonhans,
vas se·m tira com azimans
la bela cui Deus defenda.

12 Tortoreto unnecessarily emends the single MS reading 'us' to 'un'.

13 See Marcabru IX, ll. 27–8.

14 S. Gaunt, 'Marginal Men, Marcabru and Orthodoxy: The Early Troubadours and Adultery', *Medium Ævum* 59 (1990), 55–68.

15 Bernart does once claim to be in 'Fransa' (ed. Appel, poem 44, l. 36), by which poets mean the Ile-de-France, and thus separated from his beloved, but this song is undatable.

16 'Faihz es lo vers tot a randa / [. . .] / outra la terra normanda / part la fera mar prionda.'

Si·l reis engles e·l ducs normans
o vol, eu la veirai abans
que l'iverns nos sobreprenda.

Pel rei sui engles e normans,
e si no fos Mos Azimans,
restera tro part calenda. (26, 36–48)

(And though I am far from my lady, the beautiful woman whom God protect draws me to her like a magnet.
If the English king and the Norman duke allows, I will see her before winter overtakes us.
For the king's sake, I am both English and Norman, and, were it not for my Aziman, I would stay until Christmas is over.)

The *tornadas* suggest that his movements depend on the king, an indication that is supported by poem 33, where he claims to his lady 'for your sake I have left the king, and I pray that there may be no trouble for me when I, frank, gentle and humble, am ready to do your service in court among ladies and knights',[17] and by his praise of Henry II in another piece:

Fons Salada, mos drogomans
me siatz mosenhor al rei,
digatz li·m que Mos Azimans
me te, car eu ves lui no vau.
Si com a Toren' e Peitau
e Anjau e Normandia,
volgra, car li covenria,
agues tot lo mon en poder. (21, 49–56)

(Fons Salada, be my interpreter to my lord the king; tell him that my Aziman holds me, and so I do not go to him. But I wish, since it would be fitting for him, that he had all the world in his power, just as he has Touraine, Poitou, Anjou and Normandy.)

This Limousin poet depicts Henry II as the ruler of Touraine, Anjou, Normandy and Poitou and declares himself for the king's sake to be both English and Norman, in contrast, it would seem, to the attitude of many other natives of the Limousin during Henry's reign, and for Bernart, Eleanor is the queen of the Normans . . .

Was she also 'his Magnet' (*Mos Azimans*)? Bernart's editor thought not, on the grounds that it would be too daring for a low-born man like Bernart to beg to be present at and assist in the queen's disrobing, especially in songs dedicated to her husband.[18] This may or may not seem now a decisive reason for rejecting the identification, depending on one's view of the subtle interplay of social reality and the fantasy world of the courtly love-lyric and of the ideological

[17] 'No sai coras mais vos veirai, / mas vau m'en iratz e maritz. / Per vos me sui del rei partitz / e prec vos que no.m sia dans / qu'e.us serai en cort prezenters / entre domnas e chavalers / francs e doutz et umilians' (ed. Appel, poem 33, ll. 36–42).

[18] Appel, *Bernart*, p. xxxviii, and see poem 26, ll. 29–35.

manipulations for which the *canso* was the vehicle. To the thirteenth-century troubadour and composer of *vidas*, Uc de Saint-Circ, however, Eleanor did appear to be the beloved to whom some of Bernart's songs were addressed. The low-born but talented Bernart, having been allegedly ejected from Ventadorn because of an affair with the viscountess, went to the 'duquesa de Normandia', whose favour and favours he purportedly enjoyed until the king of England married her and took her to England. Uc's authority for this is of the best: 'what I have written about him was told to me by the viscount Lord Eble of Ventadorn who was the son of the viscountess Bernart loved' ('de lui so qu'ieu ai escrit si me contet lo vescoms N'Ebles de Ventadorn, que fo fils de la vescomtessa qu'En Bernartz amet').[19] Contrary to what has sometimes been asserted since the edition of the *vida*, it is quite possible that Uc, the fanatical collector of material,[20] did glean this information from Viscount Eble IV and there may have been a Ventadorn family tradition associating 'their poet' with Eleanor, one which Uc supplemented and embroidered by recourse to Bernart's own songs.[21]

However, Uc's *vidas* and *razos* had their own ideological programme, which was at once 'foundational, nostalgic and self-serving':[22] the creation of a mythology of court practice, in an idealized Occitan past, from which the lyrics and their values sprang, for the consumption of an urbanized thirteenth-century courtly public in the Veneto, that is, a culture very different from that of the first audience for which the lyrics were originally intended. It is in this context that we should see the factual error in Bernart de Ventadorn's *vida* concerning the duchess which, like the similar mistake in the biography of Duke William IX, places the duchy of Normandy in the patrimony of the house of Poitou before Eleanor's marriage to Henry.[23] More pertinently, Uc, who had spent considerable time in Gascony and Poitou,[24] clearly either did not know or did not care where Eleanor was actually duchess of, and associated her with only one troubadour.

The slim indications in Bernart's own songs evoke an association with Henry's entourage rather than with Eleanor's, and not with her supposed 'court at Poitiers'. Of course, it is difficult to tell because of the nature of the compositions: the *canso* of *fin'amor* with its particular conventions. Among those that most frustrate historical enquiry is the use of *senhals* such as 'Mos Azimans'. These

19 *BdT*, pp. 20–1.

20 Meneghetti, *Il Pubblico*, p. 182; S. Guida, 'Uc de Saint-Circ, biografo', *Studi Testuali* 4 (1996), 67–98 (pp. 72–4).

21 *BdT*, p. 25; cf. Riquer, *Los Trovadores*, I, 342–3 n. 6; on Eble, still alive in 1214, see W. D. Paden, 'Bernart de Ventadorn le troubadour devint-il abbé de Tulle?', in *Mélanges de langue et de littérature occitanes en hommage à Pierre Bec* (Poitiers, 1991), pp. 401–14; S. Guida, *Primi approcci a Uc de Saint-Circ* (Messina, 1996), pp. 102–6.

22 W. Burgwinkle, 'The Chansonniers as Books', in *The Troubadours: An Introduction*, ed. S. Gaunt and S. Kay (Cambridge, 1999), pp. 246–62 (pp. 249–50); Guida, *Primi approcci*, p. 97; E. Ghil, *L'Age de Parage: Essai sur le poétique et le politique en Occitanie au XIIIe siècle* (New York, 1989), pp. 38–56.

23 For a possible function of the references to the 'duchess of Normandy', see S. Guida, 'Le "biografe" trobadoriche: prove di agnizione autoriale', in *Studi Provenzali 98/99*, ed. S. Guida, Quaderni Romanica Vulgaria 16–17 (L'Aquila, 1999), pp. 141–98 (pp. 146–52).

24 *BdT*, p. 239.

pseudonyms seem to have had two paradoxical functions: to claim and advertise a privileged relationship between a poet and a significant figure while concealing the latter's identity from the gaze of those not within the charmed circle of courtly intimates.[25] In the *cansos*, such a ploy blurs the distinction between the object of the lover's amorous aspirations, the *domna*, in the body of the song and the patroness to whom the poet may dedicate the composition in the concluding *tornada*. The *domna* is not necessarily the same as the patroness, though part of the troubadour's art lay in flatteringly implying that she could be. Rita Lejeune thought that Eleanor might lurk concealed behind one of Bernart's *senhals*, and this idea has been often repeated. However, absolute discretion and total submission were the twin pillars of *fin'amor* and articulated in the elegant *canso* that Bernart made his poetic speciality.

If the veil of discretion slips at all, it is usually in the *tornada* of a *canso* where the real world becomes visible, where patrons, friends and other addressees may be named without a *senhal* or with some identifying mark like a location or a lordship. Conventionally, the song may be sent, sometimes via a *joglar*, to someone who may be thought to have been interested in it. This brings with it its own paradox, however, since we only know of Bernart's association with Eleanor because he was *not* in her company at the time.

When was this association? Bernart's 'career' is only very approximately datable (c.1145–c.1180), but it seems clear that these references date from a time after Henry could properly be called 'king' and Eleanor 'queen of the Normans', so not before the end of 1154. Appel considered various possibilities for dating Bernart's stay in England and put forward as a tentative hypothesis 1154–55, reasoning that the coronation of Henry and Eleanor would have been a powerful draw for a troubadour, although he *also* acknowledged that, before the queen's incarceration in 1173, a number of other times were also possible.[26] 'Queen of the Normans' has the air of a topical compliment inspired by recent developments, which may well fit with the queen's *séjour* in Normandy in the autumn of 1154, and it is possible to imagine that Bernart's praise of Henry's (newly acquired?) extensive dominions dates from the same period, but this hardly constitutes proof. Bernart's words and his *vida* are all we have to go on, and these same sources also indicate that Bernart was (later?) in the entourage of the count of Toulouse, 'lo senher de Belcaire' whom he addressed by the *senhal n'Alvernhat*.[27] Neither Henry's nor Eleanor's circles afforded Bernart a sufficiently appreciative or supportive environment.

When was Eleanor 'available', as it were, as a patron and focus of lyric activity? Stability need have little to do with it, as we have plenty of evidence of troubadours travelling with or in search of a lordly patron or in order to diffuse songs redounding to their greater glory, as long as the audience could be expected to

25 S. Kay, *Subjectivity in Troubadour Poetry* (Cambridge, 1991), pp. 146–7; A. Rieger, 'La Dialectique du réel et du poétique chez les troubadours: les quatre protagonistes de la fin'amor', *RlR* 87 (1983), 241–57; cf. L. Macé, *Les Comtes de Toulouse et leur entourage, XIIe–XIIIe siècles* (Toulouse, 2000), pp. 140 and 273.

26 Appel, *Bernart*, pp. lvi–lix.

27 Poem 12, l. 42, and see Appel, *Bernart*, pp. xlii–vii.

understand and appreciate what they sang. Using the sketchy itinerary compiled by Rita Lejeune,[28] biographers and literary scholars have focused almost exclusively on the so-called 'court of Poitiers' and Eleanor's presence in her lands in 1168–73, when she ruled Poitou and Aquitaine as duchess and in the company of the future heir, Richard.[29]

On the face of it, all the conditions were apparently right for a cultural flourishing: a ruler, back in her native lands with presumably an entourage of people for whom Occitan was not a foreign language nor the troubadour lyric an unfamiliar quantity; a duchess presumably familiar with the subtle symbolic economy of the courtly lyric, which offered a tool and a forum for poets and other followers seeking recognition of all kinds (fame, advancement, security, reward) and for rulers desirous of enhancing their own reputations as upholders of courtly values and gracious living, attracting the cream of poets, nobles and followers, and fostering the public image of themselves as valuing and rightly inspiring devotion, service and absolute loyalty.[30] Troubadour song in this respect was a powerful political tool in the broadest sense, which the counts of Toulouse and Barcelona were currently exploiting to the full.[31]

Much has been written along these lines about Eleanor's cultivated and attractive court, although the reality may well have been a good deal more prosaic.[32] Nevertheless, if her entourage was so influential and teamed with troubadours, where is the evidence? I reject here the criteria proposed by Karen Broadhurst for identifying relationships of patronage. While these may be admirably rigorous for a consideration of narrative works, they seem to me to be far too restrictive and generally inappropriate for identifying such associations of poet and lord/lady in the different culture of Occitan lyric poetry. Broadhurst insists on the contractual nature of literary patronage, with a specific work being commissioned and evidence of remuneration in money or in kind being received by the poet for performing this task, criteria that are rarely all fulfilled as she admits, but which she holds to be much more telling than dedications or praise that may be merely speculative and hopeful of an interest in the work on the part of the individual addressed.[33] It seems to me that this model assumes a rather different relationship between the creators and consumers of cultural artefacts from that which students of the Occitan lyric believe to have pertained in that social milieu.[34]

28 Nicholas Vincent's forthcoming edition of Eleanor's charters may shed a good deal of light on this question.

29 Lejeune, 'Rôle littéraire d'Aliénor', pp. 50–7.

30 See Macé's crisp reformulation of notions propounded by Duby: *Les Comtes*, pp. 140–8 and 160–4.

31 See M. de Riquer, 'La Littérature provençale à la cour d'Alphonse II d'Aragon', CCM 2 (1959), 177–201; M. Aurell, 'Les Troubadours et le pouvoir royal: l'exemple d'Alphonse I (1162–1196)', *RlR* 85 (1981), 53–67.

32 See M. Hivergneaux, 'Aliénor d'Aquitaine: le pouvoir d'une femme à la lumière de ses chartes (1152–1204)', in *La Cour Plantagenêt*, ed. Aurell, pp. 63–87 (p. 71 on the court's mobility and the lack of Gascons attested in her charters – precisely those who still were supporting troubadour lyric poetry).

33 Broadhurst, 'Henry II', pp. 54–5.

34 Apart from the brevity of the form and its essentially performative nature, one significantly

What sort of evidence *would*, then, indicate or confirm that there was a centre of lyric activity around the figure of Eleanor?

So far, documentary evidence associates only one troubadour with Eleanor during the period 1168–73: Arnaut Guilhem de Marsan, author of the *Ensenhamen al cavalier*.[35] He is one of the Gascon notables witnessing the marriage settlement made at Bordeaux in July 1170 between Henry's daughter Eleanor and Alfonso VIII of Castile.[36] As Saverio Guida has shown, Arnaut Guilhem, lord of Roquefort and Montgaillard in the Landes, also appears at the side of Richard when the duke of Aquitaine crushed the rebellion of 1177 in Dax and granted a charter of privileges to the town, and he was again with King Richard at La Réole in February 1190, along with many of the greatest lords of Gascony, when the questions of Richard's marriage and arrangements for defence during his absence *outremer* may well have been discussed.[37] Together with Arnaut's appearances as witness to grants made by Gaston of Béarn and others in Aquitaine, these suggest that he was a loyal 'man' of the dukes of Aquitaine, in their following when their political and military concerns required their physical presence in their southern lands. It also suggests that Arnaut's attendence on them had nothing to do with a search for patronage of his own poetry.[38]

Secondly, there are the references in the songs of the poets themselves: their inclusion of personal names (such as Bertran de Born's addresses to 'Richartz') or more frequently those such as we have found in the songs of Bernart de Ventadorn ('queen' plus name of the people; 'king' or 'lord' plus a place-name); or *senhals* for a lord, protector or friend, which other evidence suggests may be identified with a particular individual (such as *Linhaure* used of Raimbaut d'Aurenga, *n'Albert* employed as a mutual *senhal* by Bernart de Durfort and Count Raymond V of Toulouse, or *Rassa*, Bertran de Born's *senhal* for Geoffrey of Brittany).[39] A number of *senhals*, of course, resist such pinning down; it is not clear to whom the very frequent pseudonym *Sobre-totz* refers in the works of Giraut de Borneil – Aimar V of Limoges or King Alfonso II of Aragon.[40] There were troubadours active at this time who might have been found in 'Poitiers': Peire d'Alvernhe, Peire Rogier, Lemozi/Arnaut de Tintinhac,[41] Giraut de

different feature of the Occitan lyric is the creative participation of the aristocracy from the very beginning

35 'Qui comte vol aprendre', in *Testi didattico-cortesi di Provenza*, ed. and trans. G. E. Sansone (Bari, 1977), pp. 119–80.

36 J. Gonzalez, *El reino de Castilla en la epoca de Alfonso VIII*, 3 vols. (Madrid, 1960), I, 185–90 and insert between pp. 192–3.

37 S. Guida, 'Cartulari e trovatori', *CN* 59 (1999), 71–127 (pp. 79–83); J. Gillingham, *Richard I* (New Haven and London, 1999), pp. 124–7.

38 This should be dated no earlier than the 1180s (rather than the 1160s–1170s); all the indications are that it was destined for a local audience of Gascon notables: Guida, 'Cartulari', pp. 83–6.

39 Macé, *Les Comtes*, p. 273; *L'Amour et la Guerre: L'oeuvre de Bertran de Born*, ed. and trans. G. Gouiran, 2 vols. (Aix-en-Provence, 1985), I, lxix.

40 *The 'Cansos' and 'Sirventes' of the Troubadour Giraut de Borneil*, ed. and trans. R. V. Sharman (Cambridge, 1989), pp. 7–8.

41 S. Guida, 'Il limousino di Briva', *CN* 57 (1997), 167–97.

Borneil, Gaucelm Faidit, to name only a few 'from Eleanor's lands', although I have found no such indication in the surviving works of any of these to suggest that they were drawn to Eleanor's entourage. Instead, their contacts indicate that they found a welcome further south, in Narbonne and especially in the Crown of Aragon. Those from the Limousin were amply catered for in the following of the Limousin lords' frequent ally, the count of Toulouse. The rivalry between Raymond V and Alfonso II as rulers in Provence may explain why Limousin troubadours such as Giraut de Borneil and Gaucelm Faidit were so often visitors there.[42] In all, the focus of traceable troubadour activity appears to be consistently to the south and east, sustaining existing centres in the Limousin and perhaps the Auvergne, but not responding to a supposed return of the countess of Poitou.

A third type of evidence of a more indirect sort might be supplied by *sirventes* that allude to situations or events that concern Eleanor's interests or songs that praise a relevant region, Poitou perhaps, such as we find in the works of Marcabru.[43] However, the only *sirventes* I can identify from this time that might touch directly on the political interests of Eleanor was composed at the court of the count of Barcelona by a poet who had just come from Toulouse. Peire d'Alvernhe addresses Count Raymond Berenguer IV and produces provocatively fulsome praise of Raymond V as a valiant young opponent who is not afraid of 'those betailed English' ('aquelhs Engles coutz') in a song that is thought to evoke the count of Barcelona's imminent participation at the side of Henry II in the siege of Toulouse.[44] The implications that may be drawn from this admittedly difficult piece do not point to loyalty or confidence of 'men from Eleanor's lands' in her or in the prospect of finding a suitable audience and appreciation in Poitou. It is as if she has been forgotten.

Granted, such 'pièces de circonstance' are by their very nature ephemeral and perhaps escape being preserved by the manuscript tradition,[45] but it is hard to imagine that, if some were indeed composed for Eleanor, every last one of them failed to get into the record, especially in the light of the *tenso* involving Cercamon cited earlier. This can be regarded as having a quintessentially transient appeal; the direct topical interest of its subject-matter would have had a shelf-life of less than eight weeks in the spring of 1137, but it was nevertheless still available for a scribe in the Languedoc to copy over a century and a half later.

Nor are there any further identifiable references in *cansos* to Poitou or Eleanor. It is theoretically possible that troubadours actually present at a court have no need to 'send' their songs to a named protector elsewhere, but it is telling that a sample of references to other famous female patrons of lyric – Ermengarde and Maria de Ventadorn – produces around a dozen possible references to the former and even more for the latter.[46] However fragile some of those interpretations may

42 *Les Poèmes de Gaucelm Faidit*, ed. and trans. J. Mouzat (Paris, 1965), pp. 31–2.

43 See for example XXXIII, ll. 19–24.

44 *Peire d'Alvernhe: Poesie*, ed. and trans. A. Fratta (Rome, 1996), poem 5, l. 34 and see pp. xiii–xiv.

45 See D'A. S. Avalle, *I manoscritti della letteratura in lingua d'Oc*, rev. ed. L. Leonardi (Turin, 1993), pp. 25–30, 61–2, 105–6, and Aurell, 'La Cour Plantagenêt', pp. 34–6.

46 See F. M. Chambers, *Proper Names in the Lyrics of the Troubadours* (Chapel Hill, 1971).

be, the very volume of possible allusions seems to justify the reputation of these two women as cultured patrons of *trobar*. The basis for Eleanor's modern reputation, in contrast, evaporates the harder one looks.[47]

It is quite true that mere name-dropping of the rich and powerful does not of itself indicate patronage or the presence of the poet at the court of the great figure evoked.[48] Such allusions nevertheless hint at the prominence of figures such as Maria de Ventadorn or the Plantagenet men as bywords for gracious living, lordly generosity and the courtly qualities desirable in a prince. Does their absence in Eleanor's case speak of her *lack of prominence* in this world? If it does, was it only because she was locked up for such a long time?

There remains one last, intriguing composition to consider. It has often been suggested that Peire d'Alvernhe's 'Cantarai d'aquestz trobadors' was composed for an occasion involving Eleanor of Aquitaine. This is a satirical piece of some fourteen stanzas in which Peire reviews, one by one, the performance quirks and personal failings of eleven contemporary poets, ending with himself as the twelfth, and his presentation of them often involves very clever parodic play on existing compositions by his targets. Exploration of this satire has long been directed by the supposition that all the poets mentioned were actually present, and that the occasion that brought them together must have been a spectacular festive court assembly. All the song itself tells us is that it was composed and performed for amusement at a place called Puivert: 'Lo vers fo faitz als enflabotz / a Puioch-vert, tot jogan rizen'.[49] Since the poets mentioned include Auvergnats, Limousins, Provençaux, a possible Catalan, a possible Castilian and maybe even a Lombard, critics have searched for an 'international fixture' that took place before 1173, the date of the death of Raimbaut prince of Orange, pilloried in ninth place.[50] The 'Castilian' Gonzalbo Roitz – who incidentally, like a few others in this rogues' gallery, has left no extant verse – is thought to be the same as Count Gonsalvo Ruiz de Azagra, part of the Castilian party sent to escort Eleanor's daughter Eleanor from Bordeaux to her marriage to Alfonso VIII of Castile.[51]

The literature on this piece is extensive and inconclusive: a number of Puiverts, both real and imaginary, have been proposed and found wanting. A number of different royal and comital weddings have been suggested as the focus of this glittering assembly.[52] None is really convincing. The most recent suggestion is that the satire was composed at Poitiers, in spring 1170, and it involves an

47 R. R. Bezzola, *Les Origines et la formation de la littérature courtoise en Occident (500–1200)*, 3 vols. (Paris, 1944–67), III, 249–50.

48 Thus for example Peire Vidal, Raimon Vidal, Guiraut de Calanson and Guiot de Provins are all implausibly said to have frequented the court of Geoffrey of Brittany (Lejeune, 'Famille', p. 323); this continues to be repeated.

49 *Peire d'Alvernhe*, ed. Fratta, poem 8, ll. 85–6.

50 *The Life and Works of the Troubadour Raimbaut d'Orange*, ed. and trans. W. T. Pattison (Minneapolis, 1952), pp. 218–19.

51 See Riquer, *Los Trovadores*, I, 338–9 and n. 36 above.

52 For a critical summary of previous work on both these questions, see S. Guida, 'Dove e quando fu composto il sirventese "Cantarai d'aquestz trobadors"?', *Anticomoderno* 3 (1997), 201–26 (pp. 201–5).

ingenious palaeographical explanation of how, at a key point in the manuscript transmission, the crucial place-name became transformed from *poitiers* into *poi uert*.[53] This hypothesis is supported firstly by linguistic arguments in favour of the use here of a northern or gallicized form of the place-name *Poitiers*, rather than Occitan *Peitieus*, and secondly by contextual arguments concerning the existence of a whole series of plenary courts in the early summer of 1170 connected with Richard's investitures as lord of Poitou and Aquitaine and with the ceremonial preparations for the departure for Bordeaux of the marriage cortège of young Eleanor. Her escort of Poitevin lords and prelates may be supposed to have first assembled at Poitiers where there would already have been a festive court of *le beau monde* gathered for Richard's investiture.[54]

However, Richard's investiture is more plausibly dated to 1172.[55] It may be that a cortège did depart from Poitiers,[56] but it seems less likely that the Spaniards, including Gonsalvo Ruiz, known to be present at Bordeaux had previously gone all the way to Poitiers to collect the bride, then retraced their steps: why should they when, by a similar hypothesis, Arnaut Guilhem de Marsan did not,[57] and when Bordeaux was a more significant location for the formal handover of a girl whose dowry was Gascony? More difficult to accept is the notion that Raimbaut, prince of Orange and all his life in the *mouvance* of King Alfonso II of Aragon,[58] would have travelled halfway across France to be present at the nuptials of a Plantagenet princess to a Castilian king.[59]

This hypothesis does, however, serve to underline the continuing puzzlement of literary specialists faced with the apparent absence of troubadours from the entourage of Eleanor and the young Richard at this time.

Several different points seem to arise from this. It is beyond doubt that such *plaids* and ceremonial court occasions like those held at Limoges and Bordeaux produced large festive assemblies, for this was part of the pomp of lordship.[60] Musical entertainments very probably formed part of these, although we have no evidence that the duchess was able to field a team of her own troubadours as did

53 *Ibid.*, pp. 210–13.

54 *Ibid.*, pp. 221–2 (Easter 1170 plenary court at Niort; investiture at Poitiers 31 May; investiture at Limoges in June).

55 See Gillingham, *Richard I*, p. 40 n. 52 and Daniel Callahan's chapter in this volume. The dating of 1170 by A. Richard, *Histoire des comtes de Poitou*, 2 vols. (Paris, 1903), II, 150–5 is not decisively supported by any of the evidence he actually cites.

56 The image of Eleanor's court at Poitiers, buzzing with artists and *jeunesse dorée*, which supplies a seductive part of this context, derives from A. Kelly, *Eleanor of Aquitaine and the Four Kings* (Cambridge, Mass. and London, 1950), chapter 15, which offers little convincing supporting evidence. Contrast Hivergneaux, 'Aliénor d'Aquitaine'.

57 Guida, 'Dove', pp. 224–5; Guida, 'Cartulari', p. 84.

58 See A. Krispin, 'Espace féodal et espace politique: Raimbaut d'Aurenga entre Toulouse et Aragon', in *Les Troubadours et l'état toulousain avant la Croisade (1209)*, ed. A. Krispin (Bordes, 1995), pp. 177–82.

59 A better candidate than Poitiers for a splendid assembly that could have acted as a draw for magnates and poets alike, as the occasion of Peire d'Alvernhe's satire (assuming that such an occasion would still be identifiable by us today), is Henry II's sumptuous court at Montferrand and Limoges in February 1173. I hope to return to this question in another study.

60 Cf. R. Harvey, 'Occitan Extravagance and the Court Assembly at Beaucaire in 1174', *CN* 61 (2001), 55–74.

the count of Toulouse. Equally, there is no reason to doubt that Eleanor would have enjoyed music as part of the refinement of court life: Richard the Poitevin at least thought she should have and thus evokes her as surrounded by an entourage of female musicians.[61] What of troubadours and *joglars*? Saverio Guida's study alerts us to the possibility that, while all twelve poets of Peire d'Alvernhe's satire may not have been present at the one occasion, their songs were known by the courtly audience of 'Cantarai d'aquestz trobadors'. Indeed the skit loses much of its spice if not its whole point if they were not. So might we assume that *joglars* conveyed to Eleanor's circle songs by the important Occitan poets, even though the latter apparently never went there themselves?

Was this because she was not in her lands often enough, but rather her itinerary took her so frequently to Anjou, Normandy and England, where troubadour lyric poetry was an unfamiliar tradition in an alien language? Was it because she had been absent from the land of *trobar* since 1137, so that, notwithstanding the apparent continuity of Poitevin administrators of her domains under Louis VII, later poets identified no active patron in Poitou worth approaching, while a return of the duchess some thirty years later had left too long a gap? Was it that she was not perceived as possessing the power to dispense a patronage worth having? Was it possibly because she was no longer seen as 'one of us', but too readily identified with distant and unsympathetic authority?

One might wonder how thoroughly 'Poitevin' the troubadour phenomenon had been.[62] We have to wait till the maturity of Savaric de Mauléon (c.1200–11)[63] to find a troubadour native to the northern parts of Eleanor's domains. Marcabru and Cercamon had certainly referred to Eleanor's father using the terms 'Poitevin' and 'Poitou', although Cercamon had also been aware of differences of interests and populations within the lands of the last duke: his lament for William X enumerates the men of the Limousin, Angoulême, Aunis and 'renowned courtly Gascons'.[64] According to their *vidas*, however, these two early troubadours had been 'Gascons', and Gascons similarly predominate in the list of poets whom Rita Lejeune optimistically connected with Eleanor herself. If this information is accurate, might Marcabru and Cercamon's origins shed a different light on why they called William X 'the Poitevin'? Had the focus of lyric poetry always been further south, among local centres in Aquitaine whose literary life persisted?[65] We do find troubadours such as Gaucelm Faidit and Bertran de Born associated with Eleanor's *sons* when – even in war – they spend time in the Limousin and Gascony.[66] Perhaps rather than supposing that the

61 'juvenculae tuae cum tympanis et citharis suavem tibi cantilenam decantabant: tu vero gaudebas ad sonitum organi, et lusibus tympanistriarum tuarum exultabas' (*RHGF*, XII, 420).

62 On the nomenclature, see John Gillingham's chapter in this volume.

63 M. Cao Carmichael de Baiglie, 'Savary de Mauléon (c.1180–1233), chevalier-troubadour poitevin: traîtrise et société aristocratique', *Le Moyen Age* 105 (1999), 269–306 (pp. 287–91). It is commonly thought that, even by the time of William IX, Occitan was not the vernacular of Poitou and that the 'first troubadour' chose to compose in a literary *koiné*: see M. Pfister, 'La Langue de Guilhem IX, comte de Poitiers', CCM 19 (1976), 91–113.

64 Ed. Tortoreto, VII, ll. 31, 44, 48.

65 Compare Meliga, 'L'Aquitania trobadorica', p. 245.

66 Gaucelm's association with Geoffrey of Brittany, for example, may well have begun when the

Plantagenet court must have been an attractive and propitious environment for so many troubadours to travel all that way to get there, it may be better to consider that when Eleanor's family came to the troubadours in their usual regions, the poets showed up in their vicinity, like other courtiers.[67] The literary evidence suggests that the troubadours knew and frequented Eleanor's husband and sons, her daughters, her vassals and her enemies, but not her. In marked contrast to modern writers, the medieval Occitan poets – with the single exception of Bernart de Ventadorn – seem to have accorded her no importance at all.

latter was in the Limousin in 1183, although this poet also visited 'Count Geoffrey's courtly land': *Les Poèmes de Gaucelm Faidit*, ed. Mouzat, no. 35, ll. 37–8, and see p. 383.

67 Compare N. Vincent, 'Henry II and the Poitevins', in *La Cour Plantagenêt*, ed. Aurell, pp. 103–35 (pp. 112–13). As Meliga observes ('L'Aquitania trobadorica', p. 247), there undoubtedly were Oc–Oïl cultural contacts in the Norman-Limousin-Poitevin ambit; the general assumption, however, that these poetic exchanges must have required the patronage of Eleanor lacks supporting evidence.

The Stripping of a Queen: Eleanor of Aquitaine in Thirteenth-Century Norman Tradition[1]

DANIEL POWER

Eleanor of Aquitaine became duchess of the Normans by marriage to Henry of Anjou on 18 May 1152. She retained that title until her death on 1 April 1204, a period of nearly fifty-two years, apparently longer than any other consort of the rulers of Normandy.[2] Two or three decades after her death it was as 'the duchess of the Normans' that Uc de Saint-Circ remembered her in his fanciful description of Bernart de Ventadorn's love affair with her, and Bernart himself addressed one of his poems to 'la reina dels Normans'.[3] Yet at first sight Normandy seems the least significant of all the regions where she spent her long life. Duchess of the Aquitanians in her own right, queen of the French and then of the English by marriage, she played a leading role in the high politics of the age, notably in Syria and Palestine in 1147, in England in 1189–94 and in Aquitaine between 1199 and 1202. Hardly any significant event in her life took place in Normandy. Her famous attempt to flee in disguise at the outbreak of her sons' revolt in 1173 is perhaps the only one, and even this more probably happened in Anjou or

1 I wish to thank Jane Martindale for encouraging me to write this chapter, and the British Academy for its generous support; for suggestions, references and guidance I am indebted to the participants of the Bristol conference, especially Linda Paterson, Ruth Harvey, Catherine Léglu, and John Gillingham, as well to Penny Eley, Penny Simons, Mario Longtin and Katariina Nara. My interest in the vernacular histories discussed below arises from research for a planned new edition and English translation of the Béthune *Estoire des reis d'Engleterre* by Penny Eley, with historical notes by the present author.

This chapter observes the Anglo-Normanist practice of referring to individuals by an Anglicized first name but Gallicized surname except where convention dictates otherwise.

2 Gunnor (d. January 1031), concubine of Count (Duke) Richard I from c.966, married him at an unknown date before 996, and so was countess for between c.34 and c.65 years: see E. van Houts, 'Countess Gunnor of Normandy (c.950–1031)', *Collegium Medievale* 12 (2000 for 1999), 7–24. Leutgardis, wife of William I Longsword (at least 42 years); Berengaria, wife of Richard the Lionheart (39 years), and Isabella of Angoulême, wife of King John (46 years).

3 *BdT*, pp. 20–1 and 27; cf. p. 7, the confused genealogy in the *vida* of Guilhem de Peitieus (William IX of Aquitaine). For discussion, see J. Martindale, 'Eleanor of Aquitaine', in *Richard Cœur de Lion in History and Myth*, King's College Medieval Studies 7, ed. J. Nelson (London, 1992), pp. 17–50 (p. 37).

Aquitaine.[4] Yet although her career left remarkably few traces in her husband's duchy, after her death some Normans appear to have preserved her memory in interesting and suggestive ways. They show that even here she acquired a reputation as a beguiling figure, and that her southern origins may have been commemorated in a very particular way in northern France.

Eleanor, Duchess of the Normans

Eleanor's second marriage brought her titles, power and influence throughout her second husband's possessions. In England, she held numerous dower lands, from which she made many gifts; she also spent long periods there as queen consort, mother,[5] prisoner, and eventually queen-mother and co-regent. It is not surprising that the 'golden age of English historiography' found time to say much about Eleanor, queen of the English.[6] In Anjou, she was a lavish patron of the abbey of Fontevraud, which had so many connections with her own nearby homeland of Poitou, but she was also prepared to devastate the region when the magnates of Anjou sided with her grandson Arthur against her last surviving son John.[7] In Maine she sometimes presided over the *curia regis* in the first half of Henry's reign and possibly resumed this role during the reigns of her sons.[8] Most probably the acts placing her in Maine dated from Eleanor's residence in her husband's French lands between May 1165 and March 1166, when according to Robert of Torigni she encountered serious insubordination from the barons of

4 Gervase of Canterbury, *Historical Works*, ed. W. Stubbs, RS 73, 2 vols. (London, 1879–80), I, 242–3, mentions Eleanor's plotting but not the location of her flight. Cf. Ralph Diceto, *Opera Historica*, ed. W. Stubbs, RS 68, 2 vols. (London, 1876), I, 355. E.-R. Labande, 'Pour une image véridique d'Aliénor d'Aquitaine', *Bulletin de la Société des Antiquaires de l'Ouest*, 4th ser. 2 (1952), 174–234 (p. 213), dates it to November 1173, when she was certainly further south than Normandy.

5 Only three of Eleanor's nine children by Henry II were born in France: William (1153), before her first visit to England (Labande, 'Pour une image véridique', p. 199); Eleanor, at Domfront (1161); Joanna, at Angers (1165). See R. W. Eyton, *The Court, Household and Itinerary of King Henry II* (London and Dorchester, 1878), pp. 54–5, 86; Robert of Torigni, *Chronique*, ed. L. Delisle, 2 vols. (Paris, 1871–72), I, 280, 334, 357.

6 See the papers by John Gillingham and Richard Barber in this volume.

7 Roger of Howden, *Chronica*, ed. W. Stubbs, RS 51, 4 vols. (London, 1868–71), IV, 88 (s.a. 1199).

8 E.g. (i) *Recueil des actes des comtes de Pontieu (1026–1279)*, ed. C. Brunel (Paris, 1930), no. LXXX (1154 × 71), a dispute first heard before the local magnate, Count William Talvas, and afterwards in Queen Eleanor's court.
(ii) Le Mans, AD Sarthe, H 977, no. 1, a dispute concerning the abbey of Tironneau: 'Cum ergo dominus rex Henr(icus) tunc temporis transfretaret, et domina regina monachos illos pro controuersia ista ad audientiam suam uocaret (. . .) Cognita ergo a domina regina et ministerialibus suis partis monachorum iusticia, et eorundem humilitate et simplicitate, in curia domine regine coram ministerialibus suis Hugone de Cla[r]eis et multis aliis, monachi illi et supradicti calumpniantes, in hanc compositionem conuenerunt.' (s.d., 1154 × 80).
(iii) *Liber Controversiarum Sancti Vincentii Cenomannensis*, ed. A. Chédeville (Paris, 1968), no. 91, an act of 'I.' queen of the English concerning a Manceau court case, was most probably issued by Eleanor.

Maine: Henry was compelled to intervene against a major conspiracy that involved many barons of Brittany as well.[9]

Normandy, by contrast, although probably the most important of the Angevin provinces in strategic terms, seems to have been the most inconsequential of all for the greatest Plantagenet queen. Apart from when crossing the duchy *en route* to or from England, she is recorded infrequently in Normandy except for the period 1158–62, when she and Henry spent a succession of Christmas feasts in the duchy.[10] She exercised viceregal powers in the other Angevin lands on the Continent and in England,[11] but until 1167, as Lewis Warren noted, a more appropriate vice-gerent in Normandy was the Empress Matilda.[12] Eleanor's only genuine regency in Normandy may have been in 1170, at the height of the Becket dispute. That summer she remained in Caen while Henry II took their son Henry to England to be crowned; with the constable of Normandy she hindered the bishops of Worcester and Nevers who wished to prevent the Young King's coronation.[13] Between her capture in 1173 and her release in 1189 she appears only once in Normandy, issuing a Poitevin act at Alençon in 1185.[14] After Richard's accession she attended his great council at Nonancourt in south-east Normandy before his departure on crusade;[15] but thereafter she rarely appeared in royal acts in the duchy.[16]

It is true that Normandy represented an important source of income for Eleanor during her widowhood. Her dower, assigned by Henry II and confirmed soon after his death by Richard the Lionheart, included the important Norman ducal fortresses of Falaise, Bonneville-sur-Touques and Domfront.[17] It was at Bonneville that she held her Christmas court when she returned from her Sicilian journey in 1191,[18] and at Domfront she gave birth to the only one of her

9 Torigni, I, 361; for her authority in France, see also *The Correspondence of Thomas Becket, Archbishop of Canterbury, 1162–1170*, ed. and trans. A. Duggan, 2 vols. (Oxford, 2000), I, no. 51.

10 Eyton, *Itinerary of Henry II*, pp. 43 (1158), 49 (1159), 55 (1161), 58 (1162); their next Christmas in Normandy was in 1170 (p. 150).

11 Cf. H. G. Richardson, 'The Letters and Charters of Eleanor of Aquitaine', *EHR* 100 (1959), 193–213.

12 W. L. Warren, *Henry II* (London, 1973), p. 121.

13 *Becket Correspondence*, II, nos. 286, 296–7; *Materials for the History of Thomas Becket, Archbishop of Canterbury*, ed. J. C. Robertson and J. B. Sheppard, RS 67, 7 vols. (London, 1875–85), III, 103.

14 P. Marchegay, 'Chartes de Fontevraud concernant l'Aunis et La Rochelle', *Bibliothèque de l'École des Chartes*, 4th ser. 19 (1858), 132–70, 321–47 (pp. 330–1); Richardson, 'Letters', pp. 198–9; M. Hivergneaux, 'Aliénor d'Aquitaine: le pouvoir d'une femme à la lumière de ses chartes (1152–1204)', in *La Cour Plantagenêt (1154–1204)*, ed. M. Aurell (Poitiers, 2000), pp. 63–87 (p. 74); cf. *Recueil des actes de Henri II*, ed. L. Delisle and E. Berger, 3 vols. and intro. (Paris, 1909–27), II, no. DCLV. This undated act must be from the period 1183–86. For her visit to France in 1185, see *Gesta Regis Henrici Secundi*, ed. W. Stubbs, RS 49, 2 vols. (London, 1867), I, 337–8.

15 *Ibid.*, II, 106; Howden, III, 32.

16 *The Itinerary of Richard I*, ed. L. Landon (London, 1935), no. 268: act for Silly (Argentan, 6 April 1190). She may, however, have acted as regent in Normandy immediately after her return from Sicily: *Gesta Regis Henrici Secundi*, II, 236–7; cf. Richard of Devizes, *Chronicle*, ed. and trans. J. T. Appleby (London, 1963), p. 58. I am grateful to John Gillingham for his views on this point.

17 *Veterum Scriptorum et Monumentorum, Historicorum, Dogmaticorum, Moralium Amplissima Collectio*, ed. E. Martène and U. Durand, 9 vols. (Paris, 1724–33), I, cols. 995–7.

18 Howden, III, 179 (*Gesta Regis Henrici Secundi*, II, 235, says simply 'in Normandy'); Hivergneaux, 'Aliénor d'Aquitaine', p. 75.

children certainly born in Normandy, her daughter Eleanor, in 1161. After the fall of Normandy to Philip Augustus in 1204, separate inquests were held into the dower rights of the Angevin queens at these three fortresses. The jurors stated that the 'old queen' had been entitled to nearly 800 *livres* (presumably *livres angevins*, i.e. £200 sterling) in annual revenues from these three towns as dower.[19] The Norman exchequer rolls show that at Domfront at least the 'old queen' received significantly more cash in practice,[20] and her rights consisted of rights in land as well, for she and her son Richard made two gifts to the ducal *bailli*, Robert le Sausier, an act that shows that her rights extended well beyond the town walls.[21] At Bonneville, too, she was receiving substantial revenues and made a gift there to her almoner.[22] Apart from these gifts she issued very few acts concerning the duchy.[23]

Normandy concerned Eleanor in other ways. Her Aquitanian towns of Poitiers, Niort, Saintes and Saint-Jean d'Angély came to be governed by the customs of Rouen.[24] At various times her inheritance was governed by Norman officials whose unpopularity is well documented, and her household included some Anglo-Normans as well.[25] She also had extended dealings with prominent

19 *Registres de Philippe Auguste*, ed. J. W. Baldwin (Paris, 1992), pp. 54–5: discounting fixed alms, approximately 145 l. at Bonneville, 450 l. at Falaise, and 175 l. at Domfront (a total of about 770 l.); the jurors were unsure about another 38 l. The coinage of assessment is not specified. The epithet 'vetus regina' can refer only to Eleanor.

20 In 1198 the *bailli* of Domfront paid Eleanor 340 l. 7d, drawn from the farms of the *bailliage*, three forests and ducal escheats; she had used this income to make extensive grants: *Magni Rotuli Scaccarii Normanniæ*, ed. T. Stapleton, 2 vols. (London, 1840–44), II, lix, 352, 354 (cf. I, 220). Richard's grant of the mills of Domfront and Fontaine-Ozanne to Andrew de Domfront, a servant of his sister the queen of 'Spain' (i.e. Castile), may also have been his mother's gift.

21 Paris, Archives Nationales, L 967, no. 141: confirmation by Renaud, count of Boulogne, of various gifts of the ducal dynasty to Savigny, edited in B. Poulle, 'Une charte inédite d'Aliénor d'Aquitaine?', *Le Domfrontais Médiéval* 5 (1987), 16–26. Eleanor's gifts to Robert at Montfrilous (Orne, cant. Passais, comm. Mantilly) lie 17 km from Domfront.

22 *Magni Rotuli*, I, 233–4 (about 307 l.); II, 369–70.

23 She confirmed gifts of Henry II and Richard I to the abbey of Le Valasse near Lillebonne: Rouen, AD Seine-Maritime, 18 HP 7 (given at Bordeaux, 1189 × 99). She also issued an act, now lost, for the monks of Saint-Étienne de Caen (*Rotuli Chartarum in Turri Londonensi asservati (1199–1216)*, ed. T. D. Hardy (London, 1837), p. 6). The forthcoming publication of Eleanor's acts by Nicholas Vincent will furnish a far more comprehensive view of Eleanor's activities than is possible here.

24 *Registres*, p. 336; J. Martindale, 'Eleanor of Aquitaine: The Last Years', in *King John: New Interpretations*, ed. S. D. Church (Woodbridge, 1999), pp. 137–64 (pp. 150, 162–3). G. Pon and Y. Chauvin, 'Chartes de libertés et de communes de l'Angoumois, du Poitou et de la Saintonge (fin XIIe–début XIIIe siècle)', *Mémoires de la Société des Antiquaires de l'Ouest* 58 (2000), 25–149 (pp. 30, 36), note that Eleanor's acts for these towns were phrased in very vague terms; it was Philip Augustus who defined their customs as those of Rouen.

25 P. Boissonnade, 'Administrateurs laïques et ecclésiastiques anglo-normands en Poitou à l'époque d'Henri II Plantagenet (1152–1189)', *Bulletin de la Société des Antiquaires de l'Ouest*, 3rd ser. 5 (1919), 156–90. William de Tancarville as seneschal: Walter Map, *De Nugis Curialium: Courtiers' Trifles*, ed. and trans. M. R. James, rev. C. N. L. Brooke and R. A. B. Mynors (Oxford, 1983), pp. 490–2. William Malet: Torigni, II, 11 (cf. p. 4). Household officials with Norman connections may include her constable Geoffrey de Wanchy (although he should be regarded as primarily English) and her steward Henry de Bernaval.

Normans such as Guy de Dives, constable of Chinon in 1200,[26] and most notably the English-born archbishop of Rouen, Walter de Coutances. In 1191 the queen and archbishop travelled back together from Sicily to England via Rome,[27] and they restored order in the kingdom the following year; in 1193 they manipulated the election of the archbishop of Canterbury;[28] and in 1194 they journeyed together to Germany to the captive King Richard, whose ransom was guarded in England under the authority of their seals.[29] But in the first half of Richard's reign Eleanor made her greatest impact in England, in particular in curbing the ambitions of her youngest son John and later reconciling him to King Richard; and for the rest of her life she concentrated upon Anjou and Aquitaine. In 1198 she went to Rouen to confer with the captive bishop of Beauvais, Richard I's most prized prisoner-of-war, and nearly allowed him to escape, much to the horror of his captors.[30] She may have visited Domfront in the same year and was certainly with her son John in eastern Normandy in July and August 1199, when over several weeks the new king of England issued many acts concerning her household and her inheritance.[31] Thereafter, however, Eleanor dwelt south of Maine:[32] Roger of Howden explicitly tells us that after her journey to Castile to fetch her granddaughter Blanche as bride for Louis of France, the exhausted queen brought the girl only as far as Fontevraud, leaving others to escort Blanche to her wedding in Normandy.[33] The northern duchy nearly always appears a secondary concern of Eleanor of Aquitaine.

In the Latin sources at least, the queen's apparent indifference to Normandy was reciprocated after her death. In Anjou, where she died and was laid to rest, the annalist of Saint-Aubin d'Angers regarded Eleanor's death as the chief reason for John's disastrous failure to return to France in the spring of 1204.[34] By

26 *Rot. Chart.*, p. 102 (2 John, probably autumn 1200?); Martindale, 'Last Years', pp. 151–2.

27 *Itinerary of Richard I*, pp. 48, 192. On her return journey from Sicily Eleanor was also accompanied by Gilbert de Vascœuil, the treasonous constable of Gisors.

28 *Gesta Regis Henrici Secundi*, II, 237; Diceto, II, 107–9; Gervase of Canterbury, I, 516–19. Also involved was the Norman-born William de Sainte-Mère-Église, later bishop of London (*Itinerary of Richard I*, pp. 74–6).

29 Martindale, 'Last Years', p. 147. The archbishop also witnessed several acts of King John concerning Eleanor's gifts in summer 1199, and with Eleanor and the archbishops of Canterbury and York he advised the king to grant 100m. of revenues to his sister Queen Joanna of Sicily to make her will (*Rot. Chart.*, pp. 6, 10, 13).

30 Howden, IV, 40–1; cf. A. Richard, *Histoire des comtes de Poitou 778–1204*, 2 vols. (Paris, 1903), II, 319.

31 *Rot. Chart.*, pp. 4–8, 10–11, 13, 25; *Layettes du Trésor des Chartes*, ed. A. F. Teulet, H.-F. Delaborde and E. Berger, 5 vols. (Paris, 1863–1909), I, no. 508 (cf. no. 499); Martindale, 'Last Years', pp. 150–1. For the visit to Domfront, see Poulle, 'Une charte inédite', p. 24.

32 The contrast is noted by Martindale, 'Last Years', esp. p. 153. Eleanor probably joined John in Maine in October 1199 to oversee the will of Queen Joanna (*Rot. Chart.*, p. 25); her proclamation of Joanna's will states that she set off for Gascony to ensure that the count of Toulouse executed his late wife's bequests (Angers, AD Maine-et-Loire, 101 H 55; *Calendar of Documents Preserved in France, 918–1206*, ed. J. H. Round (London, 1899), no. 1105).

33 Howden, IV, 107, 114.

34 *Annales angevines et vendômoises*, ed. L. Halphen (Paris, 1903), p. 21, misplacing her death at Poitiers. The Saint-Aubin annalist's view is curiously echoed by Shakespeare's *King John*, IV.ii: 'What! mother dead! How wildly then walks my estate in France!'

contrast, none of the extant Norman annals even registered her death: it is true that many of them are laconic in the extreme, but even the more verbose annals of Jumièges and chronicle of Rouen both overlooked the event.[35] Naturally the Normans had other concerns in the spring of 1204, when King Philip was beating on the duchy's gates; nevertheless, their complete silence regarding Eleanor's death seems telling. It cannot be attributed simply to the remoteness of her deathbed at Fontevraud from Normandy, since the event was recorded in many English houses.[36] If we had only Eleanor's charters and the Latin narrative sources, we could be forgiven for believing that she had almost no impact upon the duchy whose title she used for half a century.

Eleanor in Norman Vernacular Tradition

Yet Eleanor did not fade completely from Norman memories. While charters and annals seem to belittle her role in the duchy, we should remember that her itinerary is almost completely unknown for long periods in the late 1160s and again in the 1190s. But for the *Histoire de Guillaume le Maréchal* we would know almost nothing of her troubled time in Poitou in 1168; and it is quite possible that she spent much of her unrecorded time in Normandy. Another type of source, one that historians rarely use for the history of the Angevin 'empire' before 1200, suggests that Eleanor did make a significant impression upon the Normans.

The sources in question are the vernacular prose histories of the dukes of Normandy and kings of England that become popular in the thirteenth century. In essence these texts continue the Latin *Gesta Normannorum Ducum*, begun by William of Jumièges and continued by Orderic Vitalis and Robert of Torigni but also drawing upon Dudo of Saint-Quentin's *De Moribus et Actis Primorum Normanniae Ducum*. Elisabeth van Houts has noted that the Latin tradition of writing the history of the Norman dukes had effectively ended in 1151, when Robert failed to persuade Gervase de Saint-Cénery to continue the text with a history of Geoffrey of Anjou as duke: she interprets the end of the Latin tradition as a sign of the decline of the 'Norman myth', but it could be argued that it merely mutated into a vibrant vernacular tradition, first the later twelfth-century poems of Wace and Benoît de Sainte-Maure, and then the early thirteenth-century prose histories of the Norman dukes and kings.[37] The tradition of vernacular prose histories that arose in the decades following the break-up of the Angevin 'empire' therefore connects the Latin texts of Dudo, William of Jumièges, and Robert of Torigni to the fourteenth-century *Grandes Chroniques de Normandie*.

35 *Les annales de l'Abbaye Saint-Pierre de Jumièges*, ed. J. Laporte (Rouen, 1954), p. 87; *RHGF*, XVIII, 358 (Rouen chronicle).

36 *Annales Monastici*, ed. H. R. Luard, RS 36, 5 vols. (London, 1864–69), I, 27 (Margam), II, 79 (Winchester), 257 (Waverley), III, 28 (Dunstable), IV, 392 (Worcester); Walter of Coventry, *Historical Collections*, ed. W. Stubbs, RS 58, 2 vols. (London, 1872–73), II, 196; Ralph of Coggeshall, *Chronicon Anglicanum*, ed. J. Stevenson, RS 66 (London, 1875), p. 144.

37 Torigni, II, 338–40; E. M. C. Van Houts, 'The *Gesta Normannorum Ducum*, A History without an End', in *Anglo-Norman Studies III: Proceedings of the Battle Conference 1980*, ed. R. A. Brown (Woodbridge, 1981), pp. 106–15.

Only one such text, written by the so-called Anonymous of Béthune, has received much attention from historians.[38] Béthune lies not in Normandy but in that part of Flanders that came to be known as Artois, at the intersection of French and Flemish culture, and both R. N. Walpole and Gabrielle Spiegel have pointed out that, apart from crusading narratives such as Geoffrey of Villehardouin's account of the Fourth Crusade, the earliest known vernacular prose histories in France developed in Artois in the later years of the reign of Philip Augustus. In an illuminating work Spiegel argues that the genre's rise was a traumatic response to a crisis of aristocratic power in Flanders, in the face of an ever more aggressive French monarchy, the challenge to noble status and power from burgeoning mercantile wealth, and the impoverishing effects of rapid economic change. The crisis of the Flemish aristocracy encouraged not only the writing of Norman history, in which the Flemish had long played a prominent part, but also the development of the vernacular Pseudo-Turpin tradition (the earliest of the prose histories to appear in Flanders), as well as the composition of prose histories of ancient Rome and of the kings of France. This last group included a second text by the Anonymous of Béthune, written from a much more pro-Capetian perspective than his 'Norman' text but reflecting similar concerns.[39]

However, numerous other, shorter histories of the dukes of Normandy and kings of England survive. Gilette Labory's meticulous reconstruction of the manuscript tradition identifies four main groups: the manuscripts of the Béthune *histoire* form one such group but appear to have made use of some of the other texts.[40] Like the writings of the Anonymous of Béthune, some of the shorter histories betray Picard dialect, but others were apparently Norman and were most probably produced in Normandy itself. If the Flemish histories of the Norman dukes were composed in reaction to the difficulties of the Franco-Flemish aristocracy, the Norman aristocracy was also facing a crisis in the early thirteenth century. After decades of bitter border warfare the duchy had lost its effective independence in 1204; many families had lost lands in England. The Norman aristocracy did not face the same challenge from urban élites since Norman towns, though wealthy, could not compare in size or economic and political muscle with their Flemish counterparts; but Norman landowners also

38 *Histoire des Ducs de Normandie et des Rois d'Angleterre*, ed. F. Michel (Paris, 1840) [hereafter *HDN*]. The manuscript used by Michel (Paris, Bibliothèque Nationale, fr. 12203) describes the history as the 'li estoire des dus de Normendie et des rois d'Engletierre' (fol. 131r) or merely '[l'estoire] des rois d'Engletierre' (fol. 184v).

39 R. N. Walpole, 'Philip Mouskés and the Pseudo-Turpin Chronicle', *University of California Publications in Modern Philology* 26 (1947), 327–440 (pp. 351–2); G. M. Spiegel, *Romancing the Past: The Rise of Vernacular Prose Historiography in Thirteenth-Century France* (Berkeley, 1993). The last part of the Béthune history of the kings of France was edited by Delisle in *RHGF*, XXIV:ii, pp. 750–5.

40 G. Labory, 'Les manuscrits de la *Grande chronique de Normandie* du XIVe et du XVe siècle', *Revue de l'Histoire des Textes* 27 (1997), 191–222 (pp. 195–6); Spiegel, *Romancing the Past*, p. 231. Two texts were published as *Chroniques de Normandie*, ed. F. Michel (Paris, 1839), pp. 4–73 (Paris, Bibliothèque Nationale, fr. 24431), 77–95 (Paris, Bibliothèque Nationale, fr. 2137); Labory identifies them as respectively from Groups *B* (which also includes the first Cambridge and Arsenal *histoires* discussed below) and *A*, and assigns the Béthune *histoire* to Group *D*.

confronted some of the same economic difficulties in this period of mounting costs of war and underlying inflation.[41] Lindy Grant has detected just such a mood of introspection in the architecture of Rouen cathedral in the 1220s – a ducal coronation church and mausoleum for a lost dynasty. In the same decade Elisabeth van Houts has perceived a greater sensitivity to the Norman past within the duchy's monastic communities, manifested in the production of numerous cartularies or the recopying of texts of the *Gesta Normannorum Ducum*.[42] The taste for vernacular prose history in early thirteenth-century Normandy could also testify to introversion and a crisis of identity as it became apparent that the ducal dynasty was gone for good.

The Béthune *histoire* has normally been consulted, not for its depiction of Norman history in ages past, but as a first-hand narrative source for early thirteenth-century history. A total of 118 out of 209 pages in Michel's edition concern events after the accession of King John in 1199: it is particularly informative for the loss of Normandy, the Bouvines war and the Magna Carta crisis in England. Eleanor of Aquitaine figures prominently in the famous depiction of the battle of Mirebeau, defying her grandson Arthur until John arrives in time to rescue her and to capture Arthur, along with Geoffrey of Lusignan who is memorably caught while feasting on pigeons.[43] Little attention has been paid to its depiction of events before John's accession. Yet this is also informative, for it reveals how the Norman past was viewed in the early thirteenth century. Although the Norman histories comprise a common core of stories based upon the older Latin texts, it is the variants that attract our attention. The Anonymous of Béthune, for example, tells some lively stories about the troubles of King Stephen's reign, including a unique and vivid account of the disastrous brawl between the Normans and Boulonnais in Stephen's army in 1137.[44] It also describes the burial of Eleanor's daughter Joanna, queen of Sicily and countess of Toulouse, in Rouen cathedral, followed by her disinterment and reburial at Fontevraud with her parents and brother Richard, a tale that is confirmed by the abbey's own muniments.[45]

41 Spiegel, *Romancing the Past*, p. 49, notes that the devastation of the Bouvines war recorded in the inquests of Saint Louis of 1247 seem much worse than anything recorded in Normandy in 1202–04. Nevertheless, the *bouleversement* of 1204 surely represented a very significant political crisis for the Normans.

42 L. Grant, 'Rouen Cathedral 1200–1237', in *Medieval Art, Architecture and Archaeology at Rouen*, ed. J. Stafford, British Archaeological Association Conference Transactions 12 (Leeds, 1993), pp. 60–8 (p. 66); *The* Gesta Normannorum Ducum *of William of Jumièges, Orderic Vitalis and Robert of Torigni*, ed. and trans. E. M. C. van Houts, 2 vols. (Oxford, 1992–95), I, cxi.

43 *HDN*, pp. 93–5.

44 *Ibid.*, pp. 73–5.

45 *Ibid.*, pp. 83–4; Paris, Bibliothèque Nationale, lat. 5480, II, pp. 3–4. There is no evidence that Joanna's tomb acquired an effigy, but if it did could it conceivably be the wooden figure identified since the sixteenth century with Isabella of Angoulême? K. Nolan, 'The Queen's Choice: Eleanor of Aquitaine and the Tombs at Fontevraud', in *Eleanor of Aquitaine: Lord and Lady*, ed. B. Wheeler and J. C. Parsons (Basingstoke, 2003), pp. 377–405, argues that the other (stone) effigies were made on the orders of Eleanor herself. If so, might she not have also commissioned an effigy for her deceased daughter as well? Isabella's effigy was made after a visit of Henry III to Fontevraud and placed 'next to the royal tombs': N. Vincent, 'Isabella of Angoulême: John's Jezebel', in *King John: New Interpretations*, ed. Church, pp. 165–219 (pp. 213–14, 219). But

Apart from the Mirebeau incident, most of the Norman vernacular histories pay little attention to Eleanor and tend to depict her in very conventional terms: as the heiress of several lands (sometimes correctly listed, sometimes not); as the wife of two kings; and as the mother of numerous children whose own marriages, children and lands are also enumerated. The following extract from one of Labory's group *B* of texts is typical:

> [Henry] took to wife Eleanor, duchess of Aquitaine, who was lady of Anjou, Poitou, and Gascony, who had been separated from King Louis of France at Étampes, and her men the Poitevins came to take her away. But she had already had two daughters by her husband King Louis: Marie, the elder, who married Count Henry of Champagne, and the other married his brother Count Theobald of Chartres. King Henry married this lady at Tours, and he had Anjou, Touraine and Maine from his father, and the kingdom of England and the duchy of Normandy from his mother the Empress; from his wife Eleanor he had Aquitaine, Gascony and Poitou. By this lady the king had five sons and three daughters . . .[46]

However, two manuscripts, one in Cambridge, the other in the Bibliothèque de l'Arsenal, offer another, rather more original view of the queen. The Cambridge manuscript contains not one but two histories of the Norman dukes: a conventional *histoire* from which the passage quoted above is taken,[47] and a much shorter history of the dukes from the death of William the Conqueror to the crusade of Richard the Lionheart.[48] The latter text contains a curious story concerning Eleanor's divorce. The same story is told in a much longer and more complete history of the dukes of Normandy in the Arsenal manuscript, although like the Cambridge short history it ceases in the midst of recounting the events of the Third Crusade.[49] These texts are not completely unknown: indeed, the

Guillaume de Puylaurens, *Chronique*, ed. and trans. J. Duvernoy (Paris, 1976), p. 40 (mid-thirteenth century), placed Joanna's tomb at the feet of Eleanor's and next to Richard's. The medieval arrangement of the tombs was abandoned in 1638: A. Erlande-Brandenburg, 'Les gisants de Fontevrault', *Revue des Pays de la Loire* 18 (1988), 21–33 (p. 21).

46 Cambridge University Library [hereafter CUL], Ii.VI.24, fol. 42r: '[Henri] prist a femme Alienor Ducheise d'Aquitaingne qui dame esteit d'Angou, Petou, et de Gascoigne, qui del rei Loeis de France esteit departie per parentage a Estampes; e la furent li Peitevin si home qui l'emmenerent, mes ele aveit ia del roi Loeis son seignor .ij. filles, Marie fu leinznee qui fu mariee al conte Henri de Champaingne, l'autre a sen frere le conte Tebaut de Chartres. Li reis Henri esposa cele dame a Tors, e ot en bone pes de par son pere Angou e Toreingnei (*sic*) e le Maine, e de par sa mere l'empereriz (*sic*) le regne d'Engleterre e la duchee de Normendie, e de par Alienor sa femme Aquitaingne, et Gascoingne et Peitou. Li reis ot de ceste dame .v. fiz e iij. filles . . .' Cf. *HDN*, p. 81; *Chroniques de Normandie*, pp. 67–8.

47 CUL, Ii.VI.24, fols. 19r–49v (belonging to Labory's group *B*).

48 *Ibid*., fols. 95r–100v. According to *Répertoire des plus anciens textes en prose française depuis 842 jusqu'aux premières années du XIIIe siècle*, ed. B. Woledge and H. P. Clive (Geneva 1964), p. 75 (no. 23), it was dated to the end of the twelfth century by G. Gröber, *Grundriß der romanischen Philologie*, 2 vols. in 4 (Strasbourg, 1902), II, 719 (§ 134); but Woledge and Clive argue that this date is derived merely from the fact that the last event mentioned occurred in 1194 (the true date is 1202 or 1209). The inaccuracy of the final paragraph, which makes Constance of Sicily the wife of Frederick Barbarossa and calls Emperor Henry VI merely 'duke of Swabia' when he conquered Sicily, might suggest that it was written some years after the event.

49 Paris, Bibliothèque de l'Arsenal, 3516, fols. 304v–315r.

Cambridge version was published by Paul Meyer as long ago as 1886,[50] but the story concerning Eleanor's divorce has been ignored. A fresh look at this account is therefore amply justified, for though tantalizingly short it may reveal much about the legends surrounding Eleanor in the decades after her death:

> Then it came to pass that the king [Louis] hated his wife, who was the heir of Aquitaine and Poitou, of Gascony and Berry, by whom he had two daughters whom the king then gave to the counts of Champagne and Chartres. The king had himself separated from his wife, who was called Eleanor, at Étampes. There her men of Poitou came to her for the separation and took her away . . . After she had been divorced and she surveyed her own people, she disrobed (*se desfubla*) and said:
> 'Lords, what sort of beast am I?'
> 'By God!' they said, 'there is no more beautiful woman living in this age.'
> 'Then, lords,' she said, 'I am not the devil that the king of France called me just now.'[51]

What are we to make of this scene? The careful studies of René Labande, Jane Martindale and Martin Aurell all urge caution when dealing with the more lurid stories about Eleanor of Aquitaine but also recognize that these have much to reveal about the queen's changing reputation.[52] Despite its brevity the Norman story touches upon a number of important ideas concerning the queen. After considering the manuscripts themselves, the present discussion will focus upon Eleanor's divorce from Louis VII and depictions of her as a devil; in conclusion, it will also consider possible allusions to her southern French origins.

The Authorship and Provenance of the Manuscripts

The date of this story's composition is unclear. The Cambridge manuscript was written by a single scribe in the mid-thirteenth century and begins with a series of Latin annals in which the latest entry is 1256. The earlier part of these annals occurs in a number of French manuscripts and shows links with the abbeys of La Charité-sur-Loire near Orléans and of Valmont in the Pays de Caux.[53] In contrast, the thirteenth-century entries are distinctive and point to a connection with Caen: they include the deaths of two abbesses of the abbey of La Trinité de Caen (1229, 1237), an earthquake at Caen in 1241, and the expulsion of the

50 P. Meyer, 'Notice sur le manuscrit II,6,24 de la bibliothèque de l'université de Cambridge', *Notices et extraits* 32 (1886), II, 37–81 (pp. 65–72); cf. *Catalogue of Manuscripts Preserved in the Library of the University of Cambridge*, 5 vols. (Cambridge, 1856–67), III, no. 1903.

51 Appendix, no. 1.

52 Labande, 'Pour une image véridique', pp. 174–234; Martindale, 'Eleanor of Aquitaine', esp. pp. 37–43. M. Aurell, 'Aliénor d'Aquitaine (1124–1204) et ses historiens: la destruction d'un mythe?', in *Guerre, pouvoir et noblesse au Moyen Âge: Mélanges en l'honneur de Philippe Contamine*, ed. J. Paviot and J. Vergers (Paris, 2000), pp. 43–9; cf. F. McMinn Chambers, 'Some Legends Concerning Eleanor of Aquitaine', *Speculum* 16 (1942), 459–68.

53 Meyer, 'Notice', pp. 38–9. The last year for which events are recorded is 1254; 1255 and 1256 are inserted but blank.

town's Jews in 1252.[54] Most events further afield are of primarily Anglo-Norman significance, such as the translation of the body of Thomas Becket in 1220 and Henry III's expedition to Gascony in 1254; others had a bearing upon the broader political rivalries of western Europe, notably the imperial career of Otto of Brunswick between 1198 and 1212, which mattered hugely to the Angevin–Capetian conflict. The annals therefore testify to the continuing interest of their compiler in the history of the erstwhile 'Anglo-Norman realm'. In this regard the manuscript may be compared with the cartulary of the lazarhouse of Pont-Audemer, which contains a similarly 'Anglo-Norman' list of events and a vernacular translation of Magna Carta, both inserted in the 1220s.[55] The orthography of the Old French texts also appears to locate the Cambridge manuscript in north-western or western France.[56]

Whereas the Cambridge manuscript is small and unremarkable in appearance, the Arsenal manuscript is a much better known, beautifully illustrated codex, incorporating a great variety of religious, cosmological and historical texts.[57] Its language contains numerous picardisms, and the calendars it contains suggest that it was compiled shortly before 1268.[58] Its history of the dukes of the Normans is much longer than, and quite different from, the Cambridge short Norman history, although they have almost identical accounts of Eleanor's divorce. Although minor, a small number of variants mean that it is unlikely that one version was copied from the other.[59] The chief difference is the Arsenal text's mention of consanguinity (*parentage*) as the pretext for the royal separation and its statement that the barons of Poitou took oaths as part of the divorce proceedings.[60]

Although the two extant manuscripts recording the story of Eleanor's disrobing were not written until the second half of the thirteenth century, it is unlikely that the story itself originated nearly so late. In neither manuscript do any of the French or Anglo-Norman histories pass beyond the attempt of the

54 Fol. 17v: Joanna (1229) and Isabella (9 July 1237); this accords with the approximate dates for their deaths given by M. Chibnall, *Charters and Custumals of the Abbey of Holy Trinity Caen* (Oxford, 1982), p. 140.

55 J. C. Holt, *Magna Carta and Medieval Governance* (London, 1985), pp. 23–4, 239–57.

56 This is based upon a preliminary survey of the manuscript using A. Dees, *Atlas des formes linguistiques des chartes françaises du 13e siècle* (Tübingen, 1980), and *idem*, *Atlas des formes linguistiques des textes littéraires de l'ancien français* (Tübingen, 1987). Such spellings as *rei*, *heir*, *aveir*, *dreiture*, *mes*, *pes* and *fere* (for *roi*, *hoir*, *avoir*, *droiture*, *mais*, *paix* and *faire*) all associate it with north-western or western rather than north-eastern France, although it contains occasional picardisms.

57 *Catalogue des manuscrits de la Bibliothèque de l'Arsenal*, ed. H. Martin *et al.*, 9 vols. in 10 (Paris, 1885–94), III, 395–405; *Répertoire des plus anciens textes*, nos. 35, 44.

58 *The Anglo-Norman Voyage of St. Brendan by Benedeit*, ed. E. G. R. Waters (Oxford, 1928), pp. xix–xxii.

59 I am grateful to Penny Eley for her help here. Meyer, 'Notice', p. 64 n., believed that the Arsenal text was the purer, arguing that the scribe of the Cambridge manuscript found a lacuna in the lost original ('. . .ot') which he reconstructed as 'apelot'. However, the Arsenal scribe does not appear to have understood everything before him, since he rendered the same word as the meaningless 'cobicot' (published by Meyer, 'Notice', p. 68 n., as 'cobitot').

60 Appendix, no. 2. Among vernacular sources, consanguinity (*lignage entre eux*) is also mentioned in the fourteenth-century *Grande Chronique de Normandie* (*RHGF*, XIII, 255).

future Louis VIII to gain the English throne in 1215–17. The Cambridge manuscript's history of the kings of France, for instance, ends with Louis's election by the English rebels in 1215; the longer history of the Norman dukes in the same manuscript culminates in his arrival in England the following year.[61] When enumerating the children and grandchildren of Eleanor and Henry, the longer Norman history mentions Thomas, count of Perche, who achieved prominence as a result of his participation in Louis's expedition to England; but it does not mention his much-reported death in the climactic battle of Lincoln in 1217.[62] It is therefore tempting to believe that the two main historical texts in the Cambridge manuscript, in the Anglo-Norman and Capetian traditions respectively, were written in the context of Louis's bid for the English throne, which stood to unite the two traditions. The shorter Norman history containing the story of Eleanor's divorce may belong to the same period, although it has been assigned dates as far apart as 1194 and 1240.[63] Most probably the story was written only a couple of decades at most after Eleanor's death.

Eleanor's Disrobing

As regards the story itself, the nature of Eleanor's gesture is very unclear, for the crucial verb, *se defubler*, is highly ambiguous. It can refer to removing a single garment, normally a cloak or hat: Chrétien de Troyes states that Cligès twice comes into the royal presence *desafublé*, having removed nothing more than his cloak, and on both occasions this state of mild undress reveals his physical comeliness to the court.[64] Yet the story concerning Eleanor hardly makes sense unless she had removed enough of her clothing to prove that she was not a devil, presumably revealing significantly more of her underclothes or body than normal. Should we assume, with Cole Porter, that 'In olden days a glimpse of stocking was looked on as something shocking'? After all, even a hint of female flesh might be highly eroticized: Lanval's mysterious lady of unparalleled loveliness arrives at King Arthur's court wearing a dress laced to reveal her sides.[65] Just as important is the barons' reaction to her gesture: like Cligès's appearance at court, Eleanor's removal of her garments before an assembly reveals the beauty of

61 CUL, Ii.VI.24, fols. 49v, 69r.

62 *Ibid.*, fol. 42r. *Chroniques de Normandie*, p. 68, mistakenly calls Thomas *Ratrot* (i.e. Rotrou), which may mean that that particular text was composed while he was still a little-known child.

63 See n. 48 above. Spiegel, *Romancing the Past*, p. 231, sees a Norman history such as the first in the Cambridge manuscript as the base for the Béthune *histoire* (c.1220).

64 Chrétien de Troyes, *Cligès*, ed. C. Luttrell and S. Gregory (Woodbridge, 1993), ll. 314–35, 2732–3. For *des(a)fubler* and its antonym *(a)fubler*, see F. Godefroy, *Dictionnaire de l'ancienne langue française et de tous ses dialectes du IXe au XVe siècle*, 10 vols. (Paris, 1881–1902), I, 153–4, II, 532, 590, IV, 169; *Altfranzösisches Wörterbuch*, ed. A. Tobler *et al.*, 10 vols. (Berlin, 1925–76), I, cols. 201–2, II, cols. 1595–6. See also S. R. Goddard, *Women's Costume in French Texts of the Eleventh and Twelfth Centuries* (Baltimore and Paris, 1927), pp. 108–11, 147, 153, 164, 169.

65 *Marie de France: Lais*, ed. A. Ewert, rev. G. S. Burgess (London, 1995), p. 72, ll. 560–2, kindly drawn to my attention by Linda Paterson. M. A. Pappano, 'Marie de France, Aliénor d'Aquitaine, and the Alien Queen', in *Eleanor of Aquitaine*, ed. Wheeler and Parsons, pp. 337–67, even argues that this exotic figure was intended to represent Eleanor herself.

her body, but in her case it also testifies to her innocence of the charges levelled against her by her erstwhile husband. The queen's body was a political weapon that she used to full effect.

If the story's exact content is unclear, its historical veracity is even more problematic. It needs hardly be said that no such tale occurs in contemporary or near-contemporary accounts of the divorce of Louis and Eleanor. The earliest references to their separation, in two of Eleanor's own charters in 1152, state that consanguinity was the chief cause, although at least one implicitly criticizes the king.[66] Lambert of Wattrelos's *Annals of Cambrai*, which purports to have been written that same year, was very critical of Louis: the king of France had accused the queen childishly (*pueriliter*), summoned a council rashly (*imprudenter*) and renounced her following its unwise advice; Eleanor returned to her own people in sadness (*moesta*) but then immediately married Henry, whom Lambert still thought of as merely the son of the count of Anjou.[67] In contrast, the *Historia Gloriosi Regis Ludovici* (written 1170 × 73) and Robert of Torigni's chronicle (probably revised from his contemporary notes in the 1170s) imply that the separation was mutual, and unlike Lambert they both invoke consanguinity as the reason for the divorce; the *Historia Ludovici* in particular was keen to stress the scrupulousness of the king's behaviour when he 'discovered' his kinship to his wife.[68] By the time it was written, rumours were circulating that Eleanor's misbehaviour had provoked the royal separation. In the 1160s, John of Salisbury's *Historia Pontificalis* made a direct link between the royal couple's squabbles in Antioch, which arose from the overfamiliarity of Eleanor and her uncle, the prince of the city, and Eleanor's demand to have their marriage annulled on grounds of consanguinity.[69] These stories become progressively more lurid. A decade or so later William of Tyre mentioned allegations of incestuous adultery between Eleanor and the prince of Antioch as the source of her quarrel with Louis.[70] Gervase of Canterbury and William of Newburgh, writing near the end of the century, suggested that Eleanor had planned to marry the duke of Normandy even before her divorce,[71] and Walter Map accused her of adultery

66 *Actes de Henri II*, I, nos. XXIII*–XXIV*: the first states that Louis, without Eleanor's consent, had given away one of her woods in alms. By confirming the grant after her divorce Eleanor's act reasserted her lordship over her lands.

67 'Annales Cameracenses', *MGH SS*, XVI, 522–3.

68 *Vie de Louis le Gros et Histoire du Roi Louis VII*, ed. A. Molinier (Paris, 1887), pp. 163–4, which names Archbishop Hugh of Rouen among those responsible for the divorce; Torigni, I, 259–61. See C. B. Bouchard, 'Eleanor's Divorce from Louis VII: The Uses of Consanguinity', in *Eleanor of Aquitaine*, ed. Wheeler and Parsons, pp. 223–35. In fact, their consanguinity was known by 1143: John of Salisbury, *Historia Pontificalis*, ed. and trans. M. Chibnall (London, 1956), p. 53 and n. 1.

69 John of Salisbury, *Historia Pontificalis*, pp. 52–3, which claims that all calculations of the degrees of consanguinity between them were mistrusted.

70 William of Tyre, *Chronicon*, ed. R. B. C. Huygens, Corpus Christianorum Continuatio Mediaeualis 63, 2 vols. (Turnhout, 1986), II, 754–5: he describes her behaviour at Antioch as 'contra dignitatem regiam legem negligens maritalem'. He wrote between c.1170 and 1184: P. W. Edbury and J. G. Rowe, *William of Tyre: Historian of the Latin East* (Cambridge, 1988), p. 26.

71 Gervase of Canterbury, I, 149; William of Newburgh, *Historia Rerum Anglicarum*, in *Chronicles of the Reigns of Stephen, Henry II, and Richard I*, ed. R. Howlett, RS 82, 4 vols. (London, 1884–89), I,

with Henry's father Geoffrey, an allegation later repeated by Gerald of Wales.[72] About the same time as Gerald wrote, Helinand of Froidmont alleged that Louis had grown to detest her 'because of that woman's incontinence, for she was behaving not like a queen but almost like a prostitute'.[73]

The tale recorded in the Cambridge and Arsenal short Norman histories does accord with some basic details of the divorce. Several vernacular texts mention that Poitevin barons came to Louis's court to fetch home their duchess,[74] but only the two examined here give a further reason for their presence. In other details the Cambridge–Arsenal tale differs from more contemporary Latin accounts, which place the proceedings at Beaugency, not Étampes,[75] and which, with the exception of Lambert of Wattrelos, neither depict Eleanor as the wronged party nor imply that the divorce offended her honour.

Eleanor – a Devil?

It was clearly important to the author of the Norman text to show that Eleanor was the guiltless party. Why, though, did she need to prove that she was not a devil? The scene may simply have been intended to refute malicious accusations that stained her memory in the decades following her death. In the *Récits d'un menestrel de Reims* (1260), which drew upon earlier vernacular prose histories but also took very imaginative liberties with French history, the barons of France urge Louis VII to divorce his wife, 'car c'est uns diables, et se vous la tenez longuement nous doutons qu'elle ne vous face mourdrir'.[76] The queen's offence that provokes this advice is an attempt to elope with Saladin during the Second Crusade! While this was, of course, a historical impossibility, both Matthew Paris and a fragment of an anonymous history of Louis VII, written some decades before the *Menestrel*, had already accused her of trying to elope with a Turk.[77]

92–3. From the same decade come Richard of Devizes' dark hints concerning her behaviour in the Holy Land.

72 Walter Map, p. 474; Gerald of Wales, *Opera*, ed. J. S. Brewer, J. F. Dimock and G. F. Warner, RS 21, 8 vols. (London, 1861–91), VIII, 300–1.

73 *PL*, CCXII, cols. 1057–8: 'Hanc reliquit Ludovicus, propter incontinentiam ipsius mulieris, quæ non sicut regina, sed fere sicut meretrix se habebat.' Helinand (writing 1190 × 1215) was copied by, among others, the chronicle attributed to Aubry de Trois-Fontaines (*MGH SS*, XXIII, 841, written in the 1240s), which preferred 'like a common woman' (*fere communem se exhibebat*) and Bernard Gui (*RHGF*, XII, 231, written 1312–20).

74 E.g. *HDN*, p. 81; CUL, Ii.vi.24, fol. 42r (quoted above, n. 46).

75 *Histoire du Roi Louis VII*, pp. 163–4; Torigni, I, 259.

76 *Récits d'un ménestrel de Reims au treizième siècle*, ed. N. de Wailly (Paris, 1876), p. 6. Cf. p. 4: 'Molt fu male femme.'

77 Matthew Paris, *Chronica Majora*, ed. H. R. Luard, RS 57, 7 vols. (London, 1872–83), II, 186 (glossing Ralph Diceto): Eleanor was rumoured to have committed adultery 'etiam cum infideli, et qui genere fuit diaboli'. Matthew Paris, *Historia Anglorum*, ed. F. Madden, RS 44, 3 vols. (London, 1866–69), I, 288: 'Diffamabatur de multiplici adulterio, præcipue de quodam infideli infidelium principi in terra orientali, dum rex bellicis negotiis indulsit, perpetrato.' *RHGF*, XII, 286: 'In hoc itinere, præfata Regina Regem in pluribus graviter offendit; in hoc vero gravissime, quod Regem clam relinquere machinans, cuidam Turco adhærere voluit.' Internal evidence could suggest that this last text was written as early as c.1200. For discussion of the Saladin story,

Hence although the exact chronology of these traditions cannot be pinpointed with great accuracy, the story recorded in the Cambridge and Arsenal *histoires* may have been in dialogue with rival, pro-Capetian traditions that denigrated the queen and the Plantagenet dynasty.

However, any modern audience acquainted with Plantagenet history will find it impossible not to see in the disrobing story an allusion to the legends of the dynasty's diabolical ancestors, in particular the stories of serpentine noblewomen who prefigure Jean d'Arras's *Melusine* (1393). The connection between Melusine and Eleanor, her fellow Poitevin, has long been made, for instance by Michelet: 'La véritable Mélusine . . ., c'est Éléonore de Guyenne'.[78] In fact, as early as the 1240s Philippe Mousket's verse chronicle linked Eleanor to a Melusine-like devil, and overtly in the context of the disrobing story.

Mousket also came from the French-speaking part of Flanders, and his chronicle is an 'original' source for French history from the Bouvines war until the early 1240s; but most of the thirty-one thousand lines of his text concern a much more remote past. While R. N. Walpole analysed his sections based upon the Pseudo-Turpin traditions that concerned the Carolingian period, the portions describing events in the twelfth century have been much less studied.[79] Walpole did note the role of various Norman sources in Mousket's account; the poet was probably writing before 1245, hence before the Cambridge and Arsenal manuscripts were written, but, if, as has been argued here, the Norman *histoires* themselves had been composed around the time of Louis's invasion of England, then Mousket may well have drawn upon another manuscript containing the disrobing story.[80]

Mousket expands upon the rather coy descriptions of the queen's self-exposure as it appears in the Cambridge and Arsenal texts:[81]

> At Saint-Jean,[82] she took her rest one evening; and when she came to disrobe (*a son desfublar*), she said to them:
> 'Look, lords, is my body[83] not worthy and lovely? The king said that I was a devil, and that in all senses I was deformed and unseemly.'
> They replied: 'Lady, no, you are not! There is no one so noble in this kingdom. You have come amongst good lords,[84] and so you shall shortly have a rich and

see P. McCracken, 'Scandalizing Desire: Eleanor of Aquitaine and the Chroniclers', in *Eleanor of Aquitaine*, ed. Wheeler and Parsons, pp. 247–63.

78 Quoted by Aurell, 'Aliénor d'Aquitaine', p. 45.

79 See Walpole, 'Philip Mouskés'.

80 Meyer, 'Notice', pp. 64–5.

81 Appendix, no. 3.

82 Labande, 'Pour une image véridique', p. 196 n.100, interprets this as Saint-Jean d'Angély in Aquitaine. The alternative meaning, 'on the feast of St John the Evangelist', does not accord with 'one evening' on the following line.

83 'Mis cors'. According to *PD*, 98, 'cors' may refer to either the human body, a corpse, or a running line or course (e.g. 'cors de pena', a slip of the pen). The phrase 'ieu mis cors' is interpreted by Emil Levy as 'moi en personne', 'I myself'. The same applies to Old French, for example with Hervis de Metz's order, 'Querrez moi fame, mes cors mestier en a' (Seek me a wife, for I need one), *Garin le Loherenc*, ed. A. Iter-Gittleman, 3 vols. (Paris, 1997), I, l. 770. Admittedly, Hervis needs heirs 'of his body' (they will include Geoffrey of Anjou, his grandson), but he seems to mean simply that he himself needs to marry immediately.

84 Here I follow the translation by Mousket's editor, Reiffenberg.

worthy lord, lady: make do with your own lands until then[85] and wait.'
'By my head!' the queen said, 'My heart yields to your advice.'

Mousket revels in the scene and leaves us in little doubt as to how he understood the term *desfublar*. Moreover, the author continues: 'Now I shall not fail to tell you the reasons why the king called her a devil', and proceeds to narrate a legend of a devilish countess of Aquitaine from whom, he alleged, Eleanor was descended. Since he made the explicit connection between Eleanor's action and her supposed demonic ancestry, it is quite possible that the audiences of the Norman *histoires* were also acquainted with such a tale.

Mousket's attribution of a devilish forebear to the great duchess of Aquitaine needs to be fitted into the broader context of medival French folklore. Claude Lecouteux and Laurence Harf-Lancner have shown that Indo-European folklore contains an array of encounters between humans (usually men) and fairies or demons (usually female). They argue that the women were originally propitious, but the Church increasingly treated them as demons; they therefore remained highly ambiguous figures, both alluring and repellent.[86] More specifically, Jacques Le Goff and Emmanuel Le Roy Ladurie have argued that the best-known demon, Melusine, combines two distinct legends: a woman who cannot endure hearing Mass, and a woman who turns into a serpent (and is usually aquatic).[87] By the thirteenth century both legends were widespread across western Europe. Geoffrey of Auxerre, an erstwhile abbot of Clairvaux (writing in 1187 × 1194), mentioned a noble's mysterious wife who became a serpent in her bath, but he located her in his own diocese of Langres (in Burgundy) and described her as a distant ancestor of many of the local castellans.[88] Further south, the *Otia Imperialia* of Gervase of Tilbury, completed in 1214–15, tells how the lady of a castle called L'Épervier (*Esperuer*) – 'the Sparrowhawk' – near Valence in Provence could not bear to remain in Mass; when she was eventually forced to do so she caused the chapel to collapse.[89] The wife of Raymond, lord of Rousset near Aix-en-Provence, like Geoffrey of Auxerre's lady near Langres, forbade her husband to see her naked and turned into a snake when she bathed.[90] Yet the two legends were already linked in their earliest recorded occurrence, in Walter Map's *De Nugis Curialium* (c.1181 × c.1193). The mysterious wife of Henno *cum*

85 The meaning of this phrase is unclear. Reiffenberg translates it thus: 'Restez, dame, sur vos domaines et attendez.'

86 C. Lecouteux, 'Zur Entstehung der Melusinensage', *Zeitschrift für deutsche Philologie* 98 (1977), 73–84; L. Harf-Lancner, *Les fées au moyen âge: Morgane, Mélusine, la naissance des fées* (Geneva, 1984), esp. pp. 119–26, 138–54, 392–401, for the Latin sources discussed here.

87 J. Le Goff and E. Le Roy Ladurie, 'Mélusine maternelle et défricheuse', *Annales: Economies, Sociétés, Civilisations* 26 (1971), 587–622.

88 Geoffrey of Auxerre, *Super Apocalypsim*, ed. F. Gastaldelli (Rome, 1970), pp. 47–51 (date), 186–7 (text), and cf. pp. 183–5 for a similar story from the kingdom of Sicily; Harf-Lancner, *Les fées*, pp. 143–50.

89 Gervase of Tilbury, *Otia Imperialia: Recreation for an Emperor*, ed. and trans. S. E. Banks and J. W. Binns (Oxford, 2002), pp. 664–8; the inhabitants of *Esperuer* allegedly afterwards moved to a nearby *castrum*, Charpey. For the date, see *ibid.*, pp. xxxix–xl; Gervase had been collecting the tales for many years.

90 *Ibid.*, pp. 88–90.

Dentibus, whom he had found upon the Norman seashore, could not bear to remain in Mass, and would turn into a dragon in the bath. This woman is located in a distant but avowedly real past, for Walter claimed that some of his contemporaries were her descendants.[91]

None of these authors was describing remote or exotic lands. Gervase of Tilbury, although of English origin,[92] had reached the zenith of his career in the kingdom of Arles and compiled the *Otia Imperialia* there. He even claimed that his Provençal wife was related to a descendant of the serpentine lady of Rousset, and that the ruins of the chapel of the Sparrowhawk authenticated his other story.[93] He clearly states his purpose in narrating these tales: for the lady who flees Mass, he wishes to show devils in human form; the bathing serpent forms part of a commentary upon the most universal text linking purity and nakedness, the third chapter of the Book of Genesis. The mysogyny of the serpentine topos is obvious: before Gervase of Tilbury tells the story of the she-serpent of Rousset he first discusses the serpent in the Garden of Eden, to which he attributes a female face 'because like approves of like'.[94] Geoffrey of Auxerre had also had a similar exegetical purpose, for his anecdote of a bathing she-serpent and a similar Sicilian tale were *exempla* in a sermon commenting upon the 'Jezebel' of the church of Thyatirae (Rev. 2.18–29).[95] Taken together, the anecdotes of Walter Map, Geoffrey of Auxerre and Gervase of Tilbury demonstrate that many noble families in Eleanor's lifetime were said to be descended from she-devils: they usually dwelt in a region familiar to the author but nearly always in the distant past, and they served as moral cautions to the authors' audiences. None had so far connected these tales to Eleanor's lineage.

Within a year or so of Gervase's writing, Gerald of Wales claimed that the Plantagenets were descended from a Mass-evading she-devil who, when forced to remain in church until the consecration, left her cloak in the hands of the soldiers who sought to restrain her and flew off through the window with two of her children. Yet Gerald made her a countess of Anjou – hence Henry's ancestor, not Eleanor's. Given the widespread occurrence of the motif, it is easy to believe that Gerald simply adapted it to blacken the dynasty that he loathed so much; yet if we accept his story concerning Richard's jest that his lineage had come from the devil, then this tale may have already been applied to the Plantagenets in the late twelfth century and possibly considerably earlier.[96] Gerald's countess of Anjou, like Henno's wife, was 'of striking appearance but unknown nation',

91 Walter Map, pp. 344–8. Henno has been plausibly identified with Hamo *Dentatus*, the ancestor of Walter's contemporary Earl William of Gloucester and numerous other Anglo-Norman magnates.

92 *Otia Imperialia*, p. 578: he claimed to be a kinsman of the earls of Salisbury.

93 *Ibid.*, pp. xxviii–xxxiii, 90, 664. He was first in the service of the archbishop of Valence, and afterwards marshal of the kingdom of Arles.

94 *Ibid.*, p. 86: 'quia similia similibus applaudunt'. Gervase derived this image and phrase from the *Historia Scholastica* (1169 × 73) of the Parisian scholar Peter Comestor (*PL*, CXCVIII, col. 1072), who in turn drew upon a venerable artistic tradition of representing the serpent in the Garden as female: L. Réau, *Iconographie de l'art chrétien*, 3 vols. in 6 (Paris, 1955–59), II:i, 60.

95 Above, n. 88.

96 Gerald of Wales, VIII, 301–2; the same jibe was allegedly uttered against Henry II himself by Bernard of Clairvaux in the 1140s and by Heraclius, patriarch of Jerusalem, against Henry's sons

whom the count married 'solely for the beauty of her body'. She is of the Eucharist-avoiding but not serpentine kind, flying through a window with two of her children when forced to remain in Mass. So by c.1217 we can see the various elements of the diabolical Eleanor coming together: the most beautiful woman in the world who is said to be a devil and the ancestor of the Plantagenets. Some time in the early thirteenth century Caesarius of Heisterbach's *Dialogue on Miracles*, after discussing Merlin's demonic father, adds: 'Even the kings ruling to this day in Britain, which is now called England, are said to be descended from a phantom mother.'[97] Philippe Mousket's verse history represents a further stage in this transition, for after narrating the story of Eleanor disrobing before her barons he tells almost exactly the same tale of a Mass-evading countess, 'trop plaisant de cors, de menbres et de vis', but makes her a countess of Aquitaine rather than a progenitor of Henry II. Mousket even claims that Louis's awareness of Eleanor's diabolical ancestry prevented him from loving her.[98] By the late thirteenth century, the legend had been transferred to Eleanor herself: in the lost Anglo-Norman romance *Richard Coeur de Lion* the Lionheart's demonic mother flew away through the roof of the church when King Henry attempted to force her to stay for the consecration, taking one of her daughters but dropping her son John as she fled.[99] The tale of the bathing she-serpent, meanwhile, was adapted in the late fourteenth century (but as a demi-serpent) by Jean d'Arras, who ascribed it to the Lusignan dynasty and named the lady Melusine.[100]

Like Mousket's chronicle, the Cambridge short history and Arsenal text therefore probably reflect an intermediate step in the transfer of demonic legends from ancient ladies on Provençal crags, in Burgundian forests or on Norman shores, to an ancestor of Eleanor and then to Eleanor herself. Yet although Mousket, having narrated the same story, connected Eleanor's stripping to the legend of a Mass-evading chapel-toppler, the queen's removal of clothing as proof that she was not a devil could just as easily link Louis's allegations against her to the legend of the bathing serpent. In the sermon of Geoffrey of Auxerre and Gervase of Tilbury's story of the lady of Rousset, the mysterious lady who turns into a serpent in her bath agrees to marriage only on condition that her

in 1185: *ibid.*, pp. 211, 309. For the story's transfer to Eleanor, see also Harf-Lancner, *Les fées*, pp. 396–401; it contrasts with the other stories whose heroes were mostly from the lesser aristocracy: Le Goff and Ladurie, 'Mélusine', p. 601.

97 Caesarius of Heisterbach, *Dialogus Miraculorum*, ed. J. Strange, 2 vols. (Cologne, 1851), I, 124 (Bk III, c.12): 'de matre phantastica descendisse referuntur'.

98 *Chronique rimée de Philippe Mouskès*, ed. Le Baron de Reiffenberg, 2 vols. (Brussels, 1838), II, 2459 (ll. 18720–829). The she-devil was married to a count of Aquitaine and their children were 'heirs of Aquitaine', but Mousket depicts Eleanor as the daughter of a lord of Saint-Gilles: II, 245 (l. 18722), 249 (ll. 18810–23).

99 *Der Mittelenglische Versroman über Richard Löwenherz*, ed. K. Brunner, *Wiener Beiträge* 42 (1913), 83–91 (ll. 44–238), an early fourteenth-century Middle English translation of the lost Anglo-Norman text; see L. A. Hibbard, *Mediæval Romance in England*, 2nd edn (New York, 1960), pp. 147–53, who also notes the propensity of tales of diverse origin to become attached to the figure of Richard the Lionheart.

100 Lecouteux, 'Zur Entstehung der Melusinensage', pp. 80, 82–4. *Idem*, *Mélusine et le chevalier au cygne* (Paris, 1982), pp. 54–6, notes that creatures that are half-woman, half-serpent recur in European myths from long before the Christian era.

husband never sees her naked (and in Geoffrey's sermon, the maids are forbidden as well); the depiction of Eleanor removing her clothing could well be a veiled allusion to this demonic stipulation. Whichever tradition the authors had in mind, if they were engaged in a dialogue with such legends, then they were attempting to refute much worse allegations than an abortive elopement with Saladin.

Conclusion

Despite the longevity of her title as duchess of the Normans, Eleanor's connections with Normandy at first appear very weak. Yet, far from forgetting her, the Normans preserved a distinctive tale about Eleanor, one which to a modern audience appears as racy as any told about this much-discussed queen. To a medieval audience, with very different views of devils and of the human body, it no doubt had a rather different significance: by revealing herself Eleanor sought not to cause scandal but to refute it, at a time when much older legends of demonic ancestors were becoming attached to the queen's memory.

Both a modern and a medieval audience would recognize that the Cambridge and Arsenal histories of the dukes of Normandy were attempting to rehabilitate Eleanor, without removing some of the exotic allure that attached to her memory, at a time when it was becoming tainted with demonic tales drawn from French folklore. Richard of Devizes, describing the queen-mother who had pacified England while her son was far away in Palestine, described her as 'an incomparable woman, beautiful yet virtuous, powerful yet gentle, humble yet keen-witted, qualities which are most rarely found in a woman'. Although he then alluded knowingly to her unmentionable activities during the Second Crusade, others may have wished to remember her fondly and as innocent of the many accusations against her that were circulating both in the later years of her life and nearly a century after her divorce.[101] It is surely significant that one of the two extant texts appears in a manuscript that had strong connections with the abbey of La Trinité de Caen, better known as the Abbaye aux Dames. La Trinité had been founded by another famous duchess of the Normans, Matilda of Flanders, wife of William the Conqueror. Its community comprised one of the best-connected collections of noblewomen in Normandy. It must remain pure speculation, but it is tempting to believe that the nuns cherished and reinvented the memory of their last great duchess, whom some of them might even have remembered at the time that the Cambridge manuscript was being composed in the abbey.

Yet Eleanor was also remembered for her foreignness. Meyer believed that the Cambridge and Arsenal texts were attempting to make Eleanor and her barons converse in a form of Occitan.[102] Whether or not this was their intention, Philippe Mousket certainly spiced her conversation with Occitan words and phrases, emphasizing her otherness.[103] The cultural diversity of the Plantagenet

101 Richard of Devizes, *Chronicle*, pp. 25–6; cf. plate opposite p. xvi.

102 Meyer, 'Notice', pp. 63–4.

103 E.g. *cap*, *lou res digat*, *malostruge et cubinens*, *mis corages*, and possibly *mis cors* (cf. n. 83 above). P.

territories had been a continual source of tension within them, ultimately contributing to the ruin of the dynasty's fortunes. Friction between the Poitevins and the inhabitants of the Anglo-Norman realm recurred from the Lusignan revolt of the 1160s to the Capetian victories between 1202 and 1242. As Nicholas Vincent has shown, very few Poitevins gained lands in England and Normandy or vice versa under the Angevin kings.[104] Eleanor, countess of the Poitevins, was still remembered for her difference from the northern French who recounted the events of her life in the decades after her death – even when she revealed her body to her barons.

Appendix

For the manuscripts from which the first two passages are taken, see above, pp. 123–5.

No. 1 Cambridge, University Library, Ii.VI.24, fol. 98r (ed. in Meyer, 'Notice', pp. 69–70)

Puis avint que li rois enhai sa femme qui estoit heir d'Aquitaingne e de Peitou, de Gascoingne et de Berri, e si avoit de lié dous filles que le rois dona puis l'une au conte de Champaigne, l'autre au conte de Chartres. Li rois se fist departir de sa femme, Alienor aveit non, a Estampes. La vindrent a lui si home de Peitou au departement e l'enmenerent. Quant laissie l'ot, si prist la fille au roi d'Espaingne; .ij. filles en ot e morut, e il reprist las soer as contes a qui il aveit donées ses premieres filles, Ale ot non, e ot de lié Philippes. Quant ele fu departie e ele esgarda ses genz, si se desfubla e dist:

'Seignor, e qau (*sic*) beste sui?'

'Par Deu!' distrent il, 'non a plus bele dame en cest siecle vivant.'

'Seignar (*sic*), dict ele, 'non sui dont ges deables, que li rei de France m'apelot tut adès.'

No. 2 Paris, Bibliothèque de l'Arsenal, 3516, fol. 314r (ed. in Meyer, 'Notice', p. 68 n. 1)

En cel tans avint que li rois Loeys enhaï sa fame la roine Alyenor, qi (*sic*) estoit dame de Poitau et de Gascoigne, et de Berri, et de tote la tere qi apent (*sic*) a Aquitaigne. Et si avoit de lui ij. filles, dont l'une fu donée al conte de Campaigne, et l'autre al conte de Chartres, qi estoit frere le conte de Champaigne. Li rois ses (*sic*) fist departir a Estampes par parentage. La jurerent por lui si home et si baron de Poitau al departement, et si l'en menerent.

Quant ele fu departie et ele esgarda ses gens, si se desfubla, et si lor dist:

Meyer, 'Des rapports de la poésie des trouvères avec celle des troubadours', *Romania* 19 (1890), 1–42 (p. 3), surely went too far when he deduced from this that 'elle avait conservé à la cour du roi de France l'habitude de parler provençal ou poitevin'.

104 N. Vincent, 'King Henry II and the Poitevins', in *La Cour Plantagenêt*, ed. Aurell, pp. 103–35.

'Segnor, quau beste sui?'

'Et per Deu!", distrent il, 'et non ac tant bele dosne en tot le mont.'

'Segnar (*sic*),' dis ele, 'non sui dont giens diables, que mes sires li rois me cobicot (*sic*)[105] adès.'

Quant laisie ot li rois Loeys la roine Elienor, il prist a feme la fille le roi d'Espaigne, don't il ot .ij. filles. Et apres morut la dame. Et li rois reprist a feme la seror as .ij. contes, a qui il avoit donées ses ij. filles de la roine Elyenor.

No. 3 *Chronique rimée de Philippe Mouskès*, ed. Le Baron de Reiffenberg, 2 vols. (Brussels, 1838), II, 244–5

De la roïne Aliénor
Ot cil rois Loéys II filles,
Bieles et sages et gentilles.
L'ainsnée, ki moult gu senée,
Fu, à grant joie, mariée
Al conte Henri de Campagne.
L'autre, si com l'uevre m'ensagne,
Si ot li quens Tiebau de Blois,
Qui moult fu sage et courtois.
Cis fu li gros rois Loéys,
Si com tiesmogne li escris.
De la roïne Aliénor,
Si com jou truis el livre encor,
Se départi petit apriés,
Comme cil qui moult iert engriés;
Et ele manda sses barons,
Uns et uns, les plus haus par nons,
Si s'en rala en Aquitagne,
Moult courecie, à grant compagne.
A St.-Jéhan éwangeliste
Prist une vesprée sa giste;
Et quant vint a son desfublar,
Si leur a dit: 'Voiies, signar,
Dont n'est mis cors prou delitables?
Lou rés digat q'ere deables,
Et q'en ere riens a tos sens
Malostruge et non cubinens.'
Il respondent: 'Dosne, vous non,
Non ac tant gente en ic roion.
Vengüe iestes à bon signor,
S'aurés signar à poi de jor
Ric e prout, dosne, et vous estas
Soubre le vostre et atendas.'
'Per mon cap!' ce dist la roïne,
'Mis corages a vous s'acline.'
Or vous dirai le voir sans falle
Dont li rois le clama déable.

105 *rectior* 'cobit tot'?

Raymond VII of Toulouse: The Son of Queen Joanna, 'Young Count' and Light of the World.

LAURENT MACÉ*
(translated by Catherine Léglu)

As we know, no princely dynasty can afford to dispense with glorious ancestors. Nor can it do without cohorts of enthusiastic panegyrists and easily identifiable public symbols. That is why medievalists are increasingly addressing the history of *mentalités*, and more precisely those ideological constructions that had immediate political implications. This is evinced most strikingly in Amaury Chauou's recent study of Plantagenet ideology.[1] The aristocracy and its modes of self-representation are an object of enquiry fuelled by consideration of the image both as it is produced and as it is reflected back on its source.[2] Having already begun to address this theme in a previous study devoted to the counts of Toulouse,[3] I would like to pick up some of the threads in order to analyse the last of the Toulousan counts, Raymond VII (1222–49), who was, lest we forget, one of the grandchildren of Eleanor of Aquitaine.

By studying the hierarchy of values this comital house chose to claim as its own, and its expression of an ideological discourse, this chapter aims to discern the more or less unconscious themes and mental schemata that might have served the 'diffused propaganda' of princely power.[4] Three facets deserve to be analysed in depth: genealogical self-definition, the heroic praise of a troubadour virtue (youth), and the new construction of a quasi-mythical definition of light and of *Paratge*.

* *Translator's note*: I have Anglicized Occitan and French names in keeping with the author's use of modern French equivalents. The term 'Raymondine' refers to members of the dynasty of the counts of Toulouse named Raymond. CEL.

1 A. Chauou, *L'Idéologie Plantagenêt: royauté arthurienne et monarchie politique dans l'espace Plantagenêt (XIIe–XIIIe siècles)* (Rennes, 2001).

2 D. Crouch, *The Image of Aristocracy in Britain, 1000–1300* (London, 1992).

3 L. Macé, *Les Comtes de Toulouse et leur entourage, XIIe–XIIIe siècles: Rivalités, alliances et jeux de pouvoir* (Toulouse, 2000). See the chapter 'L'image du prince', pp. 287–327.

4 J. Le Goff, 'Conclusions', in *Le forme della propaganda politica nel Due e nel Trecento*, ed. P. Cammarosano, Collection de l'École Française de Rome 201 (Rome, 1994), pp. 519–20.

Affirmation of Royal Birth

Raymond VII was the only child of the marriage of the count of Toulouse, Raymond VI (1195–1222) and Countess Joanna (1196–99). She was the sister of Richard the Lionheart and John Lackland, one of the three daughters of Henry II and Eleanor of Aquitaine.[5] The marriage of the Raymondine and the Plantagenet ended a century of competition and conflict between the two dynasties; thanks to this alliance, Richard definitively surrendered his claims to the succession to the county of Toulouse, rights he claimed to derive from his ancestor Philippa.[6] Former enemies, the Toulousans and the Plantagenets became close allies, a connection that gave cause for concern to Philip Augustus, who was then at war with Richard.[7]

Thus the child born in Beaucaire in 1197 had Toulousan blood in his veins, along with that of the royal French line (his paternal grandmother was Constance of France, the sister of King Louis VII) and that of the Aquitanian Angevins (his maternal grandparents were Henry II and Eleanor). If one scrutinizes the family connections between the two houses, it emerges that Raymond VI and Joanna were second cousins (that is to say, that they shared a great-grandparent). In canon law, the collateral consanguinity of the two spouses marked the union out as incestuous, and therefore vulnerable to legal obstacles: they were relatives to the fifth degree. However, no ecclesiastical sanction was ever formulated against them. It is worth noting as well that Raymond VI and Eleanor of Aquitaine had Pons of Toulouse (d.1061) as their common ancestor, and that both were descended from the first troubadour, William IX of Poitiers.

Even if the great queen was no longer alive when Raymond VII began to exercise his comital power, he, by virtue of his bloodline, was undeniably part of the world of Eleanor of Aquitaine. When she died in 1204, the future Raymond VII was only seven years old. Did he ever meet his illustrious grandmother? Probably at least once, for she travelled south into Gascony in the year 1200, some time after the death of her daughter, in order to compel the count of Toulouse to recognize bequests Joanna had made in her will in favour of the abbey of Fontevraud.[8] This establishment had been founded in 1101 by the preacher

5 E.-R. Labande, 'Les Filles d'Aliénor d'Aquitaine: étude comparative', CCM 29 (1986), 101–12.

6 See R. Benjamin, 'A Forty Years War: Toulouse and the Plantagenets, 1156–1196', *Historical Research* 61 (1988), 270–85, and J. Martindale, 'An Unfinished Business: Angevin Politics and the Siege of Toulouse, 1159', *Anglo-Norman Studies XXIII: Proceedings of the Battle Conference 2000*, ed. J. Gillingham (Woodbridge, 2001), pp. 115–54, esp. pp. 143–53.

7 In a letter to the pope of April 1208, the king of France complains about Raymond VI's attitude : he married Joanna and created an alliance with an enemy who had always threatened Toulouse, and whom the Capetians had always fought ('contra nos cepit in uxorem sororem ejusdem regis Ricardi, quamvis pie memorie pater noster et nos magna constamenta et impensas miserimus ad defendendum patrem ejus et ipsum et terram ejus'). Also, Raymond helped John in 1204 by sending a body of troops to Falaise ('cum nos guerrearemus regem Johannem propter injuriam suam, invenimus homines ejus in munitione contra nos infra Falesiam'). Lastly, he did not deign to assist his overlord ('de omnibus guerris quas habuimus, nullum auxilium de eo habuimus nec per ipsum nec per gentem suam') (*HGL*, VIII, cols. 558–9).

8 J. M. Bienvenu, 'Aliénor d'Aquitaine et Fontevraud', CCM 29 (1986), 15–27 (p. 25).

Robert of Arbrissel, who was connected to Joanna's great-grandfather, the famous troubadour. It is possible to speculate that the little boy was included in the comital procession led by his father, and that the son of Joanna, the heir of the Raymondine dynasty, was taken to the Agenais to meet his venerable relative.[9]

Apart from this possible encounter, there is not the slightest reference to Eleanor of Aquitaine in the Raymondine archive.[10] Two members of the Plantagenet dynasty are, however, honoured at the comital court: Richard and, above all, Joanna. Our knowledge of this comes via distinct sources, as Richard and his brother John are evoked in a literary text, and Joanna appears in diplomatic material.

The manuscript known to traditional literary history as the *Chanson de la croisade albigeoise* (hereafter, the *Chanson*) makes no mention of the bloodline connecting Raymond and either Joanna or Eleanor, but it devotes some space to Richard and John. The emblematic figure of the knight-king accounts for three out of the nine references to the kings of England in the poem. Beyond two somewhat peripheral mentions (the former possession of Penne-d'Agenais by Richard and his entry into the city of Acre),[11] the six remaining references concern the blood-ties between the counts and the two great royal dynasties that were the houses of France and England. This connection is underlined for the first time – surely not by chance – at the point of the fleeting but promising initial appearance in the text of the young count, during the Lateran council of November 1215. In this scene, Pope Innocent III welcomes young Raymond with good will: 'For never was a more attractive young man born [of a woman]; he has good sense, he is wise and well-mannered, the offshoot of the best lineage there is, and has ever been, that of France, England and Count Alfonso.'[12]

The pope, who is impressed by the Raymondine's good manners, recognizes his prestigious lineage ('conosc lo linatge') and expresses his esteem for the worthy potential adorning the young count. During this assembly, the intervention of the archbishop of Dublin is presented by the poet as a decisive one for the future of the 'noble nephew of the king . . . the legitimate son, courtly and of good family', a boy born of 'the best lineage that could ever be named'.[13] Another representative of King John, the abbot of Beaulieu, takes his turn to defend the cause of the Toulousan prince.[14] It is indeed in the name of his oft-

9 In 1209, aged 12, he was taken to Carcassonne to be presented to the barons of France: *Chanson*, I, laisse 38, ll. 7–14.

10 Eleanor's Toulousan ancestry was not mentioned by twelfth-century chroniclers, even when she laid claim to the county on the grounds of inheritance from her grandmother Philippa: Martindale, 'An Unfinished Business', p. 148.

11 *Chanson*, laisse 114, l. 21; laisse 204, l. 83.

12 'Qu'anc no nasquesc de maire nulhs plus avinens tos, / Qu'el es adreitz e savis e de gentils faisos / E del milhor linage que sia ni anc fos, / De Fransa e d'Anglaterra e del comte n'Anfos' (*Chanson*, laisse 143, ll. 13–16); (For never was born such an attractive youth of a mother, for he is able and wise, and of noble appearance, and of the best lineage there ever was: of France and of England and of King Alfonso.). The author's reference to a *maire* may be a calculated allusion to Joan.

13 '[L]'onratz nebs del rei [. . .] filhs legismes, gentils e de bon aire / E del milhor linatge que hom poscha retraire' (*Chanson*, laisse 150, ll. 10, 17–18). Lineage is associated with *bon aire*, which in fact designates the 'nest' of offspring: the noble house functions to assert identity on both the individual and the family level.

14 N. Vincent, 'England and the Albigensian Crusade', in *England and Europe in the Reign of Henry*

cited progenitors[15] that the pope decides at last to grant the 'nephew who can find neither a friend nor a champion' (*Chanson*, laisse 150, line 36) the chance of regaining the counties of Venaissain, Argence and Beaucaire: lands that allegedly made up the dowry of his mother Joanna.

The next reference, logically enough, is framed by the siege of Beaucaire, a crucial episode for the young Raymond VII. The anonymous author of the second part of the *Chanson* imagines the comments of one of the closest advisers of the leader of the crusade, Simon de Montfort: 'He is from such a family that he will grow and push himself forward, for Richard was his uncle and Bertrand his relative' (*Chanson*, laisse 160, lines 38–9). Raymond is quite worthy of his lineage. He has inherited all the noble qualities that make him potentially a prince of great worth; this allows him to present himself as necessarily the material and cultural heir to his mother's line. These inherited qualities are the foundation of the prince's moral superiority. The siege ends with the victory of the Toulousan. The young man has proved his mettle and the anonymous author can then conclude:

> And the castle of Beaucaire stays in the hands of the count, duke and marquis because he is valiant and wise, skilful and courtly, [because he comes] from an excellent lineage, related to the powerful house of France and to that of the good king of England.[16]

Raymond's membership of the royal line and his recent victory then make him the legitimate heir, the one who is predestined to bear the triple title of his ancestors. This reiteration of essential virtues is a message of hope, and it is reaffirmed during another siege, one that is just as important for the Raymondines: the third siege of Toulouse (1217–18). Once again the crusader knights evoke the prestigious parentage of the heir presumptive, who is unequivocally, in the hearts of the Toulousans, their legitimate prince: 'Count, duke and marquis Raymond claims it [the city] by birthright, and we know he is right to do so, as is his son, the young count who is the nephew of the king of England.'[17] Finally, just as another battle and another Raymondine victory are being prepared at Baziège, the double royal lineage is stated again by the anonymous author: 'There came out of Toulouse the young count and marquis, of the lineage of the kings of France and England'.[18]

This is obviously artificial, and the author's interest in alliteration has influenced his choice of rhyme words ('marques' . . . 'Engles'), but it does not detract from his overall intent, nor from the dynamic thrust of the message. As will have become clear, the genealogical construction around parentage rests on one key

III (1216–1272), ed. B. K. U. Weiler and I. W. Rowlands (Aldershot, 2002), pp. 67–97 (pp. 77–8).

15 *Chanson*, laisse 148, l. 55; laisse 149, ll. 56–7.

16 'E'l castel de Belcaire a'l coms, dux e marques, / Car es valens e savis e adreitz e cortes / E del milhor linatge e del ric parentes / Del barnatge de Fransa e del bo rei Engles' (*Chanson*, laisse 171, ll. 6–9).

17 'E sos fils lo coms joves, qu'es nebs del rei Engles' (*Chanson*, laisse 202, ll. 77–9).

18 'Es ichitz de Toloza lo coms joves marques, / Del linhatge de Fransa e del bo rei Engles' (*Chanson*, laisse 210, ll. 61–2).

term, *linatge*, a single word that denotes the concept as it was understood by aristocratic groups frequenting the courts of the south. According to this understanding, for the anonymous author and for the princely entourage, royal lineage and political legitimacy are closely linked, and justify the inalienable rights Raymond VII could claim in order to inherit his comital crown.[19] The principle of the continuity of lineage down the direct male line is here conflated with another key word, *eretat*. If the high noble rank of the prince is constantly stated, this is also in order to ensure the enduring political role of the Raymondine dynasty. Declared blood-ties with the royal dynasties of England and of France were important, and had to be reiterated at the crucial moment when the ancestral power of the counts over their Toulousan domains was threatened by the claims of the French. They were an obligatory, categorical proclamation. As a result, the second part of the *Chanson* can be perceived as a lengthy apologia for the legitimacy of Raymond VII's relationship with his native soil, with the lands of his ancestors: that is to say, with his inherited space.

Nephew to the king, descended from the kings of England, Raymond was also the son of Queen Joanna. His father Raymond VI liked to complete his list of titles with a reference to his own maternal ancestry. The documents of his chancery show that he wished to be considered as much 'son of Queen Constance' as 'count of Toulouse, marquis of Provence and duke of Narbonne': 'Ego Raimundus, filius quondam regine Constancie, Dei gratia dux Narbonne, comes Tholose et marchio Provincie.'[20] His heir also used the reference to his royal maternal ancestry from 21 September 1222 when he succeeded his father. This followed a period between 1216 and 1222 in which the young prince's double filiation appeared in the mixed formula 'son of lord Raymond and son of the lady queen Joanna'. As he took power, the new count was to be addressed henceforward as 'the son of queen Joanna'.[21] The lineage affirmed here was that of the Plantagenets. As we have seen in the *Chanson*, this cognatic royal ancestry was foregrounded even in the lifetime of Raymond VI, and two of his charters mention with distinct pride the remarkable origins of his future heir. In an act of December 1208 intended to guarantee the young prince's marriage to the daughter of the count of Clermont and Auvergne, young Raymond is presented by his progenitor as the grandson of the late king of England: 'R. filium nostrum, quem habimus de regina Johanna, filia Henricis Regis quondam Angliæ.' A few years later, in May 1217, several months after young Raymond's victory at Beaucaire, the elderly dynast presented his scion as 'filio meo Raimundo comiti juveni, filio regine Johanne':[22] Raymond the young count, the son of Queen Joanna. Though never addressed in her own charters as the countess of Toulouse (except on her seal) and never sovereign save in the metonymic sense of being *described* as the queen [of Sicily], Joanna's symbolic capital shed dazzling light

19 On lineage as the structuring narrative principle of the epic genre, see R. Howard Bloch, *Etymologies and Genealogies: A Literary Anthropology of the French Middle Ages* (Chicago, 1983), p. 97.

20 Out of 162 tabulated comital titles, 65 state filiation, of which 60 refer exclusively to the mother.

21 Out of 81 titles extant from 1216 to 1229, 51 refer to filiation. 19 are paternal, 15 mixed and 17 maternal (1222–29).

22 Paris, Archives Nationales, J. 304, no. 41; *HGL*, VII, cols. 111–12.

upon the Raymondine dynasty. Soon after their wedding, in November 1196, when Raymond VI confirmed the privileges and customs of Toulouse before its civic representatives, he mentioned his prestigious match with the sister of the Plantagenet sovereign in the following terms: 'after having taken lady Joanna for wife, the sister of the king of England' ('postquam . . . habuit dominam Johannam, sororem Regis Anglie, ductam in uxorem').[23] The wedding ceremony had indeed been a grand occasion, according to William of Newburgh, and its majesty had impressed the minds of many.[24]

The comital entourage's carefully tended and cultivated renown bore valuable fruit for both the princes, and for their progeny. The most striking example is the name Raymond gave his own daughter, Joanna; naming her thus was undeniably the greatest homage he could pay his mother, but it also emphasized his desire to inscribe himself more fully in the Plantagenet legacy. Another echo can be found in the genealogical memory left by the counts. A lineage-based dynastic consciousness can be traced in some thirteenth-century genealogies inserted in annals composed after the death of the last Raymondine count. The first such mention appears in two chronicles composed in Toulouse by clerks who were connected to the administration of Count Raymond VII and his successor Alphonse of Poitiers, and started respectively after September 1249 and after September 1258. These two texts, the first in Occitan, the second in Latin, were included in the registers of the Raymondine chancery and were completed in 1275 and 1289.[25] Rubrics 27, 28 and 29 of both report the wedding in October 1196 of Raymond VI and 'la regina Johanna', the birth of Raymond 'fils de la regina Johanna' and the death of 'Richards, reis d'Englaterra'; rubric 64 records the death of the last Raymondine count, 'the son of Queen Joanna' at Millau in 1249.[26] What the chroniclers recorded, as did most of their contemporaries, was the prestige associated with the royal origins of the last Raymondines.

The second genealogical assertion comes in William of Puylaurens' *Chronicle*, finished in 1276, which was based on the two documents cited above, but also drew on Raymond VII's personal recollections. Of Raymond VI's five marriages, the author mentions only the three that were sanctioned by a live birth. Among all these wives, only Joanna receives extended treatment in an anecdotal passage emphasizing the princess's stubbornness. Whereas Raymond's marriage with the sister of the king of Aragon is evoked briefly, his match with Joanna is treated quite differently by the cleric. Her royal splendour and prestige are once again foregrounded: 'The same count married, in the year of the Lord 1196, the illustrious lady Joanna, the sister of the king of England, Richard.' The chronicler's preference can be explained by the fact that Raymond VI 'had of her my lord Raymond, the last count, in 1197, to whom she gave birth in Beaucaire, in the diocese of Arles'.[27] For in truth the greatest glory that came from Joanna was that

23 *HGL*, VIII, cols. 439–40.

24 J. Flori, *Richard Cœur-de-Lion: Le roi-chevalier* (Paris, 1999), p. 222.

25 P. Cabau, 'Deux chroniques composées à Toulouse dans la seconde moitié du XIIIe siècle', *Mémoires de la Société Archéologique du Midi de la France* 56 (1996), 75–120.

26 *Ibid.*, pp. 91, 104.

27 Guillaume de Puylaurens, *Chronique*, ed. J. Duvernoy (Paris, 1976), pp. 38–9.

she gave the Raymondine dynasty the male heir it needed, and succeeded where all her predecessors had failed.

Finally, the third genealogy is inserted into a *Commentary on the Customs of Toulouse* composed in 1296. It gives a glimpse of one aspect of the city's selective memory, one that recorded only the most salient traits of its rulers. A laconic succession of fourteen counts is given from the origins of the dynasty up to 1271. Raymond VII stands out from this arid, all-male list: 'Tresdecimus comes nominabatur per universum orbem Ramundus et fuit filius domine Johanne sororis Regis Anglie . . .'[28] The commentator even adds that it was in his reign that Simon de Montfort was killed, and by this slip of the pen makes Raymond VII outshine his own father, who was still, at that time, the titular count!

So Raymond was 'the son of queen Joanna' in the eyes of his contemporaries as well as in the memory of chroniclers.[29] That is also how he was described by English historiographers of the thirteenth century, especially Roger of Wendover and Matthew Paris, both of whom belonged to the Benedictine abbey of Saint Albans. The attitude of the Cistercian abbot Ralph of Coggeshall is more surprising, considering this order's passion for attacking the last members of the Toulousan dynasty. In his *Chronicon Anglicanum*, a work he composed in the first quarter of the thirteenth century, Ralph built up a rather positive image of Raymond VII.[30] Admittedly, he also left out young Raymond's expedition over the Channel in the summer of 1215, just before the Fourth Lateran Council. This journey appears in the *Chanson* and the *Chronicle* of William of Puylaurens, who says that Raymond VI 'sent his son to England to see the king his cousin ('consanguineum suum'), to take advice'.[31] His dynastic connections played an active role in the financial assistance given by the king of England to the members of the comital family. According to Ralph of Coggeshall Raymond VI, who 'had married the sister of the king, Joanna', received the sum of ten thousand marks in 1212.[32]

The Aragonese alliance, a product of the fifth and last marriage of Raymond VI, is simply ignored out of an ideologically motivated concern for appealing to the prestigious unions of the past. The *Chronicon*'s first mention of Raymond VII occurs in 1222, the year he came to power. His emergence is treated to a chapter 'De comite Sancti Aegidii'; it symbolizes the dynastic hope for a new start: 'The count of Saint-Gilles, the son of Joanna, lately the queen of Sicily, daughter of Henry II and sister of Kings Richard and John, reclaimed nearly all the cities and lands that had been captured by count Simon de Montfort.'

28 H. Gilles, *Les Coutumes de Toulouse (1286) et leur premier commentaire (1296) (Consuetudines Tholose)* (Toulouse, 1969), pp. 162–3.

29 Some dispute Raymond VII's claims by questioning his blood-tie with Joanna: see Macé, *Les Comtes de Toulouse*, pp. 209–10.

30 K. Wagner, 'La Croisade albigeoise vue par le chroniqueur Raoul de Coggeshale: Une interprétation de l'histoire sous l'angle du "patriotisme" anglais', *Heresis* 35 (2001), 83–9.

31 'There was the count of Toulouse, with his good, handsome son, who had come from England' (*Chanson*, laisse 143, ll. 7–10); *Chronique*, cc. XXIII and XXIV, pp. 90–3. For an exciting recent study, see Vincent, 'England and the Albigensian Crusade', pp. 74–6.

32 Wagner, 'La Croisade albigeoise', p. 85. For a parallel anecdote, see M. Cao Carmichael de Baiglie, 'Savary de Mauléon (*ca* 1180–1233), chevalier-troubadour poitevin: traîtrise et société aristocratique', *Le Moyen Age* 105 (1999), 269–305 (p. 280).

Ralph's portrait of the Toulousan prince is particularly laudatory: 'The count who was strong, young and Catholic, gradually reclaimed his inheritance with a strong, courageous hand.' He describes a prince of great martial valour, who shakes off his father's negative image as a protector of heretics, for Raymond VII, on the contrary, is prepared to cooperate with the Church and Pope Honorius III in their struggle to eradicate heterodoxy. Ralph concludes with an optimistic flourish: 'on the occasion of this mandate, one hoped for peace in this land'.

The Cistercian chronicler makes his sympathies for Raymond VII clear, and presents him as a prince who is closely connected to the Plantagenets thanks to the blood-tie that unites the two houses. The illustrious origins and great qualities of the Toulousan make him the worthy and legitimate heir to his lands; Ralph is forced to conclude that the crusade is no longer worth pursuing. This entry was composed in 1226, during the expedition to the south of King Louis VIII. By writing Raymond VII into his own defence of a particular form of English patriotism, Ralph, like Roger of Wendover and Matthew Paris, criticizes the basis of the crusade at the very moment the king of France is intervening personally in the matter, and threatens the king of England's interests west of the Garonne.[33] The siege and massacre of Marmande in 1219 are proof that there was such a side to the campaign. In fact, as early as 1214, when Simon de Montfort went into the Agenais (a long-standing Plantagenet possession), King John, who was in the region, took action by marching up to La Réole. In June of that year, John had sent troops led by his chamberlain to defend Marmande and, after raising an army in the region of Périgueux, threatened to take military action against the commander of the crusading army besieging Casseneuil, for he was, according to Peter of Les-Vaux-de-Cernay, 'dismayed by the dispossession of his nephew, the son of the count of Toulouse'.[34] His words were not followed up with deeds, but they show that the conflict between the Capetians and Plantagenets resurfaced, and had a strong impact on the southern regions.[35]

Lo valens coms joves (the Valiant Young Count): the Prince as Hero

Illustrious of rank, of royal birth, the last count also enjoyed youth, a physical and moral quality foregrounded by all his contemporaries. Youth (*Jovens*) was an ambiguous quality, for it was the lynchpin of the courtly system of values, and it supported the subtle construction of a heroic image for the prince – but it was also a very late attempt to fill a yawning gap in the ideological programme of the Raymondines.

The great princely houses of the twelfth century, particularly those of kings, found profit in appropriating the great figures of the past in order to root their

33 Wagner, 'La Croisade albigeoise', pp. 86–9.

34 Pierre des Vaux-de-Cernay [Petrus Sarnensis], *Histoire Albigeoise*, trans. P. Guébin and H. Maisonneuve (Paris, 1951), § 505, p. 194; § 518, p. 198; § 522, pp. 199–200. See also the recent English translation by W. A. and M. D. Sibly, *The History of the Albigensian Crusade* (Woodbridge, 1998).

35 Vincent, 'England and the Albigensian Crusade', pp. 78f.

power in ancestral memory. Thanks to a talented circle of Cluniac historiographers, the Capetians adopted the figure of Charlemagne, and gave themselves a remarkable ancestry. At the same time, Henry II and his collaborators established a far-reaching ideological construction that rested on the revival of Arthurian myth. There was no such historiographic reference to a putative dynastic hero at the court of the counts of Toulouse, just as in other courts of southern France. Thomas Bisson has shown that some genealogical lists do appear in the second half of the twelfth century, notably in Gascony, but this archival memory is nothing compared to the prologue of the *Gesta comitum Barcinonensium et reges Aragonensium* (composed before 1184), where the legendary figure of Guifred the Hairy, ancestor to the Catalan dynasty, is depicted as the victorious leader of wars against both the Franks and the Muslims.[36] This work by the Benedictines of Santa Maria de Ripoll has no equivalent on the other side of the Pyrenees, where no such historiographical 'workshops' existed. Southern scriptoria were more concerned with the history of their own churches than with those of secular rulers: none entered the service of the Raymondine counts, whether voluntarily or by command, to concoct an official history. Although Raymond V (1148–94) makes occasional appearances in the chronicles of the church of Nîmes or of the basilica of Saint-Sernin of Toulouse, there is no question here of celebrating his courage, nor of glorifying his chivalric qualities. The ecclesiastical chroniclers were engaged in compilations, not in dynastic histories. Their interests, and those of the Raymondines, did not converge to the point of generating an original text in which the leading role would have gone to some princely hero who would have allowed the lineage to adorn itself with his qualities, and to bask in his reflected and effulgent glory.

There is, however, one exception. Devoid of an epic hero or ancestral figurehead, our writers might have turned to the real, famous, and prestigious character that was Raymond IV, whose descendants always invoked his name. In this light, Raymond of Aguilers' *History of the Franks who captured Jerusalem* could be considered as an attempt at a 'heroization' of Raymond IV; but thanks to recent work by German scholars, we now know that this is a retrospective work dating from the late twelfth century, and that its primary objective is not to present the count of Saint-Gilles as the perfect model of the valiant and pious *miles Christi*.[37] There is also a question mark over another work, the epic *Canso d'Antioca*, in which Raymond IV could have been ascribed a leading role. However, only a short fragment of 707 alexandrine lines subsists of the Occitan text, composed around 1130, and attributed to the Limousin knight Gregory Bechada.[38] This poem recounting the exploits of the first crusaders in the East must have given significant attention to Raymond IV, as champion of the faith and as the leader

36 T. N. Bisson, 'L'essor de la Catalogne: identité, pouvoir et idéologie dans une société du XIIe siècle', *Annales: Économies, Sociétés, Civilisations* 39 (1984), 454–79; *idem*, 'Unheroed Pasts: History and Commemoration in South Frankland before the Albigensian Crusades', *Speculum* 65 (1990), 281–308.

37 See B. Schuster, 'Raimond d'Aguilers: Un chantre de l'hérésie générale avant l'heure?', *Heresis* 36–7 (2002), 161–81.

38 G. Hasenohr and M. Zink, *Dictionnaire des lettres françaises: Le Moyen Âge* (Paris, 1992), p. 222.

of the southern armies, and as the memorable fellow combatant of Duke Godfrey of Bouillon.[39] This glorificatory enterprise must have been still more emphatic in the *Song of Saint-Gilles*, of which only a few fragments survive. In the early thirteenth century, echoes could still be heard of these ideas: William of Tudela composed the *Chanson* with the *Canso d'Antioca* as his model, and his anonymous successor refers to the count of Saint-Gilles in the first *laisse* of his continuation.[40] They thus inscribe the Raymondines in the direct descent of that glorious prince, and in a context that is also that of another crusade, one so different from that of 1209. It is worth noting too that some fifty years later, William Anelier modelled the form of his *History of the War of Navarre* on both the *Chanson* and the *Canso d'Antioca*.[41]

In fact, the Toulousan princes did not inspire texts that could have enabled them to cite mythical ancestors whose prestige extended to the entire lineage. Their comital abbeys, such as those of Vabres and Saint-Pons-de-Thomières, were not particularly active (in literary terms) during the twelfth century and would have had trouble appropriating the legendary figure of William of Orange, who was the object of great efforts by the Benedictine abbeys of Aniane and Gellone, where the *Vita sancti Wilhelmi* was composed around 1125–29. Moreover, this holy warrior was exploited in Provence during the twelfth century by the powerful family of the Baux – Orange.[42] The Raymondine dynasty was the product of an opportunistic succession in the mid-ninth century,[43] and was built on almost permanent opposition to William's descendants, something that forbade any recuperation on their part of Charlemagne's emblematic cousin. However, a William is listed as the third count in the genealogy of the *Commentary on the Customs of Toulouse*.[44] Could this be the emperor's cousin? The

39 Raymond IV's great fame in the Midi lasts into the fourteenth century. A note inserted in the *Bazas Chronicle* reports that a knight, Gaillard de Tontoulon, followed the count of Toulouse to the East as his seneschal ('senescallus et gubernator comitis Tolosani'): F. Boutoulle, 'De La Réole à Jérusalem: Les participants à la première croisade originaires du Bazadais et du Bordelais (1096–1099)', in *L'Entre-deux-mers et son identité* (La Réole, 2002), p. 13. There is no other source for a Gaillard of Tontoulon at the time of Raymond IV, and the office of seneschal is not attested in the comital entourage until 1210. However, a certain Guilhem-Arnaud of Tontoulon was seneschal of the Agenais on behalf of Raymond VI from 1217 to 1222. This is late evidence for a crystallization of family legends around the figure of Raymond IV.

40 R. Lafont, *La Geste de Roland*, 2 vols. (Paris, 1991), II (*Espaces, Textes, Pouvoirs*), p. 223 ; E. M. Ghil, *L'Âge de Parage: Essai sur le poétique et le politique en Occitanie au XIIIe siècle* (New York, Bern, Frankfurt and Paris, 1989), pp. 184–5. There is also an allusion to crusades in the Holy Land through the mention of Raymond IV's son Bertrand, the great-uncle of Raymond VII (*Chanson*, laisse 160, l. 39).

41 Hasenohr and Zink, *Dictionnaire des lettres françaises*, p. 595.

42 F. Mazel, 'Mémoire héritée, mémoire inventée: Guilhem de Baux, prince d'Orange, et la légende de Guillaume d'Orange (XIIe–XIIIe siècles)', in *Faire mémoire: Souvenir et commémoration au Moyen Âge*, ed. C. Carozzi and H. Taviani-Carozzi (Aix-en-Provence, 1999), pp. 193–227; idem, 'Le prince, le saint et le héros: Guilhem de Baux (1173–1218) et Guillaume de Gellone *alias* Guillaume d'Orange', in *Guerriers et moines: Conversion et sainteté aristocratiques dans l'Occident medieval (IXe–XIIe siècle)*, ed. M. Lauwers (Antibes, 2002), pp. 449–65.

43 In 849, he was betrayed by Fredelon, count of Rouergue and lieutenant of marquis Guilhem. The city of Toulouse was handed to Charles the Bald, who gave him the county of Toulouse as a reward.

44 Gilles, *Coutumes de Toulouse*, pp. 161–2.

suggestion would seem to be borne out by the fact that the fourth count in the list is Raymond I, the eponymous ancestor of the lineage, who lived in the reign of Charles the Bald. This would imply that the notables of Toulouse sought to place the Raymondines in a direct line of descent from the Carolingian hero – but this is a marginal reference from the late thirteenth century, so it goes beyond the scope of this chapter.

Can this absence of writing and of epic poetry be explained by there being no clergy attached to the Raymondines by blood, feudal loyalty or patronage? Was the pool of *curiales* fed only by laymen little inspired to produce court literature of any true value? Whatever the reason might have been, until the thirteenth century there is no extant text, no *Gesta*, no *Chanson de Guillaume* and no romance of *Jaufré* invented for the use of the comital court of Toulouse. If it proved unfruitful to turn to the dead, only the living remained as a suitable resource: this was the task undertaken by troubadours and Raymondine court poets.[45]

Let us then return to a real person, Raymond VII. He took centre-stage even during his father's lifetime, and presented himself to his vassals and the population of his domains years before his accession, in a clear break with the policies of the twelfth-century counts.[46] The anonymous author of the *Chanson*'s chief task was to promote the son of the reigning count as his legitimate heir, something that has led some to call the second part of the poem the *Song of Raymond VII*,[47] the equivalent of Philip Augustus' *Philippide*.

A prince of Youth in the troubadour scale of values, Raymond also embodied the ideal. His youth was sometimes underlined by changing his name to the obviously hypocoristic form *Raimondet*.[48] This altered form, 'little Raymond', is both familiar and affectionate. Indeed, the *Chanson* makes frequent references to the *tozet* (youth) and even the *enfans* (child). At the siege of Beaucaire, despite the comments of his entourage, Simon de Montfort refers to him as a child, even though he is a youth aged nearly nineteen.[49] This is clearly a literary device aiming to show a child's humiliating defeat of the head of the crusade; the image is much more apposite when it is used by the 'bishop of Rome' to recall that at the time of the massacre of Béziers, Raymond VII was an innocent child (*enfans*) who was only interested in the pleasures of hunting. Now a young man ('avinens tos'), he cannot be held responsible for the errors of his father.[50] The anonymous author's legitimizing discourse can be discerned through these effective scenes, where the terms employed are anything but chosen at random.[51] Once the references to the son (*filh*) of the count are analysed, they can be found to show that

45 Macé, *Les Comtes de Toulouse*, pp. 300–10.

46 *Ibid.*, pp. 69–70.

47 This is argued by Lafont, *La Geste de Roland*, II, 257.

48 Raymond VI states this to the circle of councillors he has appointed for his son: *Chanson*, laisse 155, l. 9.

49 Simon is annoyed by Alain de Roucy's comment that Raymond is neither 'ni tozets ni efans': *Chanson*, laisse 160, ll. 34, 40.

50 *Chanson*, laisse 149, ll. 48–53; laisse 143, l. 13.

51 L. M. Paterson, *The World of the Troubadours: Medieval Occitan Society, c.1100–1300* (Cambridge, 1993), p. 283.

until the scene at the Fourth Lateran Council, the eighteen-year-old Raymond is almost always called *enfans*.[52] There is a change of tone after Raymond leaves the papal court, for even in the same laisse the author names him 'count' for the first time (*Chanson*, laisse 152, line 66). The following laisse moves to the beginning of the military campaign in Provence and the siege of Beaucaire. After his triumphal welcome into Avignon, the prince heads for his birthplace, accompanied by Gui de Cavaillon. Their discussion is, significantly, about *Paratge*, but even before this subject is addressed, the prince has acquired new stature, no longer a mere child, for he is now the *coms joves*, the 'young count' (*Chanson*, laisse 154, lines 7 and 18). As the vassals of Provence gather, the anonymous author promotes Raymond to 'count, duke and marquis, of the lineage of Alfonso'. This is a count barely emerging from childhood, but possessed of sufficient mettle to lay claim to the lands of his lineage: 'He fights for the right to his land, that still-adolescent (*tozetz*) count-duke.'[53]

Indeed, in the anonymous section, the description of the siege of Beaucaire sets the scene for Raymond's future exploits as a knight, introduced at the start of laisse 154 'by a troubadour lyric incipit, featuring a spring morning, as the youth of the world greets the youth of the hero'.[54] Count Raymond VII is born in Beaucaire physically, then (at this point, undeniably) militarily, politically and in literary terms. His prestige takes shape at the foot of the rocky peak overlooking the Rhône, even if the success he finds there is debatable in many ways.[55] He is haloed by his glory at Beaucaire and becomes the hope of the Midi, a vision of the future embodied by new blood. The heir to his father's hopes, his apprenticeship over, he is now 'lo valens coms joves'.[56]

There is no need to expand on the topos of *Joven*, a multi-stranded courtly virtue oft-defined by the troubadours,[57] save in analysing the use and representation made of it by the comital entourage through the anonymous section of the *Chanson*. This author interprets reality through a strongly defining filter of poetic licence. He uses Raymond's physical and moral youth to construct an image of him as a knightly prince, a warlike man of action; this is set in opposition to the sedentary, word-dealing ruler, his pale reflection. He becomes Raymond the Younger, opposed to the excommunicated, defeated and disinherited Raymond the Elder. His courage and prowess are at loggerheads with his father's 'elderly' prudence. The *Chanson* illustrates, embellishes and amplifies these binary oppositions. For example, the author contrasts Raymond VI's unsuccessful

52 *Chanson*, laisse 38, l. 7; laisse 150, ll. 16, 32 (*totz*), 38 (*hom joves*), 40; laisse 151, l. 33; laisse 152, ll. 1, 14, 17, 38, 51.

53 '[C]oms dux e marques, del linatge n'Anfos; le coms dux qu'es tozetz' (*Chanson*, laisse 154, l. 82); 'La terra li calomja le coms dux qu'es tozetz' (laisse 155, l. 1) (my emended translation).

54 Lafont, *La Geste de Roland*, II, 253 (trans. above by translator).

55 L. Macé, 'Beaucaire (fin mai–24 août 1216)', in *Les grandes batailles méridionales: Mieux vaut mort que vif vaincu (XIIIe siècle)* (Toulouse, 2004) (forthcoming).

56 'Coms jove': *Chanson*, laisse 154, l. 59; laisse 155, ll. 4, 47; laisse 160, l. 34; laisse 162, ll. 11, 79; laisse 204, l. 117; laisse 214, l. 60. 'Valens coms joves': laisse 160, l. 7: laisse 161, l. 30; laisse 162, l. 74; laisse 167, l. 37; laisse 198, l. 12; laisse 208, l. 101; laisse 212, l. 1.

57 G. M. Cropp, *Le vocabulaire courtois des troubadours de l'époque classique* (Geneva, 1975), pp. 413–21; C. Marchello-Nizia, 'Chevalerie et courtoisie', in *Histoire des jeunes en Occident: De l'Antiquité à l'époque moderne*, ed. G. Levi and J.-C. Schmitt, 2 vols. (Paris, 1996), I, 147–97.

attempt to stop his men making a sortie at the first siege of Toulouse, with the behaviour of his son when Foucaud of Berzy is caught near Baziège, and the valiant Raymondet's men try to stop him seeking one-to-one combat with him.[58] One stalls and the other bursts from his bonds ('es descadenatz') (*Chanson*, laisses 81–2 and laisse 211, line 116). During this battle, Raymond's personal intervention receives an epic description:

> Then came the young count, riding ahead of his men, impetuous like a lion or a leopard unchained. His black horse carries him well. He arrived, his lance carried low and his head bowed beneath the helm, right where he could see the thickest scrum and mêlée of fighters. He struck John of Berzy, who had come forward, and hit him so hard with his inlaid spear that, piercing his silken surcoat, hauberk and his undergarment, he made him fall backwards, and went past him, crying, 'Toulouse!' (*Chanson*, laisse 211, lines 115–24)

The prince's brilliant exploits set him apart from the mass of fighters while his valour is crucial to the cohesion of his *companhia*, his group, and therefore to their victory. What proves this is his success in one-to-one combat with one of the most dangerous of the Toulousans' enemies, a scene through which the text underlines the young count's potential for becoming the model hero of his era.[59] His noble entourage could project their fantasies onto this image of a leader of men, and find inspiration in it. There is a similarity with the reverse side of the comital seal, on which the combatant prince is depicted charging with his lance under his arm. His fellow combatants could identify with this ideal of being his knight-companions.

Raymond's green youth echoes the springtime renewal theme of troubadour poetry. He radiates natural strength, a power born of a spontaneity evinced by the speeches he makes before Beaucaire and Baziège. In this way, the prince's youth became a major source of hope for the southern populations and the nobility at court. It was presumed to present a guarantee of moral purity, as Raymondet was not compromised by heresy and could not be saddled with the sins of his predecessor. So the future count is inscribed once more in continuity of both lineage and dynastic legitimacy. But he is also a sign of change. His special association with *Paratge*, a virtue he will maintain and revive, is a promise of a new era; the anonymous author's count is a unifying figure whose authority goes beyond the basic fidelity owed him by his disparate vassals. His subjects now include those who believe him to be the incarnation of the value system threatened by the invading crusader-knights and those churchmen who accompany them. The poem presents a reassuring image, also found in the poems of Guilhem

58 King Richard's entourage are equally anxious before the battle of Arsuf (Flori, *Richard Cœur-de-Lion*, pp. 383–4). The Plantagenet shares Raymond VII's high idea of the personal, exemplary involvement of the prince (see Raymond's speech before the battle).

59 Does this passage allude to another 'young man', Henry the Young King? See L. M. Paterson, 'La *Chanson de la croisade albigeoise*: mythes chevaleresques et réalités militaires', in *La Croisade: Réalités et fictions*, ed. D. Buschinger (Göppingen, 1989), pp. 193–203 (p. 196). Paterson's suggestion that there is no 'professional' ethic in the *Chanson* (p. 198) is debatable, as before the battle at Baziège, Raymond's entourage tries to dissuade him from fighting a social inferior, Foucaud of Berzy. A reassessment of the concept of chivalry in this work is needed.

de Montanhagol, of a strong, just and worthy ruler: 'Every man must love with a pure love ('amistat pura') and loyally serve his good lord. As for the lord, he must truly ('bonamen') love his people, for Loyalty bids them love one another so sincerely that there might be no room for Falsehood between them.'[60]

The Radiance of *Paratge*

Raymond does more than conform to the accepted idea of honour, and the anonymous author's construction goes beyond any conventional view of a 'horizon of expectations'. He is the standard-bearer for courtly and chivalric values, and he is a prince who, unlike his father, asserts his rights with his sword in his hand. The qualities of the count of Toulouse also take on a dimension that is not shared by his fellow princes, for in the anonymous author's poem, the Raymondines are the only noble line closely connected with *Paratge*. This abstraction, known to the troubadours, acquires a new meaning in the *Chanson*, for it contributes an ideological complement to the idea of innate nobility of blood, by adding qualities of the heart and mind. The early studies by Bagley and Rostaing have been developed by Peter Ricketts, Eliza Ghil and Francesco Zambon, to show that the notions found in the concept of *Paratge*, those of nobility, lineage, high rank and attachement to inherited lands, take on the dimensions of an allegorical conflict.[61] The term appears over fifty times, unglossed, in the anonymous poem.

One passage in the poem seems to summarize the polysemic nature of this umbrella term. At the start of laisse 154, Gui de Cavaillon and Raymondet engage in a *tenson* (debate) as they prepare to enter Avignon. The frame is that of an initiatory journey for the count from Rome to Beaucaire, via Marseille and Avignon.[62] It heralds the start of his adventure in the medieval sense of the word, for the siege of Beaucaire is outlined for him. The young count will have to prove himself before the battle, by solving the questions put to him by someone who is, remarkably, a troubadour-knight.[63] Gui opens by stating, 'Now is the time where

60 *Les Poésies de Guilhem de Montanhagol: troubadour provençal du XIIIe siècle*, ed. P. Ricketts (Toronto, 1964), 'Per lo mon fan li un dels autres rancura', *PC* 225, 12, XIV, ll. 35–40. On love between the prince and his men, see L. Macé, 'Amour et fidélité: le comte de Toulouse et ses hommes (XIIe–XIIIe siècles)', in *Les Sociétés méridionales à l'âge féodal (Espagne, Italie et sud de la France X^e–XIIIe s.): Hommage à Pierre Bonnassie* (Toulouse, 1999), pp. 299–304.

61 C.-P. Bagley, '*Paratge* in the Anonymous', *French Studies* 21 (1967), 195–204; C. Rostaing, 'Le vocabulaire courtois dans la deuxième partie de la *Chanson*', in *Mélanges de linguistique, de philologie et de littérature offerts à Albert Henry* (Strasbourg, 1970), pp. 249–63; P. Ricketts, 'The *Chanson* of the Albigensian Crusade: Literature and Patriotism', in *Proceedings of the Second Conference on Medieval Occitan Language and Literature* (Birmingham, 1982), pp. 63–82; Ghil, *L'Âge de Parage*, pp. 151–218; F. Zambon, 'La notion de *Paratge*, des troubadours à la *Chanson de la croisade albigeoise*', in *Les Voies de l'hérésie: le groupe aristocratique en Languedoc (XIe–XIIIe siècles): Actes du 8e colloque du Centre d'Études Cathares-René Nelli, Carcassonne, 28 août–1er septembre 1995*, 3 vols. (Millau, 2001), III, 9–27.

62 G. Gouiran, 'De *Joven* à *Paratge* ou l'intégration du futur Raimond VII dans l'univers des troubadours', in *Terres et hommes du Sud, 126e congrès du Comité des Travaux Historiques et Scientifiques (Toulouse, avril 2001)* (forthcoming).

63 Ghil, *L'Âge de Parage*, pp. 185–6; M. Aurell, 'Le troubadour Gui de Cavaillon (vers 1175–vers 1229): un acteur nobiliaire de la croisade albigeoise', in *Les Voies de l'hérésie*, II, 9–36.

Paratge needs you to be both good and wicked', and ends with the remark, 'Either all *Paratge* will have to die, or you will have to be valorous!' Raymond's reply is wise and firm: 'My right is so great, my cause so just that, if my enemies are steadfast and brave, for each one of them that is a leopard, I shall be a lion!' (*Chanson*, laisse 154, lines 7–8, 17, 25–7). Raymond will defend his inherited lands and will also safeguard the ethic produced by that land. *Paratge* is cited eight times in this twenty-line exchange, seven times by Gui de Cavaillon, with a single goal: once the term becomes part of Raymondet's speech, it can be said to have been formally taken on by him. This reveals the initiatory aspect of the conversation, and it allows the transition between childhood and the adult defence of courtly, chivalric and political values thought by the population as a whole to be threatened by the crusading forces. Raymondet can now draw together all the living forces that share the values he has reaffirmed. The pact that unites him with *Paratge* allows him to transcend mere fealty, and its consequences appear at once, as he makes a triumphant entry into Avignon. The crowd is so dense that it has to be beaten away with sticks, and a courtly banquet underlines the collective joy. The laisse concludes with a list of noblemen prepared to fight at the young count's side to force the French out of Beaucaire.

It is worth noting that the association between Raymond and *Paratge* is set in a springtime context replete with metaphors of flowering and light.[64] What in French is termed the *reverdie* is a topos of seasonal renewal, one of the key themes of troubadour poetry, but here it has an Edenic quality, giving hope of reunion in the terrestial paradise. Raymond VI and his son's actions are given an undeniably messianic, almost christological character, as can be seen in their entries into Toulouse in 1217 and 1218. As Zambon has shown, the anonymous author's concept of *Paratge* is built on unambiguously orthodox Christian ideas. Zambon's religious interpretation can be capped with another, compatible gloss. It is striking that the two Raymonds are often associated with such images as 'the morning star (*estela*), a planet that has acquired new light, for here is our long-lost lord', 'the ray of the star ("lo rays de l'estela") has lit up the darkness'. We find 'a flower (*flor*) that illumines the darkness and spreads its light', and 'all fixed their gaze upon the count, as on the flower of the rose bush'; we also find 'the young count who is our light ("nostra clardatz")', and finally: 'the valiant young count, who restores the colour green to the world, who makes shining and golden that which was darkened'.[65] It would be both inadvisable and unnecessary to indulge in esoteric speculation, for these images allude to established themes in courtly lyric poetry, and more significantly to the binary symbols visible for the most part on the seals and coinage of the counts: the moon and the sun.[66] (The Raymondine sun is rather protean, as we know from an extant *vidimus*, as it was also read as a star with either six or eight rays.)[67] The counts of Toulouse are not

64 Cited by Zambon, 'La Notion de *Paratge*', pp. 22–3.

65 *Chanson*, laisse 182, ll. 74–5; laisse 188, l. 81; laisse 191, ll. 51–2; laisse 201, l. 61; laisse 204, l. 117; laisse 208, ll. 101–2.

66 The cross, star and crescent moon feature on the counts' *deniers*. For discussion of the *raimondins* minted in the Rhône valley, and of comital seals, see Macé, *Les Comtes de Toulouse*, pp. 292–300.

67 A vidimus of 1278 states: 'quoddam cancellum lune et stellam . . . quædam stella et quidam cancellus lunæ': A. Laval, *Velorgues au comté Venaissin* (Avignon, 1919), p. 231. A vidimus of

the only princes in Europe to use the sun and the moon on their seals but their entourage seems to have been unique in exploiting them. These themes appear to have been familiar to members of the southern aristocracy. The Raymondine seals travelled widely and visibly: for example, before the siege of Beaucaire, the young count sends sealed letters to call his allies (*Chanson*, laisse 155, line 47). Allusions of this kind would have been clear to some of the poem's listeners.

While extravagant theorizing has to be avoided, it seems that in these very specific instances the symbolic and the emblematic met and were conflated. Traditional allegories borrowed from the troubadour system of values are augmented in the *Chanson* with allegories based on heraldry,[68] and this is used to develop a simple psychomachia ('Battle of the Vices and Virtues') between the two key protagonists, the cross of the house of Toulouse and the lion of the Montforts.[69] The opposition between the emblems is reinforced by religious connotations; the anonymous author is quick to point out the remarkable fact that this revered cross is the emblem of those who are attacked by the crusade;[70] but this cross is 'la crotz ramondenca': the Raymondine cross.[71] So a basic allusion to the planets depicted on the comital seal is inscribed in the symbolic development of this 'war of abstractions',[72] which becomes a near-dualist opposition between the Raymondines and Simon de Montfort. The poem's description of the count's theophanic entry into Toulouse of 1218 resumes these ideas in a few lines: 'a luminous star, the star that rises in the morning above the mountain: the valiant young count, the light and the heir, enters by the gate, bearing the cross and the sword with him' (*Chanson*, laisse 201, lines 47–9). The anonymous author presses the point, as there follows the only miracle in the second part of the poem, a sign announcing the death of the 'murderous lion'. As the prince enters the city, Simon's lion banner falls into the Garonne, the city's natural defence. Once more, the heraldic combat turns to Toulouse's advantage: light has burst forth and blinded the proud animal.

Such images make it possible to see allusions to seals and coinage, and perhaps even a form of onomastic allegory, in the anonymous author's section, for the prince has a duty to honour the name he has inherited from his ancestors. This is discernible in a *sirventes* composed after 1229 by the troubadour Peire Cardenal.

1275 describes 'at the top a sun or a star': Latin text in J. Chevalier, *Mémoires pour servir à l'histoire des comtés de Valentinois et de Diois*, 2 vols. (Paris, 1897), I, 195.

68 The anonymous poet treats heraldic figures with much more attention than colours. This could be because the colours of the arms of the Montforts and the Raymondines were similar: *gules* (red) with cross in *or* (gold) for Toulouse, *gules* with lion in *argent* (silver) for Simon de Montfort.

69 'The cross progresses and the lion loses ground', *Chanson*, laisse 160, l. 9; 'For the cross alone feeds the lion with blood, and fills him up with freshly spilt brains', laisse 188, ll. 79–80; '. . . and the lion falls into the water and the riverbed', laisse 201, l. 54.

70 Ghil, *L'Âge de Parage*, p. 174.

71 *Chanson*, laisse 109, l. 5. The *deniers* of the marquisate of Provence, which bore a cross, were also called *raimondins*. The close connection between the name of the count and his emblem was the locus of monetary rivalry, with a marked heraldic element, during the later twelfth century: see J.-C. Moesgaard, 'Surfrappes en Provence au XIIe siècle: la guerre monétaire entre le comté et le marquisat', *Bulletin de la société française de numismatique* 6 (1994), 874–6.

72 Zambon, 'La Notion de *Paratge*', p. 18.

In the *tornada* (short closing stanza) of 'Ben volgra, si Dieus o volgués', he presents a short etymological and aural gloss on the name of Raymond:

> And since his valour stands up to everything,/ his nobility rises so high above the world,/ that he is known as the 'count-duke';/ For his very name signifies it,/ that says: Light-of-the-World.[73]

Rai-mon, the light of the world, makes for a powerful, allusive etymology and its lexical field seems most accessible to this troubadour. It is a simple analogy, and one that proclaims the count's destiny. Could this light pouring from him and enlightening the world not be the christological light radiating through the anonymous poem? The light of the star shining in the darkness refers at once to the *Paratge*-count, his symbolic name and the two planets of his seal, evoking the light of both day and night: the light of the world. This alludes to the count as springtime (as the reference to a star as a flower shows), the count of renewal. It also refers to the light that restores the truth of the legitimate and ancestral rights of a dynasty over its lands and people. This positive light symbolizes the moral purity and perfection in the image of the young count. There is an echo of this idea of a beam of radiant light in the *Commentary on the Customs of Toulouse*, where Raymond VII is described thus: 'Tresdecimus comes nominabatur per universum orbem Ramundus.' Such playful images, also based on fragmenting the sound of the names of princes to derive a moral meaning, appear in other court poets' *sirventes*. For example, the anonymous troubadour who addresses a *conselh* to King Frederick III of Sicily (1296–1337) reminds the sovereign that 'Frederick means: the bridle on the powerful' ('Fredericx/ vol aitan dir com fres de ricx').[74]

The anonymous poem is original in more than one respect, as well as being a conduit for a new aristocratic ideology. Where Richard the Lionheart created a new type of sovereign by becoming the archetype of the knightly king through his assimilation and incarnation of knightly values,[75] Raymond VII's entourage of intellectuals drew on this model but went beyond it to construct another archetype, that of the prince as light, a compound image based on profane and sacred features. Indeed, Ghil has noted the lack of clergy in the southern camp, whereas prelates are found in the crusader army.[76] This does not make our Toulousan author anti-clerical,[77] but it deserves a mention because it confirms a

73 'E pos sa valors tot afron, / Sobremonta tant sobre-l mon / La sia senhoria, / Que de comte-duc a renom, / Que-l noms o signifia, / Que ditz: Rai-mon,' in *Poésies complètes du troubadour Peire Cardenal (1180–1278)*, ed. R. Lavaud (Toulouse, 1957), *PC* 335, 12, XV, ll. 51–6; for suggested interpretations, see p. 68 n. 56. In the famous poem against Rome by Guilhem Figueira, 'D'un sirventes far en est son que m'agenssa' (*PC* 217, 2), Christ the saviour is called the Light of the World: 'Cel qu'es lutz del mon' (l. 106): M. de Riquer, *Los Trovadores: Historia literaria y textos*, 3 vols. (Barcelona, 1999), III, 1272–9.

74 M. Aurell, *La Vielle et l'épée: Troubadours et politique en Provence au XIIIe siècle* (Paris, 1989), pp. 231–2 and p. 338 n. 99.

75 Flori, *Richard Cœur-de-Lion*, p. 282.

76 Ghil, *L'Âge de Parage*, pp. 170–3.

77 Troubadours had a double education, both secular and clerical; it would be a mistake to treat the two as diametrical opposites: see C. Amado, 'Clercs et moines dans la sphère courtoise

conclusion I had already reached in my study of administrative documents: the comital entourage had few clerics. It is therefore easy to understand that the Raymondines may have felt the need to call on God, the Virgin or St Sernin directly, while also needing to fill a gap by creating an 'ideological and stylistic subterfuge' that led in the *Chanson* to the image of a prince of light endorsed by a god of *Paratge*.[78] *Paratge* becomes the God that protects the heir, and in return, Raymond VII is entrusted with protecting *Paratge*. This non-clerical universe allows religious concepts to slide into the secular domain. The count of Toulouse is invested with a transcendental project, thanks to the deployment of messianic hyperbole, of being the saviour of his vassals. He becomes the mediator and bearer of the cross, the equal of Christ, simply by virtue of being the natural lord, and natural count, as the author states repeatedly.[79] Such a daring, original project illustrates the unique political situation of the Toulousan dynasty, for the relationship the young count enjoys with his God is not the same as that of his opponent, Simon de Montfort, *miles Christi*, champion of the institutional Church and of the Cistercian order. The Toulousan restores *Paratge*, the receptacle of transferred courtly values, while the Frenchman restores the peace and faith of Rome. As the light of the moon and the sun, essential to the birth and the continuation of the world, Raymond is set in opposition to the dark forces that threaten to swallow him up.

This 'light of the world' was still a source of hope in the 1240s, when Raymond VII and his cousin Henry III tried to oppose the king of France, but it dwindled thereafter and vanished for good in September 1249. In his will, the count of Toulouse asked to be buried at Fontevraud, 'where there lie King Henry our grandfather, King Richard our uncle and Queen Joanna our mother, at the feet of this our mother'.[80] The Toulousan prince wished to be buried outside his native soil, in the necropolis of his prestigious ancestors. Should we see Raymond VII as an Aquitanian Toulousan? Or as a Toulousan Angevin? More importantly, the affirmation of lineage matters most in this last gesture. Shortly before his death, Raymond VII had had the tombs of his ancestors in Saint-Sernin rearranged. Four early Christian sarcophagi were placed on columns bearing the shield of the cross of Toulouse.[81] This is a late but undeniable construction of dynastic sentiment, one involving the use of the Raymondine cross as an emblem of Toulouse, and as dynastic affirmation. A genuine as well as an ideal Toulousan identity, experienced both collectively and individually, is built around the count, who is

(XIIe–XIIIe siècle)', in *Église et culture en France méridionale (XIIe–XIVe siècle)*, CF 35 (2000), 127–36; G. Brunel-Lobrichon, 'La formation des troubadours, hommes de savoir', in the same volume, pp. 137–48.

78 *Paraticum*, which could be the source of *paratge*, has connotations of defence, protection and guarantee.

79 Ghil, *L'Âge de Parage*, pp. 177–81.

80 Teulet, III, no. 3802, p. 78. In fact, he was buried a few metres away from her: see A. Erlande-Brandenburg, 'Les gisants de Fontevrault', *303: Revue des Pays de la Loire, Arts, Recherches et Créations* 18 (1988), 27.

81 H. Débax and M. de Framond, 'Les comtes de Toulouse aux Xe et XIe siècles et leurs lieux d'inhumation', in *Le comte de l'an mil, Aquitania, Supplément* 8, ed. C. Dieulafait and E. Crubézy (Talence, 1996), pp. 11–49 (p. 44).

presented as a prince who can gather the population around him. Such was the project of the entourage of Raymond VII, especially of the anonymous poet.

Let us return then to that anonymous author: his narrative aim is to construct a hero capable of inciting his men to defeat his opponents, and thus to live in an unbroken continuity with his ancestral past. This desire however is part of a project linked to a specific historical context. The date of this work is a key issue, for it changes the perspective of the author's message, and the image he constructs when he develops a work set in opposition to the first part of the poem. The proposed date of composition is traditionally given as 1228, because of a reference it contains to the death of Guy de Montfort on 31 January 1228.[82] There has never been a real debate over the suggestion that this passage may be an interpolation, but it can be mentioned here, because in my opinion 1228 is simply too late. By that time, the nobility and population of Toulouse were weakened by nearly twenty years of warfare and were no longer in any position to support their legitimate prince. The poem would no longer have been of immediate interest to its audience. On the other hand, the anonymous author's enterprise makes much more sense in the context of the years 1219 and 1220, when Raymond the Younger was still an emblem of hope for many. For him, it was a question of ensuring the future at a time when his dynasty and his own inheritance were compromised by the crusade. The death of the titular count, Simon de Montfort, gave him the possibility of changing the situation, because Amaury de Montfort had not yet handed his rights over to the king of France. A reinvention of *Paratge* at that date would make ideological and political sense. All was still possible for the Raymondine, and he could accordingly encourage the composition of a hopeful poem, one that turned him into an exceptional and exemplary figure.

The *Chanson* gives much space to the young, and to youth. The men cited among the protagonists are the sons of the counts of Foix, Toulouse and Comminges, the flower of the southern nobility: they constitute a new generation of princes.[83] If 1219 is accepted as the revised date of composition for this poem, the presence of these young men can be easily explained by the anonymous author's verses: they ensure the continuity and the perennial quality of the alliances between the three counties. They are also, however, the future bases of political legitimacy which will reign in the lands freed from the French. The young men are the hope of that period; what they offered still seemed possible in 1219, when Toulouse was preparing to resist Prince Louis, another young man, albeit the son of the king of France. This new wave of promising men, less compromised than their fathers had been, had legitimate claims and courage on their side. By 1228, the future looked less promising, and the military situation of that moment would have given the *Chanson* a touch of nostalgia it simply does

82 *Chanson*, II, xiv.

83 Ghil suggests that by 1228, the fathers of these young men were dead, thus making it necessary to praise the living (*L'Âge de Parage*, pp. 192–3). This is true, but by the time of negotiations for the treaty of Meaux-Paris, these men were no longer regarded as *iuvenes*. See the discussion of this material by J. Rüdiger, *Aristokraten und Poeten: Die Grammatik einer Mentalität im tolosanischen Hochmittelalter* (Berlin, 2001).

not possess. In 1219, the poem's hopeful tone made sense; in 1228, the people of the south could only dream of an end to the conflict: the poem's reign of *Paratge* is set in a context of long-term ambition and hope, not in the approach of an inevitable and conclusive treaty.[84]

84 Vincent notes that negotiations began in the autumn of 1228, which worried the entourage of King Henry III: 'England and the Albigensian Crusade', p. 80.

Troubadours and History

WILLIAM D. PADEN

The phenomenon represented by the troubadours is large and complex. We have poetry by about 360 troubadours whose names we know.[1] We have about 2,500 of their poems. If we figure that these poems tend to run about 50 lines apiece, we have something on the order of 125,000 lines of lyric poetry, which, together with other Old Occitan literary forms such as narrative, theatre and prose comes out to a corpus that I am told is comparable in extent with the body of ancient Greek literature. Recently we have become more aware of some very short, archaic Occitan texts that go back to about A.D. 950.[2] We are also becoming more interested in Occitan literature of the later Middle Ages. But the production of the troubadours themselves, within the context of earlier, later, and contemporary forms, remains at the hub of this activity, essentially the twelfth and thirteenth centuries.

History: A Hypothesis

Friedrich Diez, who may be regarded as the founder of both Romance philology and troubadour studies, declared in 1826 that 'If one compares a series of poems by different [troubadours], one will immediately observe that collectively they show one and the same poetic character. One could imagine this entire literature as the work of one poet, only brought forth in varying moods.'[3] A century later Alfred Jeanroy, drawing up a synthesis of his life's work on the troubadours, attempted to write two distinct histories of their poetry, one external and the

1 Not 460, as is often said. Although the listing in *PC* extends to item 461 for the anonymous texts, it skips more than a hundred integers while inserting less than twenty (*PC* 6a, etc.). The provisional figures that I have, subject to further scrutiny, are 122 integers skipped and 18 inserted for a total of 356 named troubadours or trobairitz whose work we have. There are also other troubadours and trobairitz whose names we know, but whose work is not extant.

2 L. Lazzerini, *Letteratura medievale in Lingua d'Oc*, 'Subsidia' al 'Corpus des troubadours' 2 (Modena, 2001), pp. 11–42.

3 'Vergleicht man eine Reihe von Gedichten verschiedener Verfasser, so wird man sogleich die Wahrnehmung machen, dass sie sämmtlich einen und denselben poetischen Charakter offenbaren. Man könnte sich diese ganze Literatur als das Werk eines Dichters denken, nur in verschiedenen Stimmungen hervorgebracht.' F. Diez, *Die Poesie der Troubadours* (Zwickau, 1826), pp. 122–3; 2nd edn (Leipzig, 1883), p. 107.

other internal, but Jeanroy's withering scorn for their supposed lack of originality, their repetition of clichés and formulas, essentially continued Diez's attitude that they had no history.[4] Other scholars such as Ernest Hoepffner have stressed the individual personalities of leading figures, but by implication have left the lesser poets in the shadows of an unchanging mediocrity.[5] The recent introduction to the troubadours edited by Simon Gaunt and Sarah Kay devotes separate chapters to the early troubadours, the classical period, and the later troubadours, but does not provide a clear, unified perception of how their poetry evolved.[6] Indeed Gérard Gouiran seems to echo Diez when he writes that in the classical period, 'The songs of the troubadours become one song.'[7]

By invoking a larger framework, however, we can see the troubadours against an evolving background that leads us to regard change as natural or even inevitable. We can see the Middle Ages as a whole as the gradual transition from one sociolinguistic situation to another. In the first phase the high language throughout Western Europe was Latin, and the low language in each place was the local vernacular, developing out of spoken Latin or Germanic sources but leaving as yet few traces. The transition witnessed the gradual elevation of the vernaculars, first into writing at various times in various places, and then gradually into further functions of high language. The transition culminated in the establishment of the vernaculars in a position competitive with Latin. This second phase may be found realized in writers of the Renaissance. For Dante and Petrarch the competition between Latin and the vernacular remained vigorous, but for Montaigne, Cervantes, and Shakespeare, with his small Latin, it was only natural to write in the vernacular.[8] In this view the humanist revivals of classical Latinity in the eighth century, the twelfth century, and the thirteenth through sixteenth centuries are seen as reactions against the steady rise of vernacular languages, and the Renaissance itself becomes the logical culmination of the Middle Ages.[9]

In terms of this synthesis, the troubadours are seen as participants in the movement of history, as innovators, because they adopted the vernacular of their

4 A. Jeanroy, *La Poésie lyrique des troubadours*, 2 vols. (Toulouse and Paris, 1934).

5 E. Hoepffner, *Les Troubadours dans leurs vies et dans leurs œuvres* (Paris, 1955). Among those who have challenged the alleged uniformity of troubadour poetry are L. M. Paterson, *Troubadours and Eloquence* (Oxford, 1975), pp. 6–7, 211–12, and A. E. Van Vleck, *Memory and Re-Creation in Troubadour Lyric* (Berkeley, 1984), pp. 4–5.

6 *The Troubadours: An Introduction*, ed. S. Gaunt and S. Kay (Cambridge, 1999).

7 G. Gouiran, 'The Classical Period: From Raimbaut d'Aurenga to Arnaut Daniel', in Gaunt and Kay, *The Troubadours*, pp. 83–98 (p. 83).

8 This preference is all the more striking if, as Montaigne says in 'De l'institution des enfans' (*Essais* I.xxvi), his first language was Latin.

9 I elaborated an earlier version of this proposal in 'Europe from Latin to Vernacular in Epic, Lyric, Romance', in *Performance of Literature in Historical Perspectives*, ed. D. W. Thompson (Lanham, MD, 1983), pp. 67–105. For more recent work on the philological background, see M. L. Meneghetti, *Le origini delle letterature medievali romanze* (Rome, 1997); Y. Cazal, *Les voix du peuple/Verbum Dei: le bilinguisme Latin/langue vernaculaire au* Moyen Age (Genève, 1998); see also the collected papers in *La transizione dal latino alle lingue romanze: atti della Tavola rotonda di linguistica storica, Università Ca' Foscari di Venezia 14–15 giugno 1996*, ed. J. Herman (Tübingen, 1998), and *Langages et peuples d'Europe: cristallisation des identités romanes et germaniques (VIIe–XIe siècle)*, ed. M. Banniard (Toulouse, 2002).

place for the purpose of artistic expression. Of course, grand changes over the arc of a millennium may be expected to translate into more modest evolution over the course of two centuries. But just as the momentum of change is implicit in the troubadours' first appearance, so we should expect it to continue to effect the development of their art. This model would lead us to expect not only that troubadour song must have changed, but also that it might have worked its way toward increasingly high cultural functions. In the early thirteenth century the *vidas* and *razos* institutionalized commentary on the songs and their composers. Around the middle of the century the surviving manuscripts began to be written, including some massive monuments to cultural prestige. In the early fourteenth century the members of the *Sobregaya companhia del Gay Saber*, in Toulouse, authorized Guilhem Molinier to draw up an elaborate book of instructions and rules for composition of songs in the traditional manner, the *Leys d'amors*. The monumentalization of troubadour poetry is beyond question.[10] But how did it affect the inner reality and the external practice of the songs?

I grant out of hand that this hypothesis of change, no matter how attractive it may seem to me, is based in large part on sweeping synthesis and intuition. It needs more evidence.

Chronology of the Composition of Troubadour Songs

The names of the major troubadours have been known since Diez and before, and the names of all the known troubadours have been listed together with the incipits of their songs since 1872.[11] The chronology of the major figures has remained mostly uncontroversial through the listings by Jeanroy in 1934, Riquer in 1975, and Gaunt and Kay in 1999.[12] Recently Saverio Guida has revised the chronology of some minor poets, and Francesca Gambino has reviewed the anonymous texts.[13] But it is one thing to agree, more or less, when each troubadour sang, and another thing to grasp the chronological profile of the phenomenon as a whole.

10 On the term *monument*, contrasted with *document*, see P. Zumthor, *Langue et techniques poétiques à l'époque romane (XIe–XIIIe siècles)* (Paris, 1963), pp. 32–43. On the 'process by which troubadour poetry became cultural capital', see W. Burgwinkle, 'The *Chansonniers* as Books', in Gaunt and Kay, *The Troubadours*, pp. 246–62 (p. 259). L. Kendrick uses the terms *valorisation* or *auteurisation*; see 'L'image du troubadour comme auteur dans les chansonniers', in Auctor *et* auctoritas: *Invention et conformisme dans l'écriture médiévale: Actes du Colloque tenu à l'Université de Versailles-Saint-Quentin-en-Yvelines (14–16 juin 1999)*, ed. M. Zimmermann (Paris, 2001), pp. 507–19 (p. 508). On the 'processus original d'autorisation' of the troubadours in non-lyric Occitan texts, see F. Vielliard, 'Auteur et autorité dans la littérature occitane médiévale non lyrique', *ibid.*, pp. 375–89 (p. 389).

11 K. Bartsch, *Grundriss zur Geschichte der provenzalischen Literatur* (Elberfeld, 1872).

12 Jeanroy, 'Liste bio-bibliographique des troubadours des origines au milieu du XIVe siècle', *Poésie lyrique*, I, 326–436. M. de Riquer, *Los Trovadores: historia literaria y textos*, 3 vols. (Barcelona, 1975). Gaunt and Kay, 'Major Troubadours', in *The Troubadours*, pp. 279–91.

13 S. Guida, 'Cartulari e trovatori', *Cultura neolatina* 59 (1999), 71–127; Guida, *Trovatori minori* (Modena, 2002). F. Gambino, 'L'anonymat dans la tradition manuscrite de la lyrique troubadouresque', CCM 43 (2000), 33–90.

To do that I suggest two strategies. First, since we know the birth and death dates of only a few troubadours (like Guilhem de Peitieus), and for others we know only the date of their death, or dates of their activity, or in some cases just one date of activity, in order to arrive at comparable information for all of them I suggest that we adopt the midpoint of their known careers. Doing so will enable us to array datable troubadours in a sequence. We will have to deprive ourselves of the sense of duration of their careers, which, I admit, can be quite interesting, for example in the case of Peire Cardenal, the longest-lived troubadour, who was active over a period of sixty-seven years from 1205 to 1272. But this provisional strategy will enable us to gain a clearer sense of the larger picture.

Second, I suggest that we array these midpoints in five conventional periods, forty years long apiece, that will stretch over the two hundred years of the twelfth and thirteenth centuries. This will enable us to group the troubadours of the earliest forty years, those of the middle forty years, and so on. The periods represent an intrinsic approximation. Peire Cardenal outlasted the limits of any forty-year period and in fact worked in three of them. Nevertheless, by considering the midpoints of troubadour activity in these five periods we shall be able to get an overview of the subject.

These two strategies group some of the major troubadours as follows:

Period 1 (from 1100 to 1140) includes the work of three major poets, Guilhem de Peiteus,[14] Jaufre Rudel, and Marcabru. Marcabru is barely included in this period; since his known activity extended from 1130 to 1149, the midpoint is half-way through 1139.

Period 2 (from 1140 to 1180) includes Peire d'Auvergne, Raimbaut d'Aurenga, his friend Azalais de Porcairagues, Bernart de Ventadorn (according to the consensus regarding his dates),[15] the Comtessa de Dia (according to Gaunt and Kay, though I suspect she was later),[16] and others.

Period 3 (from 1180 to 1220) includes Bertran de Born, Guiraut de Borneill, Arnaut Daniel, Peire Vidal, Raimbaut de Vaqueiras, and others.

Period 4 (from 1220 to 1260) includes Peire Cardenal, Sordel, Uc de Saint-Circ, and others.

14 On the late identification of the 'Coms de Peiteus' of the manuscript attributions with Guilhem IX (born 1071, died 1126), see G. Beech, 'L'attribution des poèmes du Comte de Poitiers à Guillaume IX d'Aquitaine', CCM 31 (1988), 3–16. Beech shows that the attribution, based on the *vida* ('une source sûre', p. 11), is not certain but is nevertheless reliable.

15 I have pointed out the fragility of this consensus, and the possibility that Bernart wrote later, in 'Bernart de Ventadour le troubadour devint-il abbé de Tulle?', in *Mélanges de langue et de littérature occitanes en hommage à Pierre Bec* (Poitiers, 1991), pp. 401–13.

16 Gaunt and Kay, *The Troubadours*, p. 282, following A. Rieger, *Trobairitz: Der Beitrag der Frau in der altokzitanischen höfischen Lyrik, Edition der Gesamtkorpus* (Tübingen, 1991), p. 614. But a *Beatrix comitissa* who must have been the eldest daughter of the count of Die, and hence a countess of Die by inheritance, is attested in a charter of 1212; see J. Monier, 'Essai d'identification de la comtesse de Die', *Bulletin de la Société d'archéologie et de statistique de la Drôme* 75 (1962) 265–78 (pp. 274–5), and W. D. Paden, *The Voice of the Trobairitz: Perspectives on the Women Troubadours* (Philadelphia, 1989), p. 231.

Period 5 (from 1260 to 1300) includes Guiraut Riquier, Serveri de Girona, and others.

The chronological profile of the corpus of troubadour songs is a bell curve, modified so as to be higher on the right side because there are more songs from the late periods than from the early ones. This curve is implicit in the figures contained in Table 1. The census of poems in that table does not include about three hundred poems (many of them anonymous) that have not been dated. If we prefer to think that Marcabru's activity extended a little longer, and that he 'was still composing in the early 1150s',[17] then Period 1 would look even more slender and Period 2 somewhat more substantial. But the bell curve, high on the right, would remain.

Table 1
Troubadour songs datable in periods 1–5

Period	1	2	3	4	5	Total
Years	1100–1140	1140–1180	1180–1220	1220–1260	1260–1300	
Songs	61	187	961	621	431	2261
% of Total	3%	8%	43%	27%	19%	100%

What do these numbers mean? The beginning looks like a true beginning; the slender production of Period 1 grows only relatively in Period 2 before bursting forth in Period 3. Even though we have lost all the songs by Eble de Ventadour, who was also active in Period 1, and though we have a fragmentary trace of late eleventh-century song, we can say that the extant material from the first two periods looks in profile like a nascent practice of composition.[18] The third period, in relation to what precedes and follows it, looks very much like a culmination. And the last two periods, on the present evidence, look like a progressive decline in production. I have argued elsewhere that the decline did not result from the Albigensian Crusade, as has been widely believed, because the purported cause did not match the effect in time, space, or nature; rather I see a sociolinguistic groundswell, a shift of preference from Occitan to French, and a transition from a regional language dedicated to lyric expression to an emerging national language with a broader range of subjects.[19] But however that may be, the present evidence alone is sufficient for my present purpose. The overall production of troubadour song was not constant. It grew and declined. It changed.

17 *Marcabru: A Critical Edition*, ed. S. Gaunt, R. Harvey and L. Paterson (Cambridge, 2000), p. 3.

18 On Eble, see Riquer, *Trovadores*, I, 142–7. On the fragmentary Harley lyric, Lazzerini, *Letteratura medievale*, pp. 28–34. We cannot exclude the alternative that the extant material could have been produced by a nascent practice of transcription.

19 'The Troubadours and the Albigensian Crusade: A Long View', *Romance Philology* 49 (1995), 168–91; on the shift from a regional to a national language, see my article 'The Chronology of Genres in Medieval Galician-Portuguese Lyric Poetry', *La Corónica* 26.1 (1997), 183–201 (pp. 198–9).

Historical Geography of Troubadour Regions

Jeanroy offered a list of troubadours whose *patrie*, or native region, he felt able to identify.[20] This intriguing compilation calls for several remarks. For one, it is too bad that some minor troubadours appear in more than one region.[21] For another, we might want to adjust the regions somewhat, by merging some of them so that the resulting array would assemble more major units, like those of the principal modern Occitan dialects. More importantly, perhaps, opinions may have changed about the native regions of certain troubadours.[22] In any case the term *patrie* sounds more redolent of the nineteenth century than the twelfth or thirteenth.[23] But also, supposing that a troubadour's native region may be located with confidence, does that locate the production of his poems? Not necessarily; consider, for example, the time that Guiraut Riquier of Narbonne spent at the court of Alfonso *el Sabio* in Toledo. So we need to understand that the *patrie* represents not the actual place of composition of each song, but just what it seems to represent, the region where the troubadour was presumably born.

Despite all these qualifications, I think it interesting to chart the production of the troubadours in terms of their period and their region (or *patrie*), according to Jeanroy. You have the result in Table 2.[24] The figures in that table imply a large, stylized letter R. It begins with the vertical element in the west of what is now France, running from Poitou (Guilhem de Peitieus) south to Gascony (Jaufre Rudel and Marcabru). Then in the second period it loops over to the right, through the Limousin (Bernart de Ventadorn) and Auvergne (Peire d'Auvergne) and down to Provence (Raimbaut d'Aurenga). In the third period it

20 Jeanroy, 'Liste par régions des troubadours dont la patrie est connue', in *Poésie lyrique*, I, 321–5.

21 Giraut de Salignac appears in region groups A and C, Uc de Penne in C and F, Elias de Barjols in F and H.

22 The recent editors of Marcabru find little reason to consider his *patrie* as Gascony, despite a long scholarly tradition. 'Marcabru may have come from Gascony, but there is no other evidence to support this [than the *vida* in manuscript A]': Gaunt, Harvey and Paterson, *Marcabru*, p. 1. Compare the more traditional view: 'Probably a Gascon clerk' (Gaunt and Kay, *The Troubadours*, p. 287). In general the *vidas* are considered relatively reliable as to the troubadour's place of origin: Jeanroy, *Poésie lyrique*, I, 132.

23 The word *patrie* is attested in French in the sense of a nation, as well as the regional sense (intended by Jeanroy) of 'pays natal' since the sixteenth century (1516), according to the *Trésor de la langue française: Dictionnaire de la langue du XIXe et du XXe siècle (1789–1960)*, 16 vols. (Paris, 1986), XII, 1189–90. There is no entry for *patria* in *PD* or in Ricketts, *Concordance de l'occitan médiéval* (see below, n. 27).

24 I have abbreviated the names of the regions, providing only the first term given by Jeanroy. I have modified the order in which Jeanroy lists the regions so as to proceed from west to east, first across the northern tier (regions A through E), then across the southern tier (F through H), and then abroad (I and J). (Jeanroy proceeds in boustrophedon manner: from west to east in the north, then from east to west in the south.) Jeanroy names the regions in full as follows: I. Poitou, Saintonge, Périgord; II. Limousin, Marche; III. Quercy, Rouergue; IV. Auvergne, Velay, Gévaudan, Vivarais; V. Dauphiné, Viennois, Valentinois; VI. Provence (Comté et Marquisat de); VII. Languedoc, Comté de Foix; VIII. Gascogne, Comminges, Agenais, Bordelais; IX. Roussillon, Catalogne; X. Italie. The total in Table 2 differs from the total in Table I because not all the datable poems can be assigned to a region.

Table 2
Troubadour poems by period and region

Period	1	2	3	4	5	Total
Years	1100–1140	1140–1180	1180–1220	1220–1260	1260–1300	
Region						
A. Poitou	12	11	127	32	0	182
B. Limousin	0	43	165	4	0	212
C. Quercy	0	0	33	71	10	114
D. Auvergne	0	34	95	76	5	210
E. Dauphiné	0	7	33	34	0	74
F. Gascogne	48	6	14	26	0	94
G. Languedoc	0	1	182	74	131	388
H. Provence	0	40	157	132	92	421
I. Catalonia	0	13	47	1	124	185
J. Italy	0	1	15	100	27	143
Total	60	156	868	550	389	2023

moves toward closing the loop, turning back to Languedoc (Peire Vidal) and Quercy (Raimon Jordan). In the fourth and fifth periods it sweeps outward, first to the east toward Italy (Sordel) and then toward Catalonia (Serveri de Girona).[25] In other words, the *rayonnement des troubadours* began on their native ground. Well before their art spread to Italy and Spain and inspired imitation in northern France and Germany, it had already travelled among the regions of southern France.[26] It was never a stable, fixed phenomenon. It moved.

Evolution of the Troubadour Lexicon

The year 2001 witnessed the publication of not one but two computerized concordances of the entire corpus of troubadour poetry. One was edited by Peter Ricketts of the University of Birmingham and his team, the other by Rocco Distilo of the University of Calabria.[27] Both were published on compact disk, and both, *mirabile dictu*, were offered to American buyers at the exact price of $150.

25 Other data in Table 2 do not correspond so well to the pattern I suggest. In the third period, production also spreads to Dauphiné, north of Provence, and some poems were already being produced in Catalonia and Italy.

26 I cite the title of the collection of articles on troubadour lyric influence across western Europe, *Le Rayonnement des troubadours*, ed. A. Touber (Amsterdam, 1998).

27 P. T. Ricketts, director; A. Reed, technical director; with the collaboration of F. R. P. Akehurst, J. Hathaway and C. van der Horst, *Concordance de l'occitan médiéval (COM)/The Concordance of Medieval Occitan* (Turnhout, 2001). R. Distilo, *Trobadors: concordanze della lirica trobadorica in CD-Rom* (Università degli Studi di Calabria/Università degli Studi di Roma 'La Sapienza,' 2001). I have used both concordances for this study, first the one by Distilo for my preliminary explorations and then the one by Ricketts for the present version. They produce somewhat differing data, but the same essential conclusions.

The simultaneous appearance of these two essentially identical tools is one more example of simultaneous invention in scholarship as in science, like the invention, in biology, of the evolution of species by both Charles Darwin and Alfred Russel Wallace. Clearly culture was ready for a troubadour concordance.

The availability of the corpus in electronic form, with search engines attached, offers the opportunity to investigate further the ways troubadour poetry may have changed through time. One may, for example, call for the word *canson*, and while pausing to scratch one's head one gets a complete listing of the word as the troubadours used it. One cannot exaggerate the importance of the (in principle) totality of such a result. No longer must we be satisfied with a sample of some hopefully adequate size; now we can get it all. Against this advantage there are, of course, certain reservations to be borne in mind. Both concordances give us the totality of troubadour songs in selected editions. The editions chosen differ from one concordance to the other, so insofar as different editions actually differ in the text, so do the concordances. Furthermore, if an editor has chosen not to adopt the reading of a certain word in one manuscript, that word, in that passage, will not appear in a concordance using that edition. Peter Ricketts has announced plans to go on to a concordance of all the troubadour manuscripts, which, if these plans are realized, will enable us to find every manuscript version of every text. He also envisions a concordance of the non-lyric verse texts, such as the romances. Beyond those, we can dream of works in prose, including even archival documents. While musing over our fantasies of ever more all-embracing totality, however, we have much to be grateful for already.

Once we have our complete listing of the occurrences of *canson*, we must pause to wonder about variant spellings. Neither concordance is lemmatized, since the editors judged it impossible, for very understandable reasons, to lemmatize the entire computerized text. They have left to the individual researcher the task of finding variant spellings unaided. Anyone conversant with Old Occitan will realize that *canson* may be spelled with either initial *ca-* or initial *cha-*, but it does not seem self-evident that we can also find it with an initial *xa-* (*xanço*), or, to take another example, that the word *son*, 'melody', might be spelled with an initial *z-* (*zon*). Another problem is that one spelling may conceal several different words. I was interested in this word *son*, 'melody', but daunted by finding more than three thousand occurrences of this spelling; when I added the variant *so*, without the final *-n*, I got more than five thousand hits. These spellings, *son* and *so*, may represent the word meaning 'melody', but they also include the very frequent possessive adjective *son*, 'his' and so forth, and the very frequent pronoun *so*, 'that', as in *so que*, 'that which'. (Less frequent are the identical verb forms meaning 'I am' and 'they are'.) I have not yet found a practical way to determine the occurrences of this word for 'melody'. The risk of coming up with unnoticed homonyms obliges the researcher, once he or she has got his instantaneous listing, not only to read it but to do so with enough understanding to insure that the target forms all represent the same word.

So the researcher blessed with these electronic marvels must nevertheless go through some heavy slogging. Having defined the various forms that pertain to a given word, and having read through the trove to winnow out the irrelevant homonyms, one has a complete (in principle) list of troubadour uses of that word.

One may then assign each occurrence to one of the five periods I mentioned earlier, on the basis of the midpoint of the troubadour's career. One then has a profile of the word's occurrences through the two centuries.

In order to determine whether variations in the frequency of a word's occurrences are significant, however, one must compare the profile of raw numbers with some standard of the relative frequency of usage in the various periods. The obvious standard is the production of poems in each period, which we have looked at already. Since the production of poems traces the bell curve that we have seen, if the usage of some particular word traced an identical bell curve we could say that its variation merely reflected the changing production of the poems, and not a fluctuating interest in the word itself. There is a further implication too. Since the production of poems is the obvious standard by which to measure the usage of individual words, in order to insure the comparability of the standard and what we intend to measure with it (the usage of words), we should express the frequency of word usage in terms of the number of poems in which a word occurs. This means that we should not express it in terms of the number of verses, since the word might occur in more than one verse in a given poem. If the concordance produces several verses with the same word in the same poem, we should count just one poem using the word regardless how many times it is used there. For the sake of a coherent analysis based on the number of poems in both the standard and word-usage, we shall sacrifice the admittedly interesting feature of repeated usage within one song. This sacrifice is analogous to the sacrifice of duration in the troubadours' careers for the sake of clarity in chronological sequence. Both decisions simplify the analysis by omitting certain features for the sake of coherence.

Finally, we must be alert for deceptive appearances of two kinds. If we find too small a number of occurrences, the result may not be meaningful. For example, the word *vila*, in the sense 'town', seems to occur in only eight songs in the entire corpus: three songs in Period 3, four in Period 4, and one in Period 5. It is easy to say instinctively that these occurrences are not enough to provide a meaningful result; they do not tell us anything of much importance about change in the troubadour lexicon. But even if we find a more robust number of occurrences, their distribution may or may not be such as to express significant change. If we flip a coin a hundred times, we expect in principle to get fifty heads and fifty tails; but if we actually get heads fifty-one times and tails forty-nine, the margin of one between what we expected and what actually happened will not tell us anything reliable about the coin. The variation is probably random. However, if we get heads ninety-nine times and tails just once, we should look closely to see if the coin is honest. At what point between fifty-one heads and ninety-nine does the result become significant? Or, to return to our bell curve, how far does usage of a given word need to depart from the curve traced by the production of all poems in order to become a significant departure?

Fortunately we have available a standard technique in statistics that will enable us to guard against both these sources of error. Called the chi square test, it 'may be used to determine the significance of the differences' among groups of data.[28] The test imposes a requirement of minimal size for the expected results.

[28] S. Siegel, *Nonparametric Statistics for the Behavioral Sciences* (New York, 1956), p. 175.

We shall rely on the chi square test to warn us when a sample is too small to produce a meaningful result, and to gauge, if a result is meaningful, the degree of its significance.[29]

The Project

I have investigated thirty-six words or groups of words in the concordance by Ricketts in hopes of discovering possibly significant variations in their usage through time. I began with a category of words that name songs or genres of songs: the *canson*, the *vers*, the *sirventes*, and the names of minor genres. I did so because earlier work on the distribution of the actual poems that we describe with these terms had indicated that production of the first two fell while the last two rose.[30] I continued with a category of love-words such as *domna*, 'lady', *midons*, 'my lady', and *joven*, 'youthfulness', reasoning that if the love-genres declined in favour the words associated with them probably declined as well. Because I was curious about possible changes in the delivery of troubadour texts, I then turned to words describing performance: *cantar* as a verb, 'to sing', or as a noun, 'song', and *joglar*, 'performer'; and words referring to settings such as castle or court, and the names of castles and towns in the South of France. Since it seems that the theme of love became less dominant as time passed, I wondered what might have replaced it. I therefore investigated words that express religious ideas such as *Deu*, 'God', *pecat*, 'sin', and *mort*, 'death'. Finally, reflecting that the fall of the *canson* led to the rise of the *sirventes* and, among the minor genres, particularly the *cobla*, I investigated a category of words expressing morality that might be typical of the *sirventes*, words like *drech*, 'right', *tort*, 'wrong', *onor*, 'honor', and *orgolh*, 'pride', and another category of words expressing mockery that might be typical of the *cobla* such as *avol*, 'bad', *fol*, 'fool', and *vilan*, 'peasant'. A listing of the words I have studied can be found in the Appendix, together with the forms of these words that I found in Ricketts' concordance.

Most of the thirty-six items are single words. Some of them are attested in only one invariable form (*vers*, *paradis*), while others occur in two forms by normal declension (*cobla, coblas*; *tort, tortz*), or in as many as forty-six forms (*orgolh*) because of declension, the wealth of orthographic variations available in Old Occitan, and (in this case) an alternation in the initial vowel. Other items are not words but groups of words. These groups include the names of the minor genres (Appendix, item 2: ten words), words using the root *escri-*, 'write' (item 13: three words), names of castles located in the Midi (item 16: thirty-three castles), names of towns located in the Midi (item 18: 266 towns), and words on the root *escarn-*, 'scorn' (item 33: three words). I employed groups of words when there are not enough occurrences of individual words to be statistically

29 I am grateful to my colleague Michael Dacey, Professor of Anthropology and former Director of the Program in Mathematical Methods in the Social Sciences at Northwestern University, for his advice on use of the chi square test. All shortcomings in my application are of course my own.

30 W. D. Paden, 'The System of Genres in Troubadour Lyric', in *Medieval Lyric: Genres in Historical Context*, ed. W. D. Paden (Urbana, 2000), pp. 1–67.

meaningful; by grouping words together we can create greater frequency and gain a meaningful result. For example, the word *cobla* occurs in just thirty-three poems according to Ricketts, not enough to provide a meaningful analysis in four periods, but by grouping this word with other names of minor genres we can get a valid result. The same is true of the names of towns and castles. The statistical advantage holds good provided that we group words according to principles that are clear and cogent, as these principles seem to me: the names of minor genres, of castles or of towns, or etymologically related words about writing or mockery.

Results: A Panoramic View

As Table 1 indicates, only 3 per cent of datable troubadour songs were written in Period 1. Therefore it is inevitable that only a small percentage of the occurrences of these various words will be traceable to that period. In fact, among the thirty-six words or groups of words that I have investigated, almost half (sixteen) yielded too few examples to make an analysis in terms of the five periods meaningful.[31] Since the first period appeared not to be very useful for these purposes, I simply deleted it from further consideration.[32] But Period 2, with 8 per cent of overall production, looks rather frail too.[33] In order to assure that I would have robust data for the remaining periods, I took a second step of combining Periods 2 and 3 into Period A, from 1140 to 1220, and also combined Periods 4 and 5 into Period B, from 1220 to 1300. Reformulation of the data in these two periods, each eighty years long, has the advantage of showing clearly and with statistically reliable figures which words rose and which words fell in usage between these two longer times.[34]

Table 3 shows the results. Beside each word or group of words, it gives the number of songs in which that word or group of words was found first in Period A, then in Period B, and then in total. In order to gauge the meaning of these figures, the table then gives expected figures. These expected figures are based on the assumption that the total number might have been distributed across Periods A and B in proportion to the way all poems are distributed across them. (It is the usual practice in statistics to give expected figures to one decimal place.) The total of expected figures must be identical to the total of figures observed. The table then gives the difference between the observed and expected figures (the

31 Since the expected figure for each of the five periods must be 5 or greater (Siegel, *Nonparametric Statistics*, p. 178), and since the proportion of poems produced in Period 1 is 61/2261, a word or group of words would have to be attested at least 186 times in total to produce a meaningful result (186 × 61/2,261 = 5).

32 After the deletion of Period 1, the total number of songs that remains is 2,200. The number of songs in each of the remaining periods is unchanged from those given in Table 1, but the percentages of the total are modified slightly. Period 2 had 9% of the songs in the four periods; Period 3 had 44%; Period 4 had 28%; and Period 5 had 20%.

33 In fact the expected figures for Period 2 are all over 5.0, so the results given in Table 4 are meaningful.

34 In Table 3, only 11 occurrences are necessary to insure the 5% level of significance (11 times 1,052/2,200 = 5).

Table 3
Evolution in the troubadour lexicon
Two periods of eighty years apiece

	Category	Observed			*Expected*			Observed-Expected		Chi square	Significance
	Word or words	Period A	Period B	Total	*Period A*	*Period B*	*Total*	Period A	Period B		
	song-words										
1	*canson*	262	120	382	*200.9*	*181.1*	*382.0*	61.1	–61.1	39.236	down
2	minor genres	79	106	185	*97.3*	*87.7*	*185.0*	–18.3	18.3	7.244	up
3	*sirventes*	68	107	175	*92.0*	*83.0*	*175.0*	–24.0	24.0	13.224	up
4	*vers*	126	54	180	*94.7*	*85.3*	*180.0*	31.3	–31.3	21.899	down
	love-words										
5	*cortes*	267	137	404	*212.4*	*191.6*	*404.0*	54.6	–54.6	29.555	down
6	*domna*	570	250	820	*431.2*	*388.8*	*820.0*	138.8	–138.8	94.251	down
7	*gelos*	52	28	80	*42.1*	*37.9*	*80.0*	9.9	–9.9	4.947	down
8	*joven* (noun)	168	56	224	*117.8*	*106.2*	*224.0*	50.2	–50.2	45.145	down
9	*lauzengier*	133	43	176	*92.5*	*83.5*	*176.0*	40.5	–40.5	37.292	down
10	*midons*	193	99	292	*153.5*	*138.5*	*292.0*	39.5	–39.5	21.383	down
	performance-words										
11	*cantar* (noun)	95	56	151	*79.4*	*71.6*	*151.0*	15.6	–15.6	6.463	down
12	*cantar* (verb)	285	170	455	*239.3*	*215.7*	*455.0*	45.7	–45.7	18.446	down
13	*escri-* words	30	45	75	*39.4*	*35.6*	*75.0*	–9.4	9.4	4.763	up
14	*joglar*	38	36	74	*38.9*	*35.1*	*74.0*	–0.9	0.9	0.045	n.s.
	setting-words										
15	*castel*	62	36	98	*51.5*	*46.5*	*98.0*	10.5	–10.5	4.485	down
16	castle names	83	12	95	*50.0*	*45.0*	*95.0*	33.0	–33.0	46.103	down
17	*cort*	88	67	155	*81.5*	*73.5*	*155.0*	6.5	–6.5	1.092	n.s.
18	town names	217	176	393	*206.7*	*186.3*	*393.0*	10.3	–10.3	1.093	n.s.

	Category	Observed			*Expected*			Observed-Expected		Chi square	Significance
	Word or words	Period A	Period B	Total	*Period A*	*Period B*	*Total*	Period A	Period B		
	religion-words										
19	*Crist*	23	40	63	*33.1*	*29.9*	*63.0*	–10.1	10.1	6.530	up
20	*Deu*	468	431	899	*472.7*	*426.3*	*899.0*	–4.7	4.7	0.100	n.s.
21	*maire*	33	54	87	*45.7*	*41.3*	*87.0*	–12.7	12.7	7.491	up
22	*Maria*	38	35	73	*38.4*	*34.6*	*73.0*	–0.4	0.4	0.008	n.s.
23	*mort (noun)*	161	176	337	*177.2*	*159.8*	*337.0*	–16.2	16.2	3.126	n.s.
24	*paradis*	33	34	67	*35.2*	*31.8*	*67.0*	–2.2	2.2	0.298	n.s.
25	*pecat*	99	93	192	*101.0*	*91.0*	*192.0*	–2.0	2.0	0.080	n.s.
	morality-words										
26	*drech*	300	280	580	*305.0*	*275.0*	*580.0*	–5.0	5.0	0.172	n.s.
27	*fals*	231	200	431	*226.6*	*204.4*	*431.0*	4.4	–4.4	0.177	n.s.
28	*onor*	314	279	593	*311.8*	*281.2*	*593.0*	2.2	–2.2	0.032	n.s.
29	*orgolh*	130	98	228	*119.9*	*108.1*	*228.0*	10.1	–10.1	1.798	n.s.
30	*tort*	240	172	412	*216.6*	*195.4*	*412.0*	23.4	–23.4	5.310	down
31	*valor*	306	296	602	*316.6*	*285.4*	*602.0*	–10.6	10.6	0.742	n.s.
	mockery-words										
32	*avol*	120	87	207	*108.8*	*98.2*	*207.0*	11.2	–11.2	2.410	n.s.
33	*escarn- words*	42	30	72	*37.9*	*34.1*	*72.0*	4.1	–4.1	0.955	n.s.
34	*fol*	268	175	443	*232.9*	*210.1*	*443.0*	35.1	–35.1	11.126	down
35	*paubre*	54	50	104	*54.7*	*49.3*	*104.0*	–0.7	0.7	0.018	n.s.
36	*vilan*	80	33	113	*59.4*	*53.6*	*113.0*	20.6	–20.6	15.034	down

observed minus the expected), showing, for example, that the word *canson* occurred more often than expected in Period A and less often in Period B. That is, *canson* declined in relative usage from 1140–1220 to 1220–1300. The table then gives the value of chi square, calculated according to the standard formula.[35] If the value of chi square is too small, the result is not significant, that is, it could represent merely random variation.[36] I claim as a significant result any value of chi square that will occur randomly in only 5 per cent or less of all cases. This is the usual level of significance chosen in studies in linguistic statistics.[37]

What Table 3 tells us about the song-words, then, is that the terms *canson* and *vers* did decline in relative usage from Period A to Period B, while the term *sirventes* and the words for the minor genres rose. The entire category of love-words investigated here – *cortes*, *domna*, *gelos*, *joven* (noun), *lauzengier*, and *midons* – declined as well, especially the word *domna*, which declined precipitously. The high number of songs in which *domna* occurs, more than a third of all songs occurring in Periods 2 through 5, adds to the significance of this observation. The other categories produced less dramatic changes. Although the numbers were in every case large enough to support meaningful results, the variation from expectation was not significant in sixteen words or groups of words, marked 'n.s.' in the rightmost column. That is, these words or groups of words varied from expectation within the random limit, here set at 5 per cent. Among words that departed further from expectation, most declined along with *canson*, *vers*, and the category of love-words: thus *cantar*, both noun and verb; the word *castel* and the names of castles in the Midi; and the words *tort*, *fol*, and *vilan*. That is, evolving usage moved away from the words for songs in general or love songs in particular, away from love-words, and away from a major term for sung performance (*cantar*), from words indicating a setting in a castle, and from certain words of mockery.

Aside from the word *sirventes* and the names of minor genres, only a few of the words investigated here rose in usage. Words about writing that begin with *escri-*, including *escrich*, *escriptura*, and *escrire*, rose, perhaps in alternation with the words about singing that fell. Two of the words here considered in the religious category, *Crist* and *maire* (often used of the mother of God), also rose. This may be taken as evidence for a shift from a sung artform concentrating on the theme of love to a written artform turning to religion. The evidence is fragile, however. Neither of these two words (*Crist* and *maire*), nor this group of words (*escri-*), occurred in large numbers, while other, more frequent, and highly charged words including *Deu*, *Maria*, and *pecat* did not vary significantly from expectation. *Deu* and these other words seem to be used in a stable manner over time, only as frequently as the evolving production of songs would suggest. They do not gain in relative frequency. Stable usage appears to have characterized most of the words investigated here that pertain to religion (*Deu*, *Maria*, *mort*, *paradis*, *pecat*). The

35 Siegel, *Nonparametric Statistics*, pp. 175–9; C. Muller, *Initiation à la statistique linguistique* (Paris, 1968), pp. 95–103.

36 Since there is one degree of freedom in Table 3, the value of chi square must be 3.84 or greater to assure 5% or less probability of random distribution.

37 Muller, *Initiation*, p. 76; cf. Siegel, *Nonparametric Statistics*, p. 8.

same is true of words expressing morality (*drech*, *fals*, *onor*, *orgolh*, *valor*) and mockery (*avol*, *escarn-* words, *paubre*), as well as the names of towns, the word *cort*, and the word *joglar*.

If the troubadours concentrated less on love as time passed, where did they turn their attention? To the *sirventes* and minor genres, apparently, but to what themes? Searching for new areas of interest, I have looked at some words pertaining to religion, morality, and mockery. In choosing these areas and these words, I have been guided by notions about the evolution of Occitan society in the twelfth and thirteenth centuries: the developing religious movements, criticism of unworthy clerics, the Albigensian Crusade, and the growth of satire. But I have not found evidence of increased usage in these areas. In fact, some terms of morality and mockery became less favoured, and none became significantly more popular. If my results are persuasive, they suggest that the troubadours remained more or less as concerned about these subjects as they had always been.

The apparent paradox allows one solution that I have not investigated further, and which must therefore remain for the present only a hypothesis. Perhaps the concentration on love in the earlier period yielded not to some new theme, but to a diffusion of interest among a greater variety of themes. This hypothesis has the advantage of accounting for the relative decline in usage of love-words; more important, perhaps, it frees us from the need to discover some new theme that has escaped me completely, but which actually attracted the interest of the later troubadours as strongly as love had attracted them before. I find the hypothesis plausible, but it requires further investigation.

Results: A Closer Look

To understand more clearly what happened within Periods A and B we may zoom in, and look now at Periods 2 through 5. Table 4 gives this more articulate view.[38] It presents four periods of forty years apiece, ignoring only the first period for the reasons given above. This table cannot contradict Table 3, but only add further nuance to the view given there. The same words that declined in relative frequency from Period A to Period B in Table 3 are seen in Table 4 declining from Periods 2 and 3 to Periods 4 and 5. But Table 4 allows us to see more closely what happened within Period A and, especially interesting, within Period B. We can see where the troubadours turned. For a summary comparison of the results in Tables 3 and 4, see Table 5.

For one series of words, Table 5 shows a pattern of decline from Period A to B, but decline in Period 4 followed by an upturn in Period 5. This pattern is true of *vers*; most of the love-words (*cortes*, *joven*, *lauzengier*, and *midons*); and *castel* and *vilan*. These words show a relative return in the last forty years toward the prominence they had originally enjoyed. Consistent with this pattern is its complement: the word *sirventes*, gaining in relative frequency in period B, rose in Period 4 but fell in Period 5.

38 Since there are three degrees of freedom in Table 4, the value of chi square must be 7.82 or greater to satisfy the chosen level of significance.

Table 4
Evolution in the troubadour lexicon
Four periods of forty years apiece

	Category Word(s)	Observed					*Expected*					Observed-Expected					Chi square	
		Pd 2	Pd 3	Pd 4	Pd 5	Total	*Pd 2*	*Pd 3*	*Pd 4*	*Pd 5*	*Total*	Pd 2	Pd 3	Pd 4	Pd 5	Total		
	song-words																	
1	*canson*	29	233	77	43	382	*32.1*	*168.7*	*105.5*	*75.6*	*382.0*	–3.1	64.3	–28.5	–32.6	0.0	46.565	
2	minor genres	5	74	54	53	186	*15.6*	*82.2*	*51.4*	*36.8*	*186.0*	–10.6	–8.2	2.6	16.2	0.0	15.295	
3	*sirventes*	6	62	73	34	175	*14.7*	*77.3*	*48.3*	*34.6*	*175.0*	–8.7	–15.3	24.7	–0.6	0.0	20.800	
4	*vers*	55	71	16	38	180	*15.1*	*79.5*	*49.7*	*35.6*	*180.0*	39.9	–8.5	–33.7	2.4	–0.0	128.821	
	love-words																	
5	*cortes*	30	237	78	59	404	*34.0*	*178.4*	*111.6*	*80.0*	*404.0*	–4.0	58.6	–33.6	–21.0	0.0	35.291	
6	*domna*	90	480	164	86	820	*69.0*	*362.2*	*226.5*	*162.4*	*820.0*	21.0	117.8	–62.5	–76.4	0.0	97.851	
7	*gelos*	11	41	14	14	80	*6.7*	*35.3*	*22.1*	*15.8*	*80.0*	4.3	5.7	–8.1	–1.8	–0.0	6.795	n.s.
8	*joven* (noun)	28	140	33	23	224	*18.8*	*98.9*	*61.9*	*44.3*	*224.0*	9.2	41.1	–28.9	–21.3	0.0	45.230	
9	*lauzengier*	31	102	26	17	176	*14.8*	*77.7*	*48.6*	*34.8*	*176.0*	16.2	24.3	–22.6	–17.8	0.0	44.932	
10	*midons*	46	147	45	54	292	*24.6*	*129.0*	*80.6*	*57.8*	*292.0*	21.4	18.0	–35.6	–3.8	0.0	37.223	
	performance-words																	
11	*cantar* (noun)	16	79	30	26	151	*12.7*	*66.7*	*41.7*	*29.9*	*151.0*	3.3	12.3	–11.7	–3.9	0.0	6.916	n.s.
12	*cantar* (verb)	51	234	108	62	455	*38.3*	*201.0*	*125.7*	*90.1*	*455.0*	12.7	33.0	–17.7	–28.1	0.0	20.891	
13	*escri-* words	7	23	30	15	75	*6.3*	*33.1*	*20.7*	*14.8*	*75.0*	0.7	–10.1	9.3	0.2	0.0	7.337	n.s.
14	*joglar*	4	34	19	17	74	*6.2*	*32.7*	*20.4*	*14.7*	*74.0*	–2.2	1.3	–1.4	2.3	0.0	1.326	n.s.
	setting-words																	
15	*castel*	5	57	17	19	98	*8.2*	*43.3*	*27.1*	*19.4*	*98.0*	–3.2	13.7	–10.1	–0.4	0.0	9.373	
16	castle names	11	72	10	2	95	*8.0*	*42.0*	*26.2*	*18.8*	*95.0*	3.0	30.0	–16.2	–16.8	0.0	47.704	
17	*cort*	5	83	34	33	155	*13.0*	*68.5*	*42.8*	*30.7*	*155.0*	–8.0	14.5	–8.8	2.3	–0.0	10.030	
18	town names	33	184	105	71	393	*33.1*	*173.6*	*108.5*	*77.8*	*393.0*	–0.1	10.4	–3.5	–6.8	0.0	1.336	n.s.

	Category Word(s)	Observed					*Expected*					Observed-Expected					Chi square	
	religion-words	Pd 2	Pd 3	Pd 4	Pd 5	Total	*Pd 2*	*Pd 3*	*Pd 4*	*Pd 5*	*Total*	Pd 2	Pd 3	Pd 4	Pd 5	Total		
19	*Crist*	3	20	18	22	63	*5.3*	*27.8*	*17.4*	*12.5*	*63.0*	–2.3	–7.8	0.6	9.5	0.0	10.497	
20	*Deu*	100	368	240	191	899	*75.6*	*397.1*	*248.3*	*178.0*	*899.0*	24.4	–29.1	–8.3	13.0	0.0	11.206	
21	*maire*	9	24	22	32	87	*7.3*	*38.4*	*24.0*	*17.2*	*87.0*	1.7	–14.4	–2.0	14.8	0.0	18.647	
22	*Maria*	4	34	21	14	73	*6.1*	*32.2*	*20.2*	*14.5*	*73.0*	–2.1	1.8	0.8	–0.5	0.0	0.892	n.s.
23	*mort* (noun)	25	136	100	76	337	*28.4*	*148.9*	*93.1*	*66.7*	*337.0*	–3.4	–12.9	6.9	9.3	0.0	3.312	n.s.
24	*paradis*	7	26	15	19	67	*5.6*	*29.6*	*18.5*	*13.3*	*67.0*	1.4	–3.6	–3.5	5.7	0.0	3.909	n.s.
25	*pecat*	12	87	62	31	192	*16.2*	*84.8*	*53.0*	*38.0*	*192.0*	–4.2	2.2	9.0	–7.0	0.0	3.938	n.s.
	morality-words																	
26	*drech*	48	252	157	123	580	*48.8*	*256.2*	*160.2*	*114.8*	*580.0*	–0.8	–4.2	–3.2	8.2	0.0	0.726	n.s.
27	*fals*	36	195	115	85	431	*36.3*	*190.4*	*119.0*	*85.3*	*431.0*	–0.3	4.6	–4.0	–0.3	–0.0	0.252	n.s.
28	*onor*	35	279	146	133	593	*49.9*	*261.9*	*163.8*	*117.4*	*593.0*	–14.9	17.1	–17.8	15.6	–0.0	9.557	
29	*orgolh*	21	109	62	36	228	*19.2*	*100.7*	*63.0*	*45.1*	*228.0*	1.8	8.3	–1.0	–9.1	0.0	2.721	n.s.
30	*tort*	42	198	88	84	412	*34.7*	*182.0*	*113.8*	*81.6*	*412.0*	7.3	16.0	–25.8	2.4	0.0	8.879	
31	*valor*	30	276	168	128	602	*50.6*	*265.9*	*166.3*	*119.2*	*602.0*	–20.6	10.1	1.7	8.8	0.0	9.471	
	mockery-words																	
32	*avol*	24	96	60	27	207	*17.4*	*91.4*	*57.2*	*41.0*	*207.0*	6.6	4.6	2.8	–14.0	0.0	7.629	n.s.
33	*escarn-* words	14	28	14	16	72	*6.1*	*31.8*	*19.9*	*14.3*	*72.0*	7.9	–3.8	–5.9	1.7	0.0	12.823	
34	*fol*	56	212	123	52	443	*37.3*	*195.7*	*122.3*	*87.7*	*443.0*	18.7	16.3	0.7	–35.7	0.0	25.315	
35	*paubre*	5	49	34	16	104	*8.7*	*45.9*	*28.7*	*20.6*	*104.0*	–3.7	3.1	5.3	–4.6	0.0	3.805	n.s.
36	*vilan*	18	62	18	15	113	*9.5*	*49.9*	*31.2*	*22.4*	*113.0*	8.5	12.1	–13.2	–7.4	0.0	18.534	

Table 5
Comparison of tables 3 and 4

	Category Word or Words	Table 3		Table 4			
	song-words	Chi2	Period A to B	Chi2	Period 2 to 3	Period 3 to 4	Period 4 to 5
1	*canson*		down		up	down	down
2	minor genres		up		up	up	up
3	*sirventes*		up		down	up	down
4	*vers*		down		down	down	up
	love-words						
5	*cortes*		down		up	down	up
6	*domna*		down		up	down	down
7	*gelos*		down	n.s.			
8	*joven* (noun)		down		up	down	up
9	*lauzengier*		down		up	down	up
10	*midons*		down		down	down	up
	performance-words						
11	*cantar* (noun)		down	n.s.			
12	*cantar* (verb)		down		up	down	down
13	*escri-* words		up	n.s.			
14	*joglar*	n.s.		n.s.			
	setting-words						
15	*castel*		down		up	down	up
16	castle names		down		up	down	down
17	*cort*	n.s.			up	down	up
18	town names	n.s.		n.s.			
	religion-words						
19	*Crist*		up		down	up	up
20	*Deu*	n.s.			down	up	up
21	*maire*		up		down	up	up
22	*Maria*	n.s.		n.s.			
23	*mort* (noun)	n.s.		n.s.			
24	*paradis*	n.s.		n.s.			
25	*pecat*	n.s.		n.s.			
	morality-words						
26	*drech*	n.s.		n.s.			
27	*fals*	n.s.		n.s.			
28	*onor*	n.s.			up	down	up
29	*orgolh*	n.s.		n.s.			
30	*tort*		down		up	down	up
31	*valor*	n.s.			up	down	up
	mockery-words						
32	*avol*	n.s.		n.s.			
33	*escarn-* words	n.s.			down	down	up
34	*fol*		down		down	down	down
35	*paubre*	n.s.		n.s.			
36	*vilan*		down		down	down	up

This observation suggests that after the thematic diffusion that we have hypothesized in Period 4, the last period witnessed a return to the origins of composition in the earlier troubadours. Such a return is further witnessed in the treatises of poetic composition that advised the learner to imitate prestigious models. Chief among these treatises is the *Leys d'amors*, composed in the early fourteenth century as, essentially, a book of rules for judging success in imitating canonical troubadour forms. The *Leys* formulated the principle of return to authoritative models for composition. We have discovered this principle already implicit in the practice of the late troubadours themselves.[39]

Other words, however, did not show the final upturn. Thus the word *canson* continued its retreat into relative obscurity in Period 4 and then Period 5, as did *domna*, *cantar* (verb), castle names, and the word *fol*. The troubadours of the last period returned to the word *vers* but not to *canson*, to *midons* but not to *domna*, not to *cantar* the verb, to the word *castel* but not to the names of castles, to *vilan* but not to *fol*. It is tempting to see in this evidence the trace of a return to a more traditional, more hieratic, and less realistic version of early troubadour song.

Conclusions

I hope to have shown one way in which the concordances now at our disposal can be used to understand the overall shape of the troubadour phenomenon. Provided that we include all the various forms taken by some word, and that we recognize all the homonyms included among occurrences of those forms, we can get all-inclusive information on the troubadours' use of that word. By chronological analysis of such information we can arrive at a profile of the word's use through the troubadour period. This profile will be telling insofar as the word itself was well chosen as an indication of what the troubadours wrote. We can get complete data on a word, but the choice of words to consider remains only a sample guided by insight or intuition. Other words not investigated here can be expected to provide further understanding.

The evidence of word usage presented here makes a strong case that the vocabulary of love declined in relative frequency. This evidence combines with the decline in terms for songs of love, and the independent evidence that the production of songs in the genre of the love song also declined. The *canson* lost favour as the *sirventes* and the minor genres gained. It is not clear, however, on the present evidence what words or categories of words gained favour, if any did. I have speculated that no major sector of the lexicon gained in frequency, but that there was diffusion, a broadening of thematic interest that characterized the penultimate period. Then in the last period it appears that the troubadours marked a return to the vocabulary of their early predecessors. It appears that the

39 'La mémoire poétique des troubadours se trouve comme déployée, explicitée, exacerbée aussi, à la fin du XIIIe siècle, dans une pratique poétique qui se veut le prolongement de la leur, mais qui s'en sépare par sa volonté même de fidélité': M. Zink, 'Littératures de la France médiévale', *Annuaire du Collège de France* (1996–97), 859–79 (p. 861). Zink develops this insight in relation to the poetry of Guiraut Riquier and Matfre Ermengaud.

late troubadours monumentalized their predecessors and, by employing increasingly classical expression, self-consciously monumentalized themselves. This monumentalization was the climax of the sociolinguistic elevation of the artform. The arc from expression to monument replicates the larger movement of the vernacular from low language to high language and the evolution of culture from the Middle Ages to the Renaissance.

The all-inclusiveness of this technique is both a strength and a limitation. It is a strength because, as it seems to me, the technique can provide conclusions that cannot be ignored. But it is a weakness because of its very generality. In order to understand more circumstantially the way these large changes affected individual poets or individual songs, it will be necessary to return to that level of analysis. But already the sweeping conclusions of this inclusive technique can tell us something important about individual poets. They were not all the same. Troubadour poetry changed. It had a history.

Appendix

Words and Groups of Words Investigated

The head form of each word is standardized following *PD*. After the head form I provide a translation, and then the forms attested in Ricketts, *Concordance*.

Words for songs or types of song

1. *Canson*, 'song' or 'love song': *canso*, *canson*, *cansons*, *cansos*, *cansso*, *cansson*, *chanço*, *chançon*, *chanços*, *chanso*, *chanson*, *chansons*, *chansos*, *chansso*, *chansson*, *chanssos*, *chanzo*, *chanzon*, *chanzos*, *chanzzo*, *xanço*, *xanços*.

2. Minor genres. *Alba*, 'song about the dawn': *alb'*, *alba*, *albas*. *Balada*, 'a kind of dance song': *balada*, *baladas*, *balladas*. *Cobla*, 'stanza' or 'song of mockery': *cobla*, *coblas*. *Dansa*, 'dance song': *danca*, *dança*, *dance*, *dansa*, *danz'*, *danza*, *danze*. *Descort*, 'song of disharmony': *descort*, *descortz*. *Estampida*, 'a kind of dance song': *estampida*, *estampidas*. *Partimen*, 'song about a choice': *partimen*, *partimens*, *partiment*, *partimenz*. *Planh*, 'song of lament' (tables do not include occurrences where the word means 'lament'): *plaing*, *plaingz*, *planch*, *plang*, *planh*, *plans*. *Pastorela*, 'shepherdess' (included because the presence of the shepherdess serves to identify the poem as belonging to the genre): *pastor'*, *pastora*, *pastorela*, *pastorelha*, *pastorella*, *pastoressa*, *pastoreta*. *Tenson*, 'song of debate' (tables do not include occurrences where the word means 'dispute'): *tencho*, *tenços*, *tenso*, *tenson*, *tensos*, *tensson*, *tenssos*, *tenzo*, *tenzon*, *tenzos*.

3. *Sirventes*, 'satirical song': *serventes*, *sirventes*, *sirventes-dança*, *sirventesc*, *sirventesca*, *sirventez*.

4. *Vers*, 'song', especially in early usage: *vers*.

Love-words

5. *Cortes*, 'courtly, courteous': *cortes*, *cortes'*, *cortesa*, *cortese*, *cortess'*, *cortez'*, *corteza*, *cortezas*.

6. *Domna*, 'lady': *domn'*, *domna*, *domnas*, *dompn'*, *dompna*, *dompnas*.

7. *Gelos*, 'jealous': *gelos*, *gellos*, *gilos*, *giloza*, *jalous*, *jelos*.

8. *Joven* (noun, stressed *jovén*; not the adjective, stressed *jóven*), 'youthfulness': *ioven*, *iovens*, *iovent*, *ioventz*, *iovenz*, *joven*, *jovens*, *jovent*, *jovenz*.

9. *Lauzengier*, 'nasty gossip': *lausangiers*, *lausenger*, *lausengers*, *lausengier*, *lausengiers*, *lausenjer*, *lausenjers*, *lauzengeira*, *lauzenger*, *lauzengers*, *lauzengeyra*, *lauzengieira*, *lauzengier*, *lauzengiers*, *lauzenzier*.

10. *Midons*, 'my lady': *midon*, *midons*, *midonsz*, *midontç*, *midonz*.

Performance-words

11. *Cantar* (noun), 'song': *cantar*, *cantars*, *chantar*, *chantars*.

12. *Cantar* (verb), 'to sing': *canta*, *cantad'*, *cantada*, *cantan*, *cantar*, *cantarai*, *cantarey*, *cantariam*, *cantas*, *cantat*, *cantet*, *canto*, *canton*, *chant*, *chanta*, *chantad'*, *chantada*, *chantam*, *chantan*, *chantans*, *chantant*, *chantanz*, *chantar*, *chantara*, *chantarai*, *chantaran*, *chantaray*, *chantarei*, *chantari'*, *chantaria*, *chantas*, *chantassetz*, *chantat*, *chantatz*, *chantav'*, *chantava*, *chantaz*, *chante*, *chantei*, *chantem*, *chanten*, *chantens*, *chanter*, *chanter'*, *chantera*, *chanterai*, *chanteray*, *chanterem*, *chantes*, *chantet*, *chantetz*, *chanti*, *chantiei*, *chanto*, *chanton*.

13. *Escri-* words. *Escriure*, 'to write': *escrich*, *escricha*, *escrieuria*, *escrig*, *escrigh*, *escrigz*, *escrir*, *escrire*, *escrit*, *escritz*, *escriu*, *escriue*, *escriur'*, *escriure*, *escrius*, *escriut*, *escriva*, *scriver'*. *Escriptura*, 'writing': *escrichura*, *escriptura*, *escritura*, *scriptura*. *Escrivan*, 'scribe': *escrivan*, *escrivas*.

14. *Joglar*, 'performer, entertainer': *ioglar*, *ioglars*, *joglar*, *joglars*, *juglar*, *juglars*.

Setting-words

15. *Castel*, 'castle': *castel*, *castelh*, *castelhs*, *castell*, *castells*, *castels*, *casteus*, *chastel*, *chastels*, *chasteus*.

16. Names of castles in the Midi, identified here by reference to Wiacek[40] or Chambers.[41] Babon (Bouches-du-Rhône): *Babon*. Beauregard (Vaucluse): *Belesgar*. Bellande (Alpes-Maritimes): *Belanda*. Ben-Aic (Ariège): *Ben-Aic*. Benauges (Gironde): *Benaug'*, *Benauges*, *Benaujes*. Brion (Drôme): *Brio*. Burlats (Tarn): *Burlas*, *Burlatz*, *Burlaz*. Cabaret (Aude): *Cabaretz*. Cajarc (Lot): *Cajarc*. Charlus-le-Pailloux (Corrèze): *Caslutz*, *Chasluç*. Dromons (Isère): *Dromos*. Glorieta (Vaucluse): *Gloriet'*, *Glorieta*. Hautefort (Dordogne): *Autafort*. Martel (Lot): *Martel*, *Martels*. Minerve (Hérault): *Menerba*. Mirandol (Lot): *Mirandol*. Miraval-Cabardès (Aude): *Miraval*, *Miravalh*, *Miravalhs*, *Miravals*. Monclar (Gers): *Monclar*, *Monclin*. Montaigut? (Tarn): *Montagut*. Montbolo (Pyrénées-Orientales): *Monbaulo*. Montesquieu-Volvestre? (Haute-Garonne): *Montesquiu*. Montfort (Dordogne): *Monfort*, *Monfortz*. Montrosier (Tarn? Tarn-et-Garonne? Aveyron?): *Monrosier*, *Monrozier*. Mornas (Vaucluse): *Mornatz*. Planel (Lot-et-Garonne): *Planell*. Polignac (Haute-Loire): *Polinac*, *Polinhac*. Quer (Ariège): *Quer*. Saissac (Aude): *Saissac*. Son (Ariege): *So*. Talaug (Vaucluse, Wiacek; Talau, Pyrénées-Orientales, Chambers): *Talaug*. Tour Mirmanda, La (Vaucluse): *Tor Milmanda*, *Tor Mirmanda*. Tour-Blanche, La (Dordogne): *La Tor*, *Las Tors*. Ventadour (Corrèze): *Ventadorn*, *Ventedor*, *Ventedorns*.

17. *Cort*, 'court': *cort*, *cortz*, *curtz*.

18. Names of towns in the Midi, identified here by reference to Wiacek, *Lexique*, or Chambers, *Proper Names*. Agen (Lot-et-Garonne): *Agen*, *Aien*. Aigremont

[40] W. M. Wiacek, *Lexique des noms géographiques et ethniques dans les poésies des troubadours des XIIe et XIIIe siècles* (Paris, 1968).

[41] F. M. Chambers, *Proper Names in the Lyrics of the Troubadours* (Chapel Hill, 1971).

(Gard): *Agremon*. Aiguesvives (Ariège?): *Aigaviv'*. Aire-sur-l'Adour (Landes): *Aire*. Aissa (Haute-Vienne, Chambers): *Aissa*. Aix-en-Provence (Bouches-du-Rhône): *Aics*, *Ais*, *Aixs*. Alamanon (Bouches-du-Rhône): *Alamano*, *Alamanon*. Alanson (Bouches-du-Rhône): *Alanso*. Albi (Tarn): *Albi*. Alès (Gard): *Alest*. Alion (Ariège): *Alio*. Alzonne (Aude): *Alzona*. Anduze (Gard): *Andus'*, *Anduza*. Angoulême (Charente): *Engolesme*. Annonay (Ardèche): *Anonai*. Apcher (Lozère): *Apchier*, *Apchiers*. Apt (Vaucluse): *Ates*. Arles (Bouches-du-Rhône): *Arle*, *Arles*, *Arll'*, *Arlle*. Arthès (Tarn): *Artes*. Artonne (Puy-de-Dôme): *Artona*. Aubagne (Bouches-du-Rhône): *Albaigna*, *Albainia*, *Albanha*. Aubrac (Lozère): *Albrac*. Aubusson (Creuse): *Albuso*, *Albusson*, *Albuzo*. Auch (Gers): *Aug*. Aulps (Var, Chambers): *Alms*. Aups (Var, Wiacek): *Aus*. Aureilhan (Hautes-Pyrénées): *Aureilla*. Aurel (Drôme): *Aurel*. Autaves (Bouches-du-Rhône): *Autaves*. Autier (Lozère): *Autier*. Auvillars? (Tarn-et-Garonne): *Vilans*. Avignon (Vaucluse): *Avigno*, *Avignon*, *Avignons*, *Avignos*, *Avinho*, *Avinhon*, *Avinhos*. Bachélerie, La (Corrèze): *Bachallaria*. Bar (Corrèze): *Bar*. Barbezieux (Charente): *Berbesil*. Barjols (Var): *Bariols*. Barthe, La (Aveyron): *Bart'*, *Barta*. Baux, Les (Bouches-du-Rhône): *Baus*, *Bautz*, *Bauz*. Bayonne (Pyrénées-Atlantiques): *Baiona*. Bazas (Gironde): *Basatz*. Beaucaire (Gard): *Belcaire*, *Belhcaire*. Beaumont (Dordogne? Puy-de-Dôme?): *Belmon*. Beauzac (Haute-Loire): *Bauzac*. Bergerac (Dordogne): *Bragairac*, *Braiairac*. Berre-l'Étang (Bouches-du-Rhône): *Berr'*, *Berra*. Beuil (Alpes-Maritimes): *Biolh*, *Biuelh*. Béziers (Hérault): *Bezers*. Blaye (Gironde): *Blaia*, *Blaya*. Blieux (Alpes-de-Haute-Provence): *Blieu*. Boisseson (Tarn): *Boisanso*, *Boissazo*, *Boixados*. Bonrepos (Haute-Garonne?): *Ron-Repaus*. Bordeaux (Gironde): *Bordel*, *Bordels*, *Bordeus*. Bourg? (Dordogne): *Dorc*. Bourneix (Dordogne?): *Borneill*, *Bornelh*. Bozouls (Aveyron): *Boazo*. Brens (Tarn): *Berenc*, *Berencx*. Brioude (Haute-Loire): *Briva*. Bruniquel (Tarn-et-Garonne): *Brunequelh*. Bugue, Le (Dordogne): *Albuca*. Cabries (Bouches-du-Rhône): *Chabress*. Cahors (Lot): *Caortz*, *Caorz*. Canilhac (Lozère): *Canilhac*, *Canillac*. Capendu (Aude): *Canpendut*. Capestany (Pyrénées-Orientales): *Cabestanh*. Caraman (Haute-Garonne): *Caramanh*. Carcassonne (Aude): *Carcasson'*, *Carcassona*. Cardaillac (Lot): *Cardaillac*, *Cardalhac*. Carlat (Cantal? Chambers): *Carlas*. Carlux (Hérault?): *Sarlus*. Carpentras (Vaucluse): *Carpentras*. Casalz (Lot, Jeanroy, *Poésie lyrique*, I, 380): *Casalz*. Castellane (Alpes-de-Haute-Provence): *Chastellana*. Castres (Tarn): *Castras*. Caussade (Tarn-et-Garonne): *Cauzada*. Cavaillon (Vaucluse): *Cavaillon*, *Cavaillos*, *Cavelc*. Chalais (Charente): *Chales*. Chamalières (Haute-Loire, Chambers): *Camalieiras*. Chapteuil (Saint-Julien-Chapteuil, Haute-Loire): *Capduelh*, *Capduell*. Chassiers (Ardèche): *Chassier*. Chastres (Charente): *Chartres*. Châteauneuf-de-Randon (Lozère): *Castelnou*. Chénerilles (Alpes-de-Haute-Provence): *Cananillas*. Clérans (Dordogne): *Clarent*. Clermont-Ferrand (Puy-de-Dôme): *Clarmon*. Cognac (Charente): *Conhat*. Collioure (Pyrénées-Orientales): *Cogliure*, *Coliure*. Colombier (Corrèze): *Colombier*. Comborn (Corrèze): *Comborns*. Confolens (Charente): *Cofolen*. Cornil (Corrèze): *Cornil*, *Cornilh*. Corsavy (Pyrénées-Orientales): *Cortzavi*. Courthézon (Vaucluse): *Corteson*, *Cortesos*, *Cortezo*. Cruas (Ardèche): *Cruas*. Curbans (Alpes-de-Haute-Provence): *Curban*. Damiatte (Tarn, Chambers): *Damiata*. Dax (Landes): *Aics*. Die (Drôme): *Dia*. Domme (Dordogne): *Doma*. Durban-sur-Arize (Ariège):

Durban. Durfort (Tarn-et-Garonne): *Durfort*. Egletons (Corrèze): *Glotos*. Escola (unidentified place in Vaucluse): *Escola*. Escorailles (Cantal): *Escoralha*. Esparron (Haute-Garonne): *Esparo*. Esparron (Var): *Esparnon*. Estang (Gers): *Estanh*. Étoile-sur-Rhône (Drôme): *Estela*. Excideuil (Dordogne): *Essidolh*, *Essiduelh*. Eynac (Haute-Loire): *Aenac*. Fanjeaux (Aude): *Fanjau*. Forcalquier (Alpes-de-Haute-Provence): *Folcalquer*. Fos (Haute-Garonne? Hérault?): *Fosc*. Fraisse (Hérault): *Fraisse*. Gabarret (Landes): *Gavaret*, *Gavaretz*. Gaillac (Tarn): *Galhac*. Gap (Hautes-Alpes): *Gap*. Gaubert (Alpes-de-Haute-Provence): *Galpert*. Gimel (Corrèze): *Gimel*. Gloriette, La (Drôme): *Gloriet'*, *Glorieta*. Gordes (Vaucluse): *Gorda*. Gourdon (Lot): *Gordo*, *Gordon*, *Guordo*. Grandmont (Haute-Vienne): *Granmon*. Graulhet (Tarn): *Graignolet*. Grignols (Dordogne): *Graignol*. Isle-en-Jourdain, L' (Gers): *Ilha*. Issoire (Puy-de-Dôme): *Usoir'*. Larroque (Tarn): *Laroqu'*. Laurac (Aude): *Laurac*. Lausonne? (Haute-Loire): *Lausana*. Lautrec (Tarn): *Lautrec*, *Lautresc*. Lavaur (Tarn): *Lavaur*. Lectoure (Gers): *Leitor'*. Leucate (Aude): *Laucata*, *Lieuchata*. Lignan (Hérault): *Linha*. Limoges (Haute-Vienne): *Lemotges*, *Limojes*. Limoux (Aude): *Limos*. Livernon (Lot): *Liverno*. Lodève (Hérault): *Lodev'*, *Lodeva*. Lombers (Tarn): *Lombers*. Louvière, La (Aude): *Lobera*. Luc (Aveyron?): *Luc*. Lunel (Hérault): *Lunel*, *Lunelh*, *Lunelhs*, *Lunels*. Maguelonne (Hérault): *Magalona*. Mainsat (Creuse): *Maensac*. Malemort (Corrèze): *Malamortz*. Mareuil-sur-Belle (Dordogne): *Maruelh*. Marguerides (Corrèze): *Margarida*. Marseille (Bouches-du-Rhône): *Marcelha*, *Marseilha*, *Marseill'*, *Marseilla*, *Marselha*. Maugio (Hérault): *Melguer*, *Melgur*. Mercoeur (Haute-Loire? Puy-de-Dôme?): *Mercuer*. Merdagne (Puy-de-Dôme): *Mairona*. Mévouillon (Drôme): *Meolho*, *Mezeilhon*, *Miullon*. Milan (Pyrénées-Orientales): *Milas*. Millau (Aveyron): *Amilau*, *Amilhau*, *Melhau*. Miremont (Puy-de-Dôme): *Miramons*. Mison (Alpes-de-Haute-Provence): *Meisso*, *Mison*. Moirans (Isère): *Mauren*. Mon Cenis (Hautes-Alpes): *Mon Senitz*. Mondragon (Vaucluse): *Mondrago*, *Mondragos*. Mons (Haute-Garonne): *Mons*. Montaigu-de-Quercy? (Tarn-et-Garonne): *Montagut*. Montamat (Gers): *Montamat*. Montardit (Lot-et-Garonne): *Mos Arditz*. Montauban (Tarn-et-Garonne): *Montalbainz*. Montauberon (Hérault): *Mon Albeo*. Montblanc (Hérault): *Monblanc*. Monteil (Drôme): *Monteil*, *Monteill*. Montferrand, part of Clermont-Ferrand (Puy-de-Dôme, Chambers): *Monferran*. Montgaillard (Tarn-et-Garonne): *Mongalhart*. Montignac (Dordogne, Chambers): *Montignac*. Montlaur (Drôme? Ardèche?): *Monlaur*, *Monlaurs*. Montmaureau (Charente): *Monmaurel*. Montpaon (Aveyron, Chambers): *Montpaon*. Montpellier (Hérault): *Monpellier*, *Monpesler*, *Monpeslier*, *Monpesliers*, *Monspelier*, *Monspellier*. Montrabé (Haute-Garonne): *Mon Rabey*. Montréal (Aude): *Monreal*, *Monrial*. Mozac (Puy-de-Dôme): *Mausac*, *Mauzac*. Mure, La (Isère): *La Mura*. Murs (Aveyron? Vaucluse?): *Mur*. Nahuja (Pyrénées-Orientales): *Nahuga*. Narbonne (Aude): *Narbona*. Neuvic (Dordogne? Corrèze? Chambers): *Nou-Vic*. Nieuil (Charente): *Niol*. Nîmes (Gard): *Nems*, *Nemz'*. Nontron (Dordogne): *Nontron*. Olargues (Hérault): *Olargue*, *Olargues*. Oppède (Vaucluse): *Opida*. Orange (Vaucluse): *Aureng'*, *Aurenga*, *Aurenja*. Orgon (Bouches-du-Rhône): *Orgo*. Ossau (Pyrénées-Atlantiques): *Orsau*. Ostabat-Asme (Pyrénées-Atlantiques): *Ostasvalhs*. Oupia (Hérault): *Opian*. Parisot (Tarn-et-Garonne): *Paris*. Pau (Pyrénées-Atlantiques):

Paus, Paz. Péguilhan (Haute-Garonne): *Pegulhan.* Pennautier (Aude): *Pognautier.* Périgueux (Dordogne): *Peiregos.* Perpignan (Pyrénées-Orientales): *Perpinhan.* Pierrefeu (Var): *Peirafuoc.* Pissos (Landes): *Pisson.* Posquières (Gard): *Posquieiras.* Puy Guilhem (Dordogne): *Puoig Guillem.* Puy-de-Dôme (Dordogne): *Puoi de Doma.* Puy-en-Velay, Le (Haute-Loire): *Poi, Pueg, Puei, Puey, Puoi, Puoig, Puois.* Rancon (Haute-Vienne): *Rancom, Rangos.* Riez (Alpes-de-Haute-Provence): *Res.* Robion (Vaucluse): *Robion.* Rochechouart (Haute-Vienne): *Rocacoart.* Rodez (Aveyron): *Rodes.* Rognes (Bouches-du-Rhône): *Roignas.* Roquefeuil (Var): *Rocafuelh, Rocafuoill.* Roquefort-de-Marsan (Landes): *Rochafort.* Roussillon (Vaucluse): *Rossilhos.* Saignes (Cantal): *Saigna.* Saint-Antonin (Tarn-et-Garonne): *Sanh Antoni.* Saint-Astier (Dordogne): *Saint Estier.* Saint-Ceré (Lot): *Saint-Cere.* Saint-Circ-d'Alzon (Lot): *Sain Circ, Saint Circ, San Cir, San Circ, San Sir.* Saint-Disdier-en-Velay (Haute-Loire): *Saint Deslier, San Leider, Sanh Desdier.* Saint-Félix (Vaucluse): *Sain Felitz, San Felitz.* Saint-Flour (Cantal): *Sanhflor.* Saint-Loubert (Gironde): *Saint Loberc.* Saint-Pons-de-Tomières (Hérault): *Sant Pos, Sant Pos de Tomeiras.* Saint-Sever (Landes): *San Sever.* Salles (Aveyron): *Salas.* Salon-de-Provence (Bouches-du-Rhône): *Salos.* Salses (Pyrénées-Orientales): *Salsas.* Sault (Aude): *Saut.* Sauve (Gard): *Salve.* Signes (Var): *Signha, Sinha.* Sisteron (Alpes-de-Haute-Provence): *Sestairo, Sestairon.* Sommières (Gard): *Someiras.* Soulage (Cantal?): *Solas.* Tarabel? (Haute-Garonne): *Daurabell.* Tarascon (Bouches-du-Rhône): *Tarasco, Tarascon, Tarascona.* Tersanne (Drôme, Chambers): *Tarzana.* Thézan (Hérault): *Teza.* Thor, Le (Vaucluse): *.l Tor.* Tintignac (Corrèze, Chambers): *Tintinhac.* Toulon (Var): *Tolo.* Toulouse (Haute-Garonne): *Tolosa, Toloz', Toloza.* Tournoël (Puy-de-Dôme): *Tornel.* Tournon-sur-Rhône (Ardèche): *Torcho.* Tours, Las (Haute-Vienne): *La Tor, Las Tors, Lastors.* Trans (Var, Chambers): *Trans.* Treignac (Corrèze): *Trainac.* Trets (Bouches-du-Rhône): *Trez.* Trip (Var, Chambers): *Trip.* Tudelle (Gers, Chambers): *Tudela.* Turenne (Corrèze): *Toren', Torena.* Ussel-sur-Sarzonne (Corrèze): *Uysselh.* Usson (Puy-de-Dôme? Loire?): *Usson.* Uzerche (Corrèze): *Uzerca.* Uzerna, former name for Beaucaire (Gard): *Uzerna.* Uzès (Gard): *Uzetge.* Valence-sur-Rhône (Drôme): *Valensa, Valenssa, Valentia, Valenza.* Vauvert (Gard): *Valvert.* Venasque (Vaucluse): *Vennasqu'.* Vence (Alpes-Maritimes): *Vensa.* Venerque (Haute-Garonne): *Venerca.* Verdun (Ariège? Aude?): *Verdon.* Verfeuil (Gard? Haute-Garonne? Tarn-et-Garonne?): *Vertfoill, Vertfuelh.* Vienne (Isère): *Viana, Viena.* Villaret (Alpes-de-Haute-Provence): *Viralet.* Villefranche (Alpes-Maritimes): *Villafranca.* Villemur-sur-Tarn (Haute-Garonne): *Vilamur.*

Religion-words

19. *Crist*, 'Christ': *Christ, Cris, Crist, Cristz, Critz.*
20. *Deu*, 'God': *Deu, Deus, Dex, Dieu, Dieus, Diex, Diu, Dius.*
21. *Maire*, 'mother': *mair', maire, maires, mayr', mayre.*
22. *Maria*, 'Mary': *Mari', Maria, Marie.*
23. *Mort* (noun), 'death': *mort, mortç, mortz, morz.*

24. *Paradis*, 'paradise': *paradis*.

25. *Pecat*, 'sin': *peca'*, *pecaitz*, *pecat*, *pecatç*, *pecatz*, *peccaç*, *peccas*, *peccat*, *peccatz*, *pecchatz*, *pechat*, *pechatç*, *pechatz*, *pechaz*, *pechet*.

Morality-words

26. *Drech*, 'right': *dreç*, *drech*, *drechs*, *drechz*, *dreg*, *dregs*, *dregz*, *dreich*, *dreichs*, *dreig*, *dreigs*, *dreigz*, *dreit*, *dreitç*, *dreitz*, *dreiz*, *dret*, *dretç*, *dretx*, *dretz*, *dreyt*, *dreytz*, *drez*.

27. *Fals*, 'false': *fals*, *fals'*, *falsa*.

28. *Onor*, 'honor; fief': *honor*, *honors*, *onor*, *onors*.

29. *Orgolh*, 'pride': *ergoill*, *ergoills*, *ergoils*, *ergolh*, *ergolhs*, *ergoyll*, *ergueil*, *ergueilh*, *ergueilhs*, *ergueill*, *ergueills*, *ergueilz*, *erguel*, *erguelh*, *erguelhs*, *erguell*, *erguells*, *erguels*, *ergul*, *erguoill*, *erguyll*, *erguylls*, *orgoil*, *orgoilh*, *orgoill*, *orgoills*, *orgoillz*, *orgoils*, *orgolh*, *orgolhs*, *orgoyll*, *orgueil*, *orgueilh*, *orgueill*, *orgueills*, *orguelh*, *orguels*, *orguil*, *orguill*, *orguoil*, *orguoill*, *orguoills*, *orguoils*, *orguolh*, *orguolhs*, *orguoyll*.

30. *Tort*, 'wrong': *tort*, *tortz*.

31. *Valor*, 'valor': *vallor*, *valor*, *valors*.

Mockery-words

32. *Avol*, 'bad': *avol*, *avoll*, *avols*.

33. *Escarn-* words. *Escarn*, 'mockery': *escarn*. *Escarnidor*, 'mocker': *escarnidor*, *escharnidor*. *Escarnir*, 'to mock': *escarnen*, *escarnic*, *escarnida*, *escarnir*, *escarniran*, *escarnire*, *escarnirs*, *escarnis*, *escarnisca*, *escarnisson*, *escarnit*, *escarnitz*, *escarniz*, *escharnida*, *escharnir*, *escharnirs*, *escharnis*, *escharnitz*, *escharniz*.

34. *Fol*, 'foolish': *fol*, *fola*, *folla*, *follas*, *fols*, *folz*.

35. *Paubre*, 'poor': *paubr'*, *paubra*, *paubre*, *paubres*, *paupr'*, *paupra*, *paupre*.

36. *Vilan*, 'peasant': *vila*, *vilain*, *vilan*, *vilana*, *vilans*, *vilanz*, *villan*.

Index